a **LIVING** **FREE** guide

Homemade Snacks and Staples

Kimberly Aime

ALPHA

A member of Penguin Group (USA) Inc.

ALPHA BOOKS

Published by Penguin Group (USA) Inc.

Penguin Group (USA) Inc., 375 Hudson Street, New York, New York 10014, USA • Penguin Group (Canada), 90 Eglinton Avenue East, Suite 700, Toronto, Ontario M4P 2Y3, Canada (a division of Pearson Penguin Canada Inc.) • Penguin Books Ltd., 80 Strand, London WC2R 0RL, England • Penguin Ireland, 25 St. Stephen's Green, Dublin 2, Ireland (a division of Penguin Books Ltd.) • Penguin Group (Australia), 250 Camberwell Road, Camberwell, Victoria 3124, Australia (a division of Pearson Australia Group Pty. Ltd.) • Penguin Books India Pvt. Ltd., 11 Community Centre, Panchsheel Park, New Delhi— 110 017, India • Penguin Group (NZ), 67 Apollo Drive, Rosedale, North Shore, Auckland 1311, New Zealand (a division of Pearson New Zealand Ltd.) • Penguin Books (South Africa) (Pty.) Ltd., 24 Sturdee Avenue, Rosebank, Johannesburg 2196, South Africa • Penguin Books Ltd., Registered Offices: 80 Strand, London WC2R 0RL, England

International Standard Book Number: 978-1-61564-299-1
Library of Congress Catalog Card Number: 2012953760

15   14   13   8   7   6   5   4   3   2   1

Interpretation of the printing code: The rightmost number of the first series of numbers is the year of the book's printing; the rightmost number of the second series of numbers is the number of the book's printing. For example, a printing code of 13-1 shows that the first printing occurred in 2013.

Printed in the United States of America

Note: This publication contains the opinions and ideas of its author. It is intended to provide helpful and informative material on the subject matter covered. It is sold with the understanding that the author and publisher are not engaged in rendering professional services in the book. If the reader requires personal assistance or advice, a competent professional should be consulted.

The author and publisher specifically disclaim any responsibility for any liability, loss, or risk, personal or otherwise, which is incurred as a consequence, directly or indirectly, of the use and application of any of the contents of this book.

Trademarks: All terms mentioned in this book that are known to be or are suspected of being trademarks or service marks have been appropriately capitalized. Alpha Books and Penguin Group (USA) Inc. cannot attest to the accuracy of this information. Use of a term in this book should not be regarded as affecting the validity of any trademark or service mark.

Most Alpha books are available at special quantity discounts for bulk purchases for sales promotions, premiums, fund-raising, or educational use. Special books, or book excerpts, can also be created to fit specific needs. For details, write: Special Markets, Alpha Books, 375 Hudson Street, New York, NY 10014.

Publisher: *Mike Sanders*

Executive Managing Editor: *Billy Fields*

Executive Acquisitions Editor: *Lori Cates Hand*

Editorial Supervisor: *Christy Wagner*

Senior Production Editor: *Janette Lynn*

Cover/Book Designer: *Rebecca Batchelor*

Indexer: *Johnna VanHoose Dinse*

Layout: *Ayanna Lacey*

Proofreader: *Cate Schwenk*

Contents

Appendixes

Introduction

Three years ago, my husband and I made the decision to clean up our diet. Compared to the average American, we were already healthy superstars. We ate a high-fiber cereal with a bowl of frozen and fresh berries every morning. We ate salads or light sandwiches at lunch and always had a side salad for dinner. For snacks, I loved my high-fiber, low-fat crackers, cookies, and chips. I drank water, diet sodas, and the occasional powdered light lemonade, thinking I was outsmarting the masses. We worked out every day, usually together, and were avid runners. With all this time, effort, and energy we invested, clearly we should feel great, be at our ideal weights, and be happy, right?

That wasn't exactly the case. We were tired all the time and bloated most of the time, and I was often frustrated with how I looked and those last 5 pounds I just couldn't seem to lose.

Everything changed when I read the book *Real Food Has Curves* by Mark Scarbrough and Bruce Weinstein. Scarbrough and Weinstein challenged their readers to go real or go home. They argued that when you compare the "real" version of food to the processed version, the real food always wins when it comes to nutritional value, taste, and often the time, effort, and energy put into preparation. I told my husband about the book and made him read it. As soon as he put it down, we agreed to try to eliminate all processed foods from our diet. We were already so healthy, so this would be easy, right?

It wasn't easy.

It wasn't *remotely* easy.

We phased out processed foods over 6 months. At times, we were grumpy and frustrated, but we couldn't argue with how good we felt and how much more energy we had. And yes, I did lose those final 5 pounds (and more!). Even though it's not always easy, I can honesty say we never looked back. Once you go real, you'll never look at processed foods the same way again.

This book is a collection of our go-to snack and pantry staple recipes. We had to get creative about our cooking, snacking, and eating to change this "diet" into a "lifestyle."

I think you'll be pleasantly surprised at how easy it is to re-create some of your favorite premade foods, and I know you'll like how much better real, whole foods taste.

The Cast of Characters

I apologize; I didn't introduce myself. My name is Kimberly, a.k.a. Badger Girl, and I have a cooking blog, Badger Girl Learns to Cook (learntocookbadgergirl.com). On my blog, I share recipes, clean-eating tips, guest posts from healthy bloggers, book reviews, interviews with local chefs, and other tales from the clean-eating field. Badger Girl is a shout-out to my B.A. alma mater, University of Wisconsin–Madison, home of the Badgers. I didn't take on this identity until I left Wisconsin for graduate school and felt an unexplainable longing for my home state.

In an effort to protect my poor husband's identity on my blog, I have dubbed him "Manatee." And for the record: no, I am not married to a fat, slow-moving, endangered water creature.

When we went to Sea World together, we saw manatees being fed. Have you ever seen that? Crates of lettuce are thrown into the water, and the manatees float around snacking, looking perfectly content and peaceful. Still confused? My husband consumes more spinach and lettuce than an average family of four. We seriously go through at least a pound of spinach or mixed greens every day. As soon as I saw those manatees, his cyber identity was born.

Then there's my mom. You think your kids are picky? You haven't met my mom. Seriously, trying to get this woman to eat anything that's not something she grew up eating is close to impossible. That is, unless you're Manatee or one of her girlfriends. Manatee has sweet-talked her into trying tofu, sushi, and pesto. After years of making and buying her all kinds of hummus only to have her stick her tongue out at me, I get this call from her: "Kimberly, Julie had the most amazing dip at her party. What was it, Tom? What? Well, you spell it H-U-M-M-...."

So maybe I should rephrase this: getting my mom to eat anything out of the ordinary is impossible *for me*. Parents, does this sound familiar? I would say this was payback, but I wasn't a picky eater as a child, as evidenced by my then rotund shape.

In the recipes in this book, I include notes about my mom's advice and things I've tricked her into eating, to her pleasant surprise.

Recipe Tips

Messing up recipes is one of my many talents, so no matter how much you have screwed up in the kitchen, just know I've done it all at least twice—and in most cases, more times than I'm comfortable admitting to the general public. I wanted to offer some tips, and you can trust that I've learned all these the hard way.

Third Time's the Charm

Read the recipe three times. Not once, not a quick skim-through, not as you're mixing the ingredients, and not after you've mixed half of the dough for cookies you plan to serve to guests who are on their way to your house and then realize the dough needs to chill for 8 hours.

Read the recipe three times. Then, humor me and read it three more times. Then, tell someone about what you're going to do in the recipe.

Then, read it again.

Make a List

In one of the multiple times you're reading the recipe, go to your pantry and refrigerator. Take out all the ingredients you need for the recipe. Are you missing something? If so, make a list. Double-check your list. Are you absolutely sure you have everything you need on the list? Check again.

Now, here are two very important steps: put the list into your purse before you go to the store *and* take your purse to the store. When you get to the store, take the list out of your purse (contrary to what you might think, you have not memorized the list) and use it as you shop. Before you check out, be sure you have everything on the list. Don't check when you're walking out of the store, getting into your car, or walking into your house. Check your list and your items *before* you buy your groceries.

I'm not being facetious. I am the queen of multiple trips to the store before, right before, and during the cooking of a new (or old) recipe. In our family (the Dachels), we call it the Dachel curse (we're also not known for our creativity). Our Thanksgiving dinner generally requires a minimum of four trips to the store—three of them after we've started cooking. Sometimes there are two more after we've sent one person to the store and, of course, they didn't remember their phone so we could call and ask them to get another item we forgot.

Choose Real Ingredients

All the recipes in this book call for real-food ingredients. Do not buy light or reduced-fat versions of anything. If it calls for maple syrup, use real maple syrup.

I include notes within the recipes, but it can't be said enough: to make real food, you have to cook with real food.

Make an Organized Mess

When you're cooking any recipe, set up a *mise en place,* which translates to "everything in place"—or according to Manatee, an organized mess. He never understands why I need to measure all my ingredients and put them into little bowls, but that's only because he doesn't cook and he does all the dishes.

It may seem counterintuitive, but take this extra step, and your cooking will go more smoothly, and you'll make less of a mess in the end.

Clean as You Go

On my blog, I interview local chefs in Madison, Wisconsin, and always ask for cooking advice. The best piece of advice I ever received was from Chef Julie Pryzbylski, who said, "Cook like a pro; clean as you go."

As soon as you finish with an ingredient, put it away. This prevents you from trashing your kitchen or accidentally dumping over an opened bottle of vanilla … twice. (Yes, my kitchen smelled amazing for a week, but it was also sticky and a waste of really good vanilla.)

How to Use This Book

I set up this book to guide you through some basic recipes to get you started. These "staples" serve as building blocks for the recipes later in the book. All the recipes were born out of necessity: I needed to make my own basic ingredients because I couldn't find a good whole-food substitute, or I needed a treat or goodie to get me through the day.

The following sections give you a map of the book. Although the later recipes refer to the staple recipes, you certainly can skip ahead to the Sweet Treats and Beverages section. I get it. I'm a sucker for homemade ice cream, too.

Staples, Sauces, and Spices

When I started shopping clean, I paid way more attention to the labels of some of my pantry staples than I did to the price tags. Manatee was sure to point this out when I brought home a $12 jar of marinara sauce. "You paid what?!" he exclaimed when he read the receipt. I countered with, "It was the only jar in the store with no chemicals or added sugar." He was speechless. At first I thought it was because, like me, he was shocked that there was only one jar in the store that met our criteria. Little did I know, he was counting to 10, and then 20, and then 50. Now that I think about it, he was actually quiet for a long time that night. Oh, did I mention he's a financial adviser?

Since then, we have worked hard to make as many of our staples as we can. The results are better tasting and far better for your wallet. There's nothing like whipping up your own pizza sauce, pesto, and even ketchup and peanut butter.

Although we did buy some premade sauces as we eased into clean eating, salad dressings were the first to go. I can't stress enough how bad these dressings can be for you. Not only do they add chemicals and preservatives to extend the shelf lives, there's no way to tell whether the oil in the dressing has grown rancid. Given how long those dressings have to be on the shelf (or in refrigerated cases), I have a hard time believing the oils are fresh and haven't gone bad. Dressings are so easy to whip together and so customizable. There's no reason not to make your own.

The same goes for peanut butter. I love peanut butter. As in, if-I-could-eat-one-food-for-the-rest-of-my-life-it-would-be-peanut-butter kind of love. You can make your own peanut butter in 5 minutes with two ingredients (peanuts and salt). From there, you can add oil or honey to change the sweetness or texture—but 5 minutes, people! And you've never tasted peanut butter like fresh peanut butter. Take that from someone who has tried a *lot* of peanut butter.

I end this section with a chapter on making your own spices. I love being able to customize my spice blends to get just what I want in a spice. It's so easy and saves time, effort, and energy trying to track down these blends in the store. Do you know how hard it is to find pumpkin pie spice year-round? Trust me, it's hard. And for someone who eats pumpkin year-round, it's frustrating. When I started making my own, I never had to worry about it.

Consider these chapters your whole-food toolkit for re-creating your pantry to fit your tastes, your budget, and your new, healthy lifestyle.

Snacks, Salads, and Mini-Meals

When we tell people we eat clean and avoid processed foods, we're usually met with blank stares and then this question: "So what *do* you eat for snacks?"

People are dumbfounded that we could walk away from the bulk of the grocery store: the snack aisles.

In addition to eating lots of fresh fruits and veggies, we've been able to maintain this lifestyle because we are creative in the kitchen. We don't feel deprived in any way. It's quite the opposite.

If I really want chips, there's no reason I can't bake my own. The same goes for crackers and cookies. (Let your friends believe it's a lot of hard work to do this. I do admit it's harder than ripping open a bag or box. However, it's not *that* much harder.)

I can have amazing baked tortilla chips in less than 15 minutes. I can whip together my own salsas and guacamole that completely blow processed versions out of the water. After making my own, I wouldn't even want to touch something premade and boxed.

When we entertain, we use a lot of these recipes and no one complains about our boring diet or asks where the cheese puffs are. They're too busy eating homemade nachos, taco dips, hummus, salsa, tofu dippers, and quesadillas. When they aren't eating, they're raving and asking about the recipes. Little do they know how easy it is to make your own pita chips or baba ghanoush.

Matter of fact, maybe we should keep that our little secret. What do you say?

Sweet Treats and Beverages

With your new clean-eating diet, you can have your cake and eat it, too. Literally. In Part 3, I offer a wide range of sweet treats, from baked apples to dairy-free homemade ice cream to chocolate crispy rice bars and even infused vodka!

As with all the recipes, the focus remains on real, whole-food ingredients. You'll also find that once you eliminate artificial sugars from your diet, you can truly appreciate real sugar—and you should. You'll be surprised at how much sugar you can cut out of your favorite sweet recipes. I also share some easy baking substitutions so you can make your own clean-eating recipes with your favorite desserts.

The book ends with a chapter near and dear to my heart. When you eliminate processed foods, you're also eliminating processed drinks. No soda, no fake-sugar light drinks? No worries. I walk you through making your own sodas, lemonades, hot cocoa mix, and some fun "adult" beverages that get their flavor from fruits and healthy sweeteners.

Acknowledgments

I would like to thank my husband and #1 taste-tester, Jean-Paul. I would like to thank my parents for their support, and for their patience as I routinely destroyed their kitchen and forced them to eat exotic foods. I would like to thank April Ueland and Kristen Henslin for always being on the other end of the phone line.

Thank you to Caroline and Matt Laviolette, Belena and Jason Vincetti, Kathy Paulson, Caryn Christianson, Katherine Sager, Andi Dachel, Rebecca Brokmeier, Elizabeth Krotser, Robyn Klinge, and Elizabeth Aime for testing the recipes and providing exceptional feedback.

Thank you to my blog readers, supporters, and the blogging community—you have kept it fun and exciting over the years.

Finally, I would like to thank my agent, Marilyn Allen, for her support and confidence in a new writer, my editor Lori Cates Hand for her patience, and editor Christy Wagner for her excellent feedback and contributions to the book.

Special Thanks to the Technical Reviewer

Homemade Snacks and Staples was reviewed by an expert who double-checked the accuracy of what you'll learn here, to help us ensure this book gives you everything you need to know about making your own tasty snacks and pantry staples. Special thanks are extended to Heidi Reichenberger McIndoo, MS, RD, LDN.

Heidi is a registered dietitian, freelance writer, and co-author of *The Complete Idiot's Guide to 200-300-400 Calorie Meals* and *When to Eat What.* She has spent the last 20 years helping women, men, kids, and families eat nutritiously and deliciously. Check her blog, foodiemomrd.com, for tips and recipes for you and your family.

Getting Started with Real Food  1

Welcome! If you picked up this book, my guess is that you're looking to start incorporating more whole foods in your diet and to get rid of that processed junk. In the following pages, I walk you through the why, what, and most importantly, the how of cleaning up your diet.

I share with you a little about my journey from processed to whole-food cooking, including all the benefits of this new, clean-eating way of life. Trust me, no one was more clueless than I was when it came to cooking with real food! After learning about all the health benefits and how to clean up your kitchen, we get to the bulk of the book: easy recipes for making your own pantry staples and tons of wholesome and delicious snacks and treats.

But first, we must go back to the beginning, to a distant time of convenience over quality, canned meals, and premade shortcuts. In our other words, we are going back to the 1980s ....

The Real Food Revolution

1

Growing up, vegetables came from a can and herbs came from plastic shakers. There were two kinds of cheeses: Kraft singles and, for special occasions, Colby. Sandwiches were made of bologna, mayonnaise, and white bread. Pasta sauce was supposed to be made from tomatoes, and if you were going to dip, you better be scooping something creamy and white with your chip or carrot. I grew up in the 1980s, when processed foods were the norm and quicker was always better.

This was the age of convenience. Men and women were rewarded for working overtime, and women were shunning the kitchen. With an audience determined to have it all, the food industry exploded with readymade meals, precooked shortcuts, and snacks that could outlive most household pets. Of course, we wanted boxed macaroni and cheese dinners, fruit rollups, and Twinkies. Who wouldn't?

We didn't grow up unhealthy; we grew up *unaware*. Despite our love of all things snack cake, our household prided itself on its quest for health. My mother always served a salad before dinner and fruit for dessert. Granted, it was iceberg lettuce, croutons, fat-free French dressing, and fruit cocktail floating in thick syrup, but compared to my friends, we were a bunch of tree-hugging health nuts. We even owned a juicer, and my dad would make crazy-thick concoctions and force me to drink them. As a 13-year-old, carrot-orange-apple-celery-wheat-germ juice was not on my list of favorite foods, but I respect my dad for trying.

It wasn't until I was in graduate school in California that my eyes were opened to the world of real foods. In my mind, guacamole was the ultimate Californian food, and I made it on a weekly basis. But of course, I relied on a packaged, all-chemical spice packet to make this "healthy" treat. My Mexican American roommate, Susana, was quietly appalled. One night as I was pouring my premade seasonings into a bowl with some fresh avocado and patting myself on the back for my transition to California living, Susana said (with all the patience she could muster), "You know, Kimberly, you could try using real-food ingredients to make your guacamole." A lightbulb went on, and I saw my cooking for what it was: premade, processed, and pathetic.

A New World of Whole Foods

In a doctoral program, you don't have a lot of free time. I was either in a seminar vying for attention from a professor I was desperately trying to impress, teaching undergraduates who would rather be surfing, studying esoteric texts, or trying to squeeze in a workout or a run to maintain a semblance of sanity. Despite my hectic schedule, I always made time to cook dinner. My processed upbringings notwithstanding, I had always been taught the value of a healthy diet. (Remember the dessert fruit cocktail and homemade juices I could chew?) I actually preferred to take time to make something at home instead of calling for takeout every night like many of my classmates.

After my guacamole revelation, I began experimenting with whole foods. As anxiety about graduate school grew, I began to look forward to my cooking breaks more and more. Not surprisingly, my dinners became more and more elaborate. Reading 1,000 pages a week of erudite history and theory was a chore, but reading cookbooks was a welcome break. I pored over ingredient lists, techniques, and foreign foods. I tried everything but lacked a firm foundation. When I attempted an herb garden, I was thrilled to not kill the plants but then was clueless about what to do with fresh herbs. Let's just say my fiber intake skyrocketed until a classmate informed me that you do not eat the *whole* rosemary plant, just the leaves. Oops.

A desire to eat more whole foods, coupled with a desire to avoid studying at all costs, meant I tried to make everything from scratch. Marinara sauces, pesto, salad dressings, cashew sour cream— I tried to do it all. Without that foundation, most of my experiments resulted in a destroyed kitchen, a humbler ego, and a good story for my mother, who was becoming convinced I was crazy for not just making a piece of toast and calling it a day. I was just happy to have a distraction from the rigors of academic life.

At the same time, I was blogging. During my Masters program, my blog had been about adventures in graduate school. In the doctoral program, my blog transitioned into an outlet for anxiety and angst about academia, California, and of course, cooking. As I began to doubt my place in academia, my blog chronicled what it was like to leave graduate school, move back to Wisconsin, and start over in the corporate world and in life. Dinner was still my refuge, and slowly I learned. In some cases, I exhausted all the wrong ways to do something; and sometimes I was just lucky.

Back in Madison, I met a guy who shared my passion for healthy eating, nutrition, and fitness. My blog chronicled meeting a new family, planning a wedding, and of course, new and healthier versions of my favorite foods. After our wedding, I felt I was out of writing material: no more graduate school angst, exciting 20-year-old adventures, or wedding planning. I still had the blog, but I lacked direction. With six subscriptions to cooking magazines, an ever-growing collection of cookbooks, and a dozen food blogs in my Google Reader, I decided to take the logical next step: to blog about my cooking adventures.

Deciding to Come Clean

A year after starting my blog, my husband and I began to re-examine our diet. At the time, my husband's favorite piece of cocktail party trivia was that someone once dug up a corpse, and everything was decomposed on the body except the digestive system. Why? Because that's how many preservatives and chemicals are in our food. I have no idea where he got the quote or if he just made it up, but he brought it up every single time food or diet was the topic of conversation at a social gathering. Charming, isn't it?

After about the hundreth time of killing the mood at a party, we began to rethink our own diet. On the outside, we ate very healthfully. Because of my lactose intolerance, we already avoided most premade dinners, and we had at least one salad every day. At the same time, we also knew we were eating too many processed foods. We were addicted to high-fiber cereals, granola bars, fat-free bottled salad dressings, crackers, chips, and for me, diet soda. We talked about cleaning up our diet. We strategized. We read books on a diet called "clean eating," and it seemed right up our alley: no processed foods; no white flours; very little sugar; and lots of real, natural foods.

We decided to make the change because we wanted to control what went into our bodies. If we ate sugar, we wanted to choose to eat sugar and not eat it because it was included in our ketchup or pasta sauce. If we ate salt, we wanted to season our food with it, not digest it because it was used as a preservative in our soup. We wanted to give our bodies food it could use and not chemicals that would be deposited as fat because our bodies didn't know what to do with them. We wanted to nourish our bodies so we could live an active life. Essentially, we wanted to eat to live, and not live to eat. And of course, we wanted to enjoy our food as much as possible.

Taking Steps Toward a Cleaner Life

The ideal story would be that we cleaned out our pantry and quit processed foods cold turkey. And for some of you, that could be your reality. In our reality, however, we took more than a year to fully transition to a clean diet.

I was determined to set myself up for success. I knew that for me, if I quit processed foods cold turkey, three things would happen:

1. It would be harder than I thought, and I would get crabby.

2. I would link my crabby mood with this new way of life and resent it.

3. After days of crabbiness and resentment, I would quit.

I was determined not to quit. I knew I had to find a way to make this "diet" a new way of life. I wasn't looking for a quick fix or wanting to lose weight. I wanted a healthier life.

Manatee and I approached this change in stages. As I mentioned, we already didn't eat many premade dinners, but I was a sucker for low-calorie frozen meals. We finished what we had, and that was the end. We eliminated bottled salad dressings, even the organic ones. I eliminated diet soda right away, too.

At this point, we also became more strategic in our shopping. If we bought something packaged (like salsa or hummus), we read labels and bought only foods that had all real-food ingredients. If anything convinced us we were making the right choice in cleaning up our diets, this was it. I dare you to start reading labels of foods you consider healthy. If you can't picture the ingredient, put the item back on the shelf and walk away. I talk about this more in the next chapter, but I can't impress this on you enough: *when you read labels, you become aware of how much of our food is made up of nonfood items.*

At this stage, we also eliminated any granola or cereal bars, as well as any packaged sweets. I stopped buying white flour and switched to whole-wheat flours. After we got through that stage, we eliminated chips, crackers, and other "snack-y" things. This is when I really started experimenting with homemade versions and clean eating became fun. As you'll see in this cookbook, there's so much you can make and it's so much easier than you think. It tastes much better, too!

Our final stage was cereal. We were cereal-a-holics. We loved our high-fiber cereal with frozen berries. Even though we were eating a fiber-rich meal, we were always hungry mid-morning and often felt too full after breakfast. After replacing cereal with real food and protein-packed smoothies, we were fuller longer and felt better overall than ever before.

As you move toward a whole-foods diet, I recommend creating a strategy. On one hand, by shocking your system with the complete elimination, you'll see a drastic difference in how you feel (for the better!), and that could help you keep up the momentum. On the other hand, think about this as a long-term way of life, not a crash diet. What items will be the easiest for you to eliminate? What items will be the hardest? How quickly will you adjust to a new life without your old processed favorite? What real-food substitutes can you find or make yourself? When you get used to not having something, move on to the next. Remember, this is not a race to the finish, but a gradual build toward a healthier life.

Cleaning Up Your Taste Buds

Eating clean is a lot like falling in love: apples taste sweeter, lettuce is crisper, and spices become a flavor punch. When you don't have artificial sweeteners and chemicals screwing with your taste buds, food tastes so much better.

In their book, *Real Food Has Curves,* Mark Scarbrough and Bruce Weinstein challenge their readers to compare the fake foods to real foods. When you start doing these comparisons, you realize how your taste buds have been fooled. Fake food counterparts are cheap exaggerations of the real food. Compare the eerily smooth packaged peanut butter to real peanut butter (which you can make in less than 5 minutes), and you'll see how the two aren't even in the same league. Packaged, chemically laden yogurt isn't even remotely as rich and decadent as homemade yogurt. In fact, I didn't even realize I liked yogurt until I made it myself. (I share a few terrific recipes in Chapter 3.)

When you eliminate artificial sweeteners from your diet, everything—and I mean *everything*—tastes so much sweeter. I was a self-proclaimed cereal-a-holic before, but now, I can't even eat packaged cereals anymore. Even the so-called "healthy" versions taste overly sweetened. You'll taste sweetness in crackers, breads, and other items that used to be savory. Packaged sweets will taste cloyingly, mouth-puckeringly sweet. When you get to the desserts section of this book, you'll see that I've reduced the amount of sweeteners in all my desserts, even the ice cream.

When you clean up your diet, your taste buds are sharpened and you don't need as much sugar or extra flavoring.

Counter Calorie Counting

When you start eating real food and become more attuned with your body, you can say good-bye to counting calories. You'll be fueling your body with fresh produce, whole grains, and lean proteins. You can start to trust your body's signals to let you know when to stop eating, and the new whole foods will keep you feeling satisfied longer. Your body has an "off" switch when you fuel it with whole foods. In the past, you may have scraped the bottom of your low-fat yogurt container and then ached for more. Now, you'll be able to eat less and enjoy what you eat more. Think about this way: how many cookies can you eat in one sitting to feel satisfied? How many apples? My guess is you'll reach your limit of apples long before you reach your limit of cookies.

In the recipes in this book, I encourage you to use the full-fat versions of everything (dairy products, mayonnaise, peanut butter, breads). When food manufacturers take out the fat, they replace it with sugar and chemicals that fool your taste buds and your body. You may crave more of reduced-fat foods because they won't be as satisfying—and you may think you "deserve" more because you chose a low-fat version. Whole foods are a treat, and that's how you should view them. Choose real food that will satisfy you, and you'll eat less and be happier.

Because of my strong feelings on this subject, I refuse to include nutrition information with the recipes in this book. Stop counting calories, and start enjoying your food. Trust the body you're working so hard to nourish.

As you move toward your real-food way of life, take time to really enjoy what you're putting your mouth. Don't gobble it down in a rush. Don't inhale it. Taste it. Savor it. Relish it. Your body will give you clues.

As Manatee likes to say, always end the meal a little hungry because who knows what treat will appear in the next few hours. Will I break out the homemade ice cream? Want him to sample a new sauce? If you think of ending a meal a little hungry, you'll find that by the time your mind catches up to your stomach, you'll be at the perfect level of satiety.

Keep your body—and your mind—open to the possibilities.

Dare to Come Clean

 2

You've made the decision to come clean, and you want processed foods out of your diet. But now what you do? How do you even begin to get started on this journey?

In this chapter, I share some clean-eating survival tips—everything from where to get started; to the importance of defining what clean eating means to you; to some practical matters like how to stock a "clean" pantry, approach shopping and social situations, and make some easy whole-food substitutions.

Living in the Moment

First, don't scare yourself or overwhelm yourself with this decision. Yes, you want to make a lifestyle change, but rather than think, *I'm never going to eat processed foods again for as long as I live!* approach it on a moment-to-moment basis. It can be scary to think you'll never have your beloved chips again. At least, I know it was for me.

Instead, make every time you put something in your mouth a conscious choice. Right now, at this moment, I choose carrots and hummus instead of chips. I choose them because I know I'll feel better about myself mentally and physically for making this one healthy choice. Moments add up to a lifetime.

If you slip up and go for the potato chips (it happens!), you haven't thrown your clean-eating lifestyle completely down the drain. There will be another moment when you can make a clean choice.

Defining Your Clean-Eating Diet

A whole-foods diet is one filled with real food. To clean up your diet, you need to remove processed foods. Sounds easy, right?

When I first went clean and told people about it, I tried to describe it by saying I didn't eat anything that came in a box or a bag. Then I had people ask about things like brown rice, spinach, or apples—and they weren't being smart alecks. Now I'm a little more careful with my description.

For me, clean eating is eating whole foods or foods made with whole foods. In a perfect world, I make everything myself: hummus, salsa, pasta, condiments, and bread. In reality, there are times when I do buy one of these items, but I buy items only when I can read the ingredient list and picture all the ingredients in my mind and all the ingredients are whole foods. Essentially, I look for the shortest ingredient lists possible. When you start seeing nonessential ingredients added to a food, you have to starting asking yourself why they're needed.

In my version of clean eating, I choose not to eat any premade crackers or chips. When I started reading the ingredient lists for these items, I was shocked at the hidden dairy and sugar products, even with the supposedly organic and "healthy" versions. I made similar discoveries about jarred pasta sauces. I don't eat white flour either, in any form. Because of this, it's just easier to make my own tortillas and bread. I also don't eat any packaged bars, cookies, or any other snacky food. These are my choices.

At its heart, a whole-foods diet is just that: a diet comprised of all whole foods. In some ways, I'm stricter than other clean eaters, and some clean eaters would be shocked at some of the things I do eat. Everyone has the right to define clean eating for him- or herself. With the baseline set on whole foods, how will you define it?

Cleaning House: Foods to Phase Out

In this book, I show you how to make clean versions of your favorite processed foods. Once you've tried these recipes, you'll see just how easy it is to make your own snacks and pantry staples.

If you're particularly worried about a certain food, try that recipe before you phase out the processed version. After you experience how much better the whole-food version tastes and how easy it is to make, you won't look back at your processed way of eating.

HAVE SOME CHIPS!

I will never look at bagged tortilla chips again. If you're a chip fan, go directly to Chapter 10 and make a batch of Baked Tortilla Chips. You may want to snack on them as you read the rest of this chapter.

Cleaning Out Your Pantry

The rest of the book is about all the great food you can eat, but for now let's talk about what you should phase out. Go through your pantry and find all those premade snacks and bars. Donate them to a food pantry, give them to a neighbor, or simply finish what you have and don't buy any more.

Find all your premade sauces, and read the ingredients. Do they contain chemicals? Unnecessary sugars? Gone and gone.

Do you have a bag of all-purpose flour? Don't be fooled by the packaging.

What your body sees is a bag of sugar. White flour and white sugar are simple carbohydrates: the body breaks them down quickly, blood sugar spikes, and then it crashes. You get a rush of energy, and just as quickly, it comes down, leaving you tired, hungry, and crabby afterward. You don't want that to happen in your new clean, lifestyle. Finish the flour, give it to a neighbor, or use it for flouring pans for baking. Just don't put it in recipes.

Let me know how that is. I feel very strongly that people need to see that white flour is incredibly similar to white sugar. This is a cornerstone of clean eating as defined by Tosca Reno. You may be see it as an overstatement, but I can't stress it enough. I worked really hard to eliminate white flour from all of the recipes (including pasta!), I'm really proud of that, and I did that because I do have an agenda with white flour. I don't think people should be eating it, and definitely not cooking with it. Got diet soda? Or any artificially sweetened carbonated drink? Get rid of it. Pass it off to your friends, take it to the office, or create a new bowling game with the bottles. Just don't drink it. I give you plenty of water alternatives in Chapter 17.

Cleaning Out Your Freezer and Fridge

Take a look at your freezer. You're going to need to get rid of all those frozen dinners, tater tots, artificially sweetened ice-cream treats, and meals in a bag because you'll need room for your home-made sauces (Chapter 4), pasta (Chapter 3), and of course, ice cream (Chapter 16).

Let's move on to the fridge. If you're like me, you may have more condiments in it than actual food. Look at the labels, if you dare, but I'm afraid that shock will lead to disgust. Who knew that salty sauces needed high-fructose corn syrup? Do you have low-fat dairy products? You're better off with the full-fat versions. Remember, when manufacturers 86 the fat, they replace it with sugar and chemicals. Trust me, the fat is the least of these evils. Fat satisfies you so you eat less and feel more indulgent. And wait until you see my homemade yogurt recipes (Chapter 3). You'll never load your shopping cart with those little plastic containers again.

Shopping Clean: Reading Labels

Believe it or not, shopping is about to get a whole lot easier. When you shop clean, the grocery store becomes smaller. You spend the majority of your time on the perimeter of the store and venture occasionally into the aisles for some whole-food items such as brown rice, quinoa, whole-wheat flour, etc.

On your first few trips as a clean shopper, allow yourself more time to shop, and actually read the labels on your favorite premade, processed goodies. Study the ingredient lists and see what you're *not* missing when you eat clean. Compare those labels with the recipes in this book. Do any of the flavored boxed crackers have five or fewer ingredients? Do you know what all the ingredients are? What about that bag of chips? Any of those have three or fewer ingredients?

After you've spent some time reading the labels, you discover that your options are greatly reduced. The rows of bright plastic packaging lose their siren call once you know what's actually in them.

YOUR NEW FAVORITE STORES

As you set out on your whole-food journey, explore new grocery stores in your area. Stores like Whole Foods, Trader Joe's, and Fresh Market offer shoppers more organic and clean-eating options. Remember that just because you're at a "healthy" store doesn't make everything in there fair game. Keep reading those labels!

I couldn't believe how much easier shopping became when we started eating clean. I could avoid so much of the store. And it's funny: the store seems much less crowded when you aren't going through the aisles of processed foods.

Stocking Your Clean Kitchen

I've spent a lot of time talking about what you *can't* eat, but rest assured I am going to spend a lot more time talking about what you *can* eat. In this section, I've included lists for some of the staple ingredients you'll be using to make all this incredible, clean food.

In Your Pantry

I'll share a handy pantry shopping list in a second, but first, let's talk ingredients. When stocking your clean pantry, change your focus from snacks and premade food to raw ingredients. These raw ingredients enable you to make a huge variety of real-food snacks and meals.

I've included a lot of flours in my shopping list, and each type lends itself to a different end product or purpose. Whole-wheat pastry flour replaces all-purpose flour in most recipes. Spelt flour is a nutty, whole-grain flour, perfect for homemade graham crackers (Chapter 14). Corn flour is perfect for homemade corn tortillas (Chapter 3) and for some of the spice blends (Chapter 7).

There's a wide world of sweeteners out there, and as you start to cook with agave nectar, honey, and maple syrup, you'll start to gravitate to one over the other. I tend to favor agave nectar because it doesn't spike blood sugar like its counterparts. I look for raw versions when at all possible.

THE BEST OF BOTH WORLDS

Sucanat is pure dried cane sugar. It has the nuttiness and molasses taste of brown sugar but the texture of white sugar. You can find it in the baking aisle by the sugar.

For the dry versions of sweeteners, sucanat is one of my favorites. It has the nuttiness of brown sugar but produces the same crisping and browning qualities as regular sugar. In some cases, you'll need a white sugar, and I encourage you to find the least-processed one available. Evaporated cane juice is my top pick, but it may be hard to find. Look for organic, unprocessed sugar in your regular grocery store. You can also buy these sweeteners online.

I use all parts of the coconut in clean cooking. There's no substitute for rich and salty coconut butter when it comes to making ice cream (Chapter 16). I'm never without a couple cans of coconut milk. It's great for dairy-free frostings (Chapter 15) and ice cream (Chapter 16).

I can't live without peanut butter, so I keep peanuts on hand at all times. If you can find dry-roasted unsalted peanuts in the bulk aisle, that's your best bet, but dry-roasted and lightly salted peanuts work in a pinch. Once you make your own peanut butter and see how easy it is (Chapter 6), you will never go for store-bought again.

I love having a variety of oils on hand. Like sweeteners, you'll gravitate to certain oils over others. I use a lot of canola and olive oil when I cook. Walnut oil adds a nutty flavor to your cooking. Coconut oil is great to use as a cooking oil because it has a high burning (or smoking) point. When oils reach their burning point, they start to smoke and oxidize—not good for you. Grapeseed oil is a heart-healthy, mild-tasting oil that also has a high burning point, so it's great for making homemade, baked potato chips or fries (Chapter 10).

Now, here's a list of whole-food ingredients to have on hand for the recipes in this book:

Flours and grains:

Whole-wheat pastry flour

Whole-wheat flour

Whole-wheat bread flour

Spelt flour

Corn flour

Quinoa

Popcorn kernels

Rolled oats

Brown rice

Sweeteners:

Agave nectar

Honey

Maple syrup (only the real stuff!)

Unsweetened applesauce

Unprocessed sugars: sucanat, evaporated cane juice

Oils:

Coconut oil

Canola or grapeseed oil

Extra-virgin olive oil

Vinegars:

White wine vinegar

Red wine vinegar

Apple cider vinegar

Balsamic vinegar

Other natural packaged foods:

Coconut milk

Coconut butter

Unsweetened coconut flakes

Roasted, unsalted, shelled peanuts

Sun-dried tomatoes (not packed in oil)

Canned beans (chickpea, kidney, black beans)

In the Refrigerator

Like the pantry, your fridge will hold your raw ingredients. And later, you'll fill it with all your homemade goodies.

Go full fat for your dairy products (milk and cheese), and try out some dairy alternatives. When buying almond and soy milk, look for unsweetened versions.

Here's what to look for for your refrigerator:

Whole milk

Full-fat cheeses

Unsweetened almond milk or soymilk

Fresh veggies (broccoli, lettuce, spinach, mushrooms, carrots, celery, sweet peppers)

Fresh fruit (apples, oranges, berries, melons)

Tofu (organic, non-GMO)

In the Freezer

It might seem odd to store nuts in your freezer, but this keeps them from going rancid. At any given time, you can find walnuts, almonds (whole, sliced, and slivered), and pecans in our freezer. Rolled oats stay fresh longer when stored in the freezer as well.

Here are some other ingredients you can keep in your freezer:

Raw nuts

Frozen fruit

Frozen veggies

Rolled oats

Frozen lean meat, poultry, and seafood wrapped in individual packages

Buying Fresh, Buying Local

Fresh is best, so if you live in an area that offers community supported agriculture (CSA) programs or hosts farmers' markets, you definitely should take advantage of these resources for fresh, delicious food.

A CSA is a program that allows you to buy shares of a local farmer's crop. Each week, every other week, or every month, you receive a share of what has recently been harvested. By joining a CSA, you support the farmer by paying a set price every week. In turn, you reap their harvest. There's an assumed risk with CSAs: if the crop is bad, your share may be small. But if the crop is good, your share is bigger.

For most CSAs, you don't get to hand-pick what goes in your box. This exposes you to new fruits and veggies you might have never seen before. Often, farms will also include some sample recipes and basic handling information to help you with the new produce.

In addition to supporting local farmers through thick and thin, I love CSAs because at heart, I am a very lazy person. Yes, I know I should eat seasonally, but how do I know what's in season, and what if I lack a green thumb and can't grow my own? I can go to farmers' markets, but I can't always make it at the appointed times. And let's say I do get to the store and know what's in season. I don't know about you, but I have a tendency to gravitate toward the same types of produce again and again (broccoli, tomatoes, peppers). With a CSA share, I don't have to think. I just pick it up and make the most of it. I am also introduced to produce I never would have placed in my grocery basket. It cuts down on my grocery shopping time (and often money), the produce couldn't be fresher, and I'm exposed to a greater variety of fruits and vegetables.

Not sure whether your city has a CSA? Check out the LocalHarvest CSA website, localharvest.org/csa, to find a CSA near you.

Farmers' markets are another great way to support local farmers and get high-quality produce. Farmers' markets are becoming more and more popular across the country, in cities big and small. When you go, try to make friends with the sellers. Talk to them about their crops, get their tips on preparation, and ask questions. People love to talk about themselves, and the same goes for farmers. They are a wealth of information. Learn from them!

Keeping It Clean When Out and About

As much as I would love to think that the entire world is going to start eating clean, the fact is that most people eat C.R.A.P.—*c*arbonated drinks like soda, *r*efined sugars, *a*rtificial sweeteners and colors, and *p*rocessed foods. So how can you, as a clean-eater, navigate the junk food–saturated world around you?

Parties, dinners out, meeting friends at bars—most social situations involve food in some way, shape, or form. In the following sections, I share some tips for handling the most common social eating situations.

At Potlucks and Parties

When going to a potluck or a party, offer to bring a clean dish to share. Few hosts turn down help with food. And you know you at least have one food you can eat and feel good about.

You may even turn some more people on to clean eating. You won't believe how impressed people are when you bring Baked Tortilla Chips or Baked Pita Chips (Chapter 10) to a party. Little do they know how easy they are to make!

At Restaurants

There are two main strategies for going out to restaurants. First, scan the menu and look for clean offerings, such as steamed veggies, grilled meats, and whole grains. Second, don't be afraid to ask for customization. Use your head with this. If you're at a four-star restaurant, the chef might be a little insulted if you start telling her how to cook the food. But in most situations, if you ask nicely, you'll be surprised at how accommodating people can be.

Do a quick scan of the menu to get an idea of the ingredients the restaurant has on hand. For example, if it serves a grilled chicken sandwich but doesn't offer grilled chicken on a salad, it's probably safe to assume the chef could take that grilled chicken breast and put it on a salad.

One key to this strategy is asking *nicely*. Also, be sure to reward your server for his or her help when you tip. Then, if you go back, he or she will be glad to help you again.

Being a Houseguest

When staying with other people while traveling, Manatee and I often either bring some of our favorites or spring for a small grocery trip if we're staying for multiple days. We always share our goodies with our hosts, who are usually happy they don't have to worry about finding food for us.

That way, we don't worry about eating them out of produce—or in Manatee's case, eating them out of fresh spinach and lettuce.

Clean Eating and Kids

When kids enter the picture, a whole-foods diet can seem a little intimidating. Here are some tips to help keep your whole family on track:

Focus on foods your kids like. Are they huge fans of pizza? Schedule a regular pizza night when you make the pizzas yourself. Wheat Tortillas (recipe in Chapter 3) make great thin crust, personalized pizzas, and your kids will love picking out their own toppings.

Make it easy. If weeknights are hectic with practices and extracurricular activities, use your shortcuts. Buy precut veggies you can steam in the bag, or cook chicken over the weekend to throw on salads or make into a chicken salad on a busy night.

When in doubt, make a dip. Kids love dipping things. Turn to Chapter 11 for some fun dips that will make veggies more fun to eat.

Talk it out. While you're enjoying your whole-foods goodies, make it a point to talk to your kids about how much better the real-food version tastes and then bring up how much healthier it is for them. Stress how important it is to your kids to fuel their bodies with good food.

No matter how careful you are with what you feed them at home, you can't control your kids all the time. To a certain degree, you have to let go and understand that a stray cheese puff might make it into their mouths. But let's be honest—a stray cheese puff might make its way into *your* mouth as well. Don't stress about it. One cheese puff does not a lifestyle disrail. If you've been eating clean 90 percent of the time, that cheese puff might make you or your child feel a little ill. Help connect the dots for your children: when you eat junk food, you often feel like junk. They'll catch on.

Clean-Cooking Substitutions

You can convert most recipes to clean recipes easily. The following table gives some common 1:1 substitutions for your favorite recipes.

Instead of This ...	Use This ...
All-purpose flour	Whole-wheat pastry flour or a combination of whole-wheat pastry flour and spelt flour
Oils (in baking)	Applesauce/Apple Butter (recipe in Chapter 6)/Pumpkin Butter (recipe in Chapter 6)
White sugar	Unprocessed sugar or honey (1:1)
Margarine	Unsalted butter
Regular pasta	Whole-wheat pasta or quinoa pasta (gluten-free)
White rice or jasmine rice	Brown or wild rice

Eating Whole Foods in a Processed World

We live in a world of food temptations. Once you start eating clean, many of those foods won't tempt you anymore. But no one's perfect. You might still be tempted on occasion, and yes, you may give in to those temptations.

This is not a fire-and-brimstone type of diet. A lightning bolt will not come out of the sky and strike you dead if you eat a potato chip or drink a diet soda. In all likelihood, something much worse will happen: you'll feel awful after you eat it. Not from the guilt, but physically, you'll probably feel a little sick or bloated or get that awful feeling when your mouth feels like it's covered in fuzz because something was so sweet. When you commit yourself to a clean-eating diet and then have a processed "treat," you'll be reminded why you stopped eating those foods. It's okay to eat unclean sometimes. If anything, it serves as a reminder of why you choose to eat clean.

On occasion, I have a diet soda. I may not instantly regret it, but at some point in the day, I do. Sometimes, I notice I'm bloated or I just don't feel well. Or when I'm laying wide awake in bed at 2 o'clock in the morning, I remember that half a soda I drank in the afternoon. I curse my earlier behavior and then stop drinking it for a few more months (until I forget about how awful I felt last time).

I think these slip-ups are essential to a successful change in lifestyle. If you vow to never let a diet soda touch your lips again, the extremeness of that opinion will make diet soda the forbidden fruit and drive you back to it. Or if you do slip up and have a sip, you might go to the other extreme— you've already broke your "diet," so why stop now? Remember, you have a choice every moment you put something in your mouth. Take time to think about that choice. How will you feel if you eat or drink it? Physically? Mentally? Emotionally? Make the choice, live with it, and move on.

Instituting a whole-foods diet is a long process. Have patience with yourself and enjoy the journey. The recipes in this book will help you as you transition from all your processed favorites to your new homemade favorites. Shopping will become easier. Food will taste better. And you'll be shocked at how many things you can make from scratch with real, whole-food ingredients.

Staples, Sauces, and Spices 2

Consider Part 2 your arsenal for your new whole-food diet. In the next five chapters, you learn how to make all the basics with real food ingredients.

First, I start you off with everything you need to have in your pantry, from whole-grain bread to pasta to tortillas, and even yogurt. You learn how much you can do with just a few ingredients, some patience, and a few new tricks. Then I cover the basic sauces you can make that will taste better than anything you can find in a jar—*and* save you a ton of money at the grocery store. Say good-bye to that jar of overpriced, overprocessed marinara sauce and hello to sweet simplicity.

Next, I share recipes for all your favorite go-to dressings (French, Thousand Island, Ranch, Italian) plus a few fun vinaigrettes for special occasions. I also give you recipes for super spreads, including a recipe that's near and dear to me: Peanut Butter. You also learn how to make some basic preserves and fun butters.

The last chapter in Part 2 explains how to customize your own spice blends and really take ownership in the kitchen. You learn how to make Italian seasonings and some fun sweet spices you'll use throughout the recipes in this book.

Make Your Own Staples  3

The subheading for this chapter should be "It's easier than you think!" When I started making my own staples, I couldn't believe how easy it was and how much better all my cooking tasted than the commercial versions I'd bought for years.

Of all the chapters in this book, I feel like this is the most intimidating. It's so easy to buy a bag of tortillas, a carton of yogurt, or a loaf of bread. Why take the time to make it? My response: why not?

When you make your own staple ingredients, you have complete control over what's going into your body. There are no added chemicals or preservatives, just real-food ingredients. You also can flavor your staples to go best with the dishes you'll use them in. And if complete control and customized flavor didn't close the deal, how about if I told you you would save a ton of money by DIYing it?

Pasta

For a long time, I thought it would be too hard to make my own pasta. Then I thought I couldn't make it because I'd have to use white flour. Now I regret the years wasted eating dry, tasteless commercially made pasta.

Making your own pasta is so easy—and fun! All you need is a food processor and a hand-crank pasta machine. The pasta has a richer, nuttier taste than anything you can buy in a store, and although it takes some time to make, when you're finished, the fresh pasta cooks in just a few minutes.

Bread

I've had a long, complicated relationship with bread-making. I've had loaves rise right off the pan and loaves that remained an inch high after rising. I've had beautiful loaves of bread and loaves of bread even a mother couldn't love. I've killed the innocent yeast in just about any way possible and then wondered why my bread was so dense. After exhausting all the ways to mess it up, I finally found the answer to foolproof homemade bread: Jim Lahey's no-knead method.

The problem with kneading the dough is that there are far too many variables at play. You don't fully learn how to do it without lots of experience. And until you get the experience, you're gambling with each batch. I don't know about you, but I don't have time to gamble with cooking.

All you need for Jim Lahey's method of no-knead bread is time. Time to let the bread rise, time to let all the chemistry happen, and time to enjoy what it means to prepare and eat real food.

After sharing my whole-grain version of a Jim Lahey bread, which I recommend you make in a Dutch oven, I've included some recipes to do with leftover bread. This bread doesn't contain preservatives, so it'll grow stale in a few days. Luckily, the croutons and breadcrumbs will make you crave leftover bread.

THE DUTCH OVEN

A Dutch oven is a heavy, covered pot that's essential in a clean-eating kitchen. When making bread, the Dutch oven acts as an oven within an oven and heats the bread so the crust is crusty and the rest of the bread is doughy and light.

Refrigerator Pickles

There's nothing like biting into a freshly picked cucumber, or a cuke from your local farmers' market. I've been known to nosh on raw cucumbers in the car, unable to wait to get home. I love them.

As much as I love cucumbers, I didn't even know you could make pickles until I was an adult. Even then, I associated pickling with canning, a process I've decided God does not want me to do (although I'm sure it's very easy for *other* people to do).

When Manatee and I were first married, I bought all the equipment necessary for canning and a home-preserving bible. Manatee laughed, and I got mad. I was determined to can. Then, I started reading about it. There were so many warnings, I was intimidated before I even began.

Two years later, I became determined to can ketchup. I had 100 tomatoes, and darn it, I was going to make ketchup. I cooked. I puréed. I strained. I simmered. My finished ketchup had the consistency of water. I stormed. I swore. I sobbed. I threw things. Still water—flavorful tomato water, but water nonetheless.

Determined to save the day, I decided I wouldn't give up on canning. When I went to put the canning rack in the pot, it wasn't even close to fitting. I wrestled. I finagled. I pressed. Finally, I did what I should have done 8 hours earlier: I laughed. Thank goodness you can make amazing pickles in the refrigerator, because I gave up on canning.

There's also no rule saying you have to pickle only cucumbers. Experiment with green beans, peppers, carrots, and cauliflower. After you finish making the cucumber pickles in this chapter, throw in some other veggies to see how they taste. Why waste good pickle juice?

CHOOSING YOUR CUKES

In an ideal world, you'd use small, pickling cucumbers to make your pickles. The taste will be more concentrated. I've never been able to find this platonic produce ideal, however. Instead, I get regular cucumbers and slice them into discs, or I get small (supposedly) seedless cucumbers and cut them into strips. Look for cucumbers that are firm to the touch and not shriveled on the ends.

Yogurt

I never liked yogurt until I made my own. You can't even imagine how the recipe in this chapter eclipses any premade yogurt you've eaten before. Of all the recipes in this book, I think the yogurt recipe appears the most intimidating—and I'm from Wisconsin. You'd think this whole dairy thing would be in my blood. Yet I was so sure I couldn't do it.

After prepping it at night, I was scared to get up the next morning. I was sure I was going to have a bowl of watery, smelly milk. How wrong I was! When I saw the creamy yogurt waiting for me in the oven, it was all I could do to not run around the neighborhood showing off my yogurt. Let's be honest: if I had thought my neighbors were awake, I probably would have done it.

The yogurt in this chapter is so easy to make and will save you so much money. And may I mention again that it tastes completely out of this world? Forget all the fancy equipment. All you need is a heavy-bottomed saucepan, a casserole dish with cover, a dishtowel, a thermometer, and a whole lot of patience and faith.

Depending on how long you strain the yogurt, you can make a creamy Greek Yogurt or a dense Yogurt Cheese (similar to cream cheese). You'll find these recipes in this chapter, too.

Basic Whole-Wheat Pasta

For this pasta, it's important to use whole-wheat flour as opposed to whole-wheat pastry flour or another flour blend. Given the amount of liquids in the recipe, the dough will be too wet and sticky unless you use whole-wheat flour.

Yield:	Prep time:	Cook time:	Serving size:
4 cups	1 hour	5 minutes	1 cup

2 cups whole-wheat flour	1 TB. olive oil
¾ tsp. salt	1 or 2 TB. warm water
2 large eggs	

1. Set up a lightly floured work area on your counter or a silicone mat.

2. In a food processor fitted with a chopping blade, pulse together whole-wheat flour and salt.

3. With the food processor running, crack 1 egg into a small bowl, and add egg to the food processor. Repeat with second egg.

4. With the food processor still running, add olive oil and 1 tablespoon warm water. Keep mixing until dough forms. If needed, add second tablespoon warm water.

5. Transfer dough to your workspace, and knead for 1 or 2 minutes or until you can form dough into a smooth ball. Cover dough with plastic wrap, and let sit for 30 minutes.

6. Meanwhile, set up a pasta rack (if using) or a clean dishtowel.

7. After dough has rested for 30 minutes, tear it into 2 pieces. Set 1 piece back under the plastic wrap, and shape the other half into a rectangle that will fit (width-wise) through your pasta machine.

8. Set the pasta machine to its biggest setting (1) and run dough through the machine according to the manufacturer's instructions. After the initial run, lightly sprinkle flour on dough and fold it in half. Change the setting to (2), and run dough through again. Change the setting to (3), and run dough through again. Continue until you reach the desired thickness.

9. To cut dough, run it through your pasta machine's cutting attachment or loosely roll dough into a cylinder and use a knife to cut into the desired shape.

10. To dry pasta, hang it on a pasta rack (if using), or place it on a dishtowel and lightly dust it with flour. Be sure no pieces are touching each other.

11. Repeat steps 8 and 9 with remaining pasta dough. Let noodles dry for 10 to 15 minutes. If you're not going to use pasta right away, you can either dry it by letting it sit out at room temperature overnight or freezing it (see the following sidebar for more information).

12. To cook pasta, bring 3 or 4 quarts water to a rolling boil in a large saucepan over medium-high heat. Add pasta, and cook for 2 or 3 minutes or until noodles are done.

FREEZING HOMEMADE PASTA

To freeze the pasta, line a plate or baking sheet with parchment paper. After drying the pasta for 20 to 30 minutes, place it in bundles of your desired serving size on the plate or baking sheet. Freeze for 1 to 3 hours until partially frozen. Remove frozen pasta from the plate or baking sheet and place in zipper-lock freezer bags. Don't forget to add a label and date to the bag. Freeze the pasta for up to 1 month.

Basic Bread

In this recipe, I've taken Jim Lahey's process and created a whole-grain version. Commercial bread contains white, highly processed flour. By adding vital wheat gluten to your bread, you get the gluten you need without giving up your dreams of whole-grain bread. The spelt flour provides a nutty texture and taste, while the bread flour gives the bread the rise it needs to look like those gorgeous artisanal loaves you see in European bakeries. The rise time can vary due to many factors, including the temperature of your house, the humidity, or the freshness of the yeast. After you've made bread a few times, you'll get a sense of the rhythm of the rise.

Yield:	Prep time:	Cook time:	Serving size:
1 (8×4×-3-inch) loaf	15 minutes, plus 20 to 26 hours rest time	45 to 50 minutes	1 slice

2 cups spelt flour

1 cup whole-wheat bread flour

2 TB. vital wheat gluten

½ tsp. active yeast

1 tsp. salt

1½ to 2 cups water

1. In a medium bowl, whisk together spelt flour, whole-wheat bread flour, vital wheat gluten, active yeast, and salt. Add water slowly, and stir with a wooden spoon. Dough should be wet and sticky, not soupy.

2. Cover the bowl with plastic wrap, and place pieces of tape on the outside of the bowl at the same level as dough. This helps you gauge how much dough has risen.

3. Place dough in a draft-free spot, and let it sit for 18 to 24 hours. Dough is ready when it has roughly doubled in size, and top of dough is darkened and/or has bubbles on the surface.

4. To prepare for the second rise, dust your workspace with flour and lay out a clean, plain flour sack dishtowel next to your workspace. Dust the towel with flour.

5. Remove dough from the bowl using a rubber spatula. Form dough into a small ball, tucking under the edges. Place dough on the towel, with the seams down. Continue to tuck dough into a tight ball. Lightly sprinkle dough with flour, and wrap in the towel. Let sit for 1½ to 2½ hours or until dough has doubled in size.

6. Preheat the oven to 475°F. Place dough in a covered Dutch oven in the preheated oven, and bake for 30 minutes.

7. Remove the Dutch oven. Place dough in the Dutch oven, cover, and set the Dutch oven back in the oven. Bake for 30 minutes.

8. Uncover Dutch oven, and bake for 15 to 20 more minutes or until top of bread is a dark, golden brown.

9. Transfer bread to a cooling rack, and resist all urges to cut bread while it cools. You'll hear bread crack as air bubbles release and dough finishes cooking. When the cracking has ceased and bread is room temperature to the touch, slice and enjoy.

10. Wrap in a paper bag or waxed paper. If you store in a plastic bag, bread will become soggy and lose crispness. Store in the refrigerator or at room temperature.

BREAD-BAKING NOTES

I've tried baking bread with many different kinds of flour. No matter how much gluten you add or strange combinations of ingredients you include, you need bread flour. Bread flour has extra protein, and that protein is what helps your bread rise. Without it, you can still get great-tasting bread, but it'll be flat as a pancake (and a thick, dense, chewy pancake at that!). Whole-wheat bread flour is the best option, but it's hard to find. I order mine online. You can substitute white bread flour. This is the one case where it's okay to substitute white bread flour. If you use white bread flour, you can reduce the vital wheat gluten to 1 tablespoon. Spelt flour has properties similar to all-purpose flour and is a great whole-grain alternative. If you don't have spelt flour available, substitute whole-wheat flour and add 1 more tablespoon vital wheat gluten. When you use whole-grain flours, you need to give your bread dough a little nudge, and that nudge comes from vital wheat gluten. Vital wheat gluten is another form of the protein found in the bread flours. You can find vital wheat gluten by the yeast in the baking section of the grocery store, in natural food stores, or online. And then there's yeast. When I buy yeast, I always freezer-tape a label on the jar and write down the date I opened it. After 4 months, the yeast will no longer be good and your bread may mysteriously stop rising, so it's time to get new yeast.

Croutons

Homemade bread has a limited shelf life. If you can't eat it all before it loses its freshness, don't let any of those gorgeous grains go to waste. Make croutons! Croutons are perfect to dress up salads or pop as a quick snack. Plus, they're so easy to make, you'll never want a premade crouton again. By removing the crusts, the bread will soak up more of the olive oil goodness. But don't throw out those crusts! Save them for the breadcrumb recipe that comes next.

Yield:	Prep time:	Cook time:	Serving size:
3 cups	15 minutes	30 minutes	¼ cup

3 TB. olive oil

¼ tsp. salt

¼ tsp. ground black pepper

3 cups Basic Bread, crusts removed and cut into ½- to 1-in. cubes (about ½ loaf)

1. Preheat the oven to 350°F. Line a rimmed baking sheet with parchment paper or a silicone mat.

2. In a medium bowl, whisk together olive oil, salt, and black pepper. Add Basic Bread cubes, and toss until evenly coated in oil mixture. Spread bread cubes in a single layer on the baking sheet.

3. Bake for 25 to 30 minutes or until croutons are dark brown and crispy.

4. Transfer croutons, still on the parchment paper, to a cooling rack. Croutons will continue to crisp as they cool. Transfer cool croutons to a zipper-lock plastic bag, and store in the pantry for 3 or 4 days. You can also freeze croutons and reheat them in the oven at 200°F for 10 to 15 minutes or until they're warmed through and crispy.

CHEWY OR CRUNCHY?

Feel free to adjust the cook time based on how you like your croutons. Like them a little chewy in the middle? Reduce the cooking time to 15 to 20 minutes. Like them crunchy throughout? Let them cook for the full 30 minutes.

Breadcrumbs

If you've got crusts left over from the Croutons recipe, use them to make breadcrumbs! Store-bought breadcrumbs have too many chemicals for my taste, and making your own is incredibly easy. You can decide whether to keep them soft, perfect for Clean Chicken Nuggets (recipe in Chapter 12), or make them crispy.

Yield:	Prep time:	Cook time:	Serving size:
3 cups	10 minutes	40 minutes	¼ cup

3 cups bread, with crusts, cut in large chunks

2 large cloves garlic, peeled

½ tsp. salt

½ tsp. ground black pepper

2 TB. olive oil

1. If you're making dry breadcrumbs, preheat the oven to 300°F and line a rimmed baking sheet with parchment paper or a silicone mat.

2. In a food processor fitted with a chopping blade, pulse together bread, garlic, salt, and black pepper until mixture resembles coarse meal.

3. Add olive oil, and pulse until breadcrumbs are your desired texture. If you want soft breadcrumbs, you can stop here. Store breadcrumbs in the refrigerator, and use within 3 or 4 days.

4. If you're making dry breadcrumbs, spread breadcrumbs in a single layer on the baking sheet.

5. Bake for 30 to 40 minutes or until breadcrumbs are completely dry. Let cool completely on a cooling rack.

6. If you'd like finer-crumb breadcrumbs, place dried breadcrumbs in a blender and pulse until you reach your desired consistency. Store in a zipper-lock plastic bag in the pantry for up to 1 week or in the freezer for up to 1 month.

Variation: For **Italian Breadcrumbs,** add 1 teaspoon Italian Seasoning (recipe in Chapter 7), reduce garlic to 1 clove, and only use ¼ teaspoon salt.

Whole-Wheat Cake Flour

I love to bake, but Manatee doesn't like baked goods. Although sometimes I feel like we're a match made in heaven, I also feel that we're proof God has a sense of humor. I still bake, and I have become the most popular person at Manatee's office, even though most of his co-workers haven't met me in person. When he walks into the office carrying a pan or a plastic container, people follow him like lemmings to the break room, or so I've been told. The one baked good Manatee does eat—and loves—is angel food cake. The problem? You need cake flour to make a good angel food cake, and cake flour is white flour. I didn't let that stop me. Instead, I came up with my own whole-wheat cake flour mix.

Yield:	Prep time:	Serving size:
1 quart	5 minutes	1 cup

3½ cups whole-wheat pastry flour or whole-wheat flour

½ cup cornstarch

1. In a food processor fitted with a chopping blade, pulse together whole-wheat pastry flour and cornstarch until thoroughly combined.

2. Store in an air-tight container in the pantry for up to 1 month.

Corn Tortillas

Corn tortillas are my favorite pantry staple. Once you've had homemade corn tortillas, there's no going back to those crumbly, thin things you find at the store. I love eating one of my favorite guacamoles (recipes in Chapter 11) in a corn tortilla as a snack, using them for tacos, or having them with eggs in the morning. For this recipe, a tortilla press comes in handy for flattening out the tortillas. They're handy and inexpensive, but you could also use a medium, flat-bottomed bowl in a pinch.

Yield:	Prep time:	Cook time:	Serving size:
12 (6-inch) tortillas	5 minutes	30 minutes	1 tortilla

2 cups corn flour

1 tsp. salt

1 cup warm water

Juice of 2 small limes (¼ cup)

2 TB. canola oil

1. Heat a large skillet over medium-high heat.

2. In a medium bowl, whisk together corn flour and salt.

3. In a small bowl, whisk together warm water, lime juice, and canola oil.

4. Add lime juice mixture to flour mixture, and using a wooden spoon, stir until dough forms.

5. Form dough into a log. Divide dough in half and then in thirds. Divide each third into halves to form 12 small balls, and cover balls with a damp dishtowel.

6. Prepare 2 pieces of wax paper. Dust 1 piece lightly with corn flour, shaking off any excess flour.

7. Place 1 dough ball on 1 piece of wax paper, and cover with the remaining piece. Place dough and wax paper in a tortilla press, and press into a 6-inch circle. Or using a flat-bottomed bowl, apply pressure to form the circle.

8. Carefully peel off wax paper. (I find it easier to peel the wax paper up and off dough instead of trying to peel delicate dough off the wax paper.) This can be the most difficult step, so be patient and gentle with dough.

9. Place tortilla in the hot skillet. Without leaving the skillet, cook tortilla for 2 or 3 minutes or until brown. Use tongs or your fingers to flip over tortilla, and cook for 1 to 3 more minutes or until browned on other side. Remove cooked tortillas to a plate, and repeat with remaining dough.

10. Store tortillas in an airtight container or zipper-lock plastic bag in the refrigerator for 3 or 4 days. If not eating fresh, warm tortillas for 5 to 10 seconds in the microwave to soften them.

COOL DOUGH

If you don't plan to eat all the tortillas in one sitting, you can refrigerate the dough for 2 or 3 days. Store the dough balls in an airtight container with a damp paper towel. Bring to room temperature before pressing.

Wheat Tortillas

I love whole-wheat tortillas, but I'm always shocked and dismayed when I read the ingredient lists. Why do you need so many chemicals? You don't. These tortillas, packed with flavor thanks to the lime juice and salt, are the perfect balance of light, chewy, and moist. They're perfect for stuffing with Clean Taco Filling, making into pizzas, or using them for quesadillas (recipes in Chapter 12). They're just as good with a little butter, Avocado Butter (recipe in Chapter 6), or guacamole (recipes in Chapter 11).

Yield:	Prep time:	Cook time:	Serving size:
8 (8-inch) tortillas	1 hour	45 minutes	1 tortilla

½ cup warm water

¼ cup canola oil

Juice of 2 small limes (¼ cup)

1½ cups whole-wheat pastry flour

1 cup whole-wheat flour

1 tsp. salt

1 tsp. baking powder

1. Set up a lightly floured work area on your counter or a silicone mat.

2. In a small bowl, whisk together warm water, canola oil, and lime juice.

3. In a food processor fitted with a chopping blade, pulse together whole-wheat pastry flour, whole-wheat flour, salt, and baking powder.

4. With the food processor running, pour in lime juice mixture, and mix until dough forms.

5. Transfer dough to your workspace, and knead for 2 or 3 minutes or until air bubbles form.

6. Divide dough in half, and repeat until you have 8 balls. Cover dough balls with plastic wrap, and let sit for 1 hour.

7. Heat a large skillet over medium-high heat.

8. Set 1 dough ball on your workspace, and cover with waxed paper. Using a rolling pin, roll out dough to a 6-inch circle.

10. Carefully peel wax paper off tortilla.

11. Hold your fists up chin-level in the front of you, with your knuckles up and together. Place tortilla on top of your fists, and slowly pull your fists apart to thin dough. Move your fists in small circles away from your body, similar to making a hand-tossed pizza crust. If you prefer a thicker tortilla, you can skip this step.

12. Place tortilla in the hot skillet. Cook for 1 to 3 minutes on each side or until bubbles start to form in tortilla. Err on the side of flipping sooner than later. You can always flip it back to a side. To encourage more bubbles, press down on dough next to a formed air bubble. Remove cooked tortillas to a plate, and repeat with remaining dough.

13. Store tortillas in an airtight container or zipper-lock plastic bag in the refrigerator for 4 or 5 days.

PERFECT TORTILLA POINTERS

To roll dough into a circle, put more pressure on your left side when you roll it out and then put more pressure on your right side when you roll the dough back. This will "rock" the dough into a circle and help you create a perfectly shaped tortilla. When using wax paper, be sure to use a fresh sheet each time, or you may be eating waxy tortillas. Also, the more flour you use to dust your workspace, the more likely your tortillas will burn, so use flour sparingly.

Dill Pickles

Growing up, ours was a family divided. My father, sister, and I liked tangy dill pickles, while my brother and mother favored their sweet cousins. I love the tang of the dill, and luckily, these may just be the easiest pickle to make. No precooking is required. All you need are fresh ingredients infusing the crunchy cucumbers with natural flavors. Whole-food cooking doesn't get any better than this!

Yield:	Prep time:	Marinate time:	Serving size:
2 quarts	15 minutes	24 hours	¼ cup

2 cloves garlic, peeled and halved

1 medium sweet onion, peeled and cut in eighths

¾ cup fresh dill

5 cups cucumbers, ends removed and sliced ¼-in. thick

2 cups boiling water

2 TB. salt

2 TB. sugar

2 TB. whole black peppercorns

1 tsp. ground coriander

1. In the bottom of a quart jar, layer ½ garlic clove, followed by ¼ onion, ¼ dill, and ¼ cucumbers. If you divided the jar into fourths, place dill at every fourth between cucumbers. The layers should be garlic, onion, dill, cucumbers, dill, cucumbers, dill, cucumbers, dill, onion, and garlic.

2. In a small saucepan over medium-high heat, combine water, salt, sugar, black peppercorns, and coriander. Bring to a boil.

3. Pour boiling water over cucumber mixture, and top with additional water if necessary. All cucumbers and fixings should be submerged in water.

4. Cover and seal the jar, and let cool for 30 minutes until at room temperature. Refrigerate for 24 hours and then taste. Store in the refrigerator for up to 3 weeks. (I doubt they'll last that long.)

THE PATIENCE FOR PICKLES

The pickles will taste better if you wait at least 24 hours before you try them. However, Manatee doesn't have the iron-clad willpower I have, so he digs in hours after I make them. He loves them just the same. Patience will pay off, but no one is going to know if you sneak a taste a little early.

Bread-and-Butter Pickles

This recipe is based on a family recipe held by my Aunt Ellen and Uncle Paul. When I called to get the recipe, my uncle began, "Well we're not experts, but we do make the *best* pickles." As you can see, modesty runs in the family. These really are the best pickles I've ever had. I normally don't like pickles that aren't dill, but these balance the sweet and tangy divide with a precision that inspires speeches, poetry, and other great works of art.

Yield:	Prep time:	Marinate time:	Serving size:
2 quarts	3 hours, 10 minutes	24 hours	¼ cup

5 cups cucumbers, sliced in ½-in. slices	2 TB. salt
2 medium sweet onions, peeled and thinly sliced	½ cup unprocessed sugar
	½ cup brown sugar, firmly packed
1 cup water	¼ tsp. ground turmeric
1 cup white vinegar	2 tsp. mustard seeds
	½ tsp. celery seeds

1. Place cucumbers and onions in a colander or strainer, and set the colander in the sink. Cover cucumbers and onions with ice, and let sit for 3 hours. Keep replacing ice as it melts. Unless it's unusually hot, you should have to do this only once or twice. Keep cucumbers and onions covered in ice until you're ready to use them.

2. After 3 hours, in a large saucepan over medium-high heat, whisk together water, white vinegar, salt, unprocessed sugar, brown sugar, turmeric, mustard seeds, and celery seeds, and bring to a boil. Add cucumbers and onions, return to a boil, and remove the saucepan from heat.

3. Place the saucepan on a cooling rack, and let cool for about 2 hours or until room temperature.

4. Transfer pickles to jars, and store in the refrigerator. Pickles will be ready after 24 hours. Store in the refrigerator for up to 3 weeks.

COOLING THE CUKES

Icing the cucumbers and onions makes the finished pickles crisper. I like to cut these pickles into ½-inch-thick slices. I'd err on the side of thicker (up to 1 inch) over thinner any day.

Spicy Pickles

These pickles pack just the right amount of punch, thanks to the crushed red pepper flakes and cayenne. These are Manatee's favorite. A few bites of our first several batches had me running to the sink and putting my head under the faucet because they're so spicy. Be forewarned: there's a fine line between a little warming heat and eye-watering-hiccuping-stuffing-bread-and-pouring-water-into-your-mouth heat. Proceed with caution.

Yield:	Prep time:	Marinate time:	Serving size:
1 quart	20 minutes	24 hours	¼ cup

6 mini-cucumbers, ends removed and quartered lengthwise, or 2½ cups cucumbers, cut into ½-in. slices

1 medium onion, peeled and thinly sliced

1 clove garlic, peeled and smashed

1 cup apple cider vinegar

1 cup water

½ cup unprocessed sugar

½ tsp. mustard seed

¼ tsp. ground turmeric

⅛ to ¼ tsp. cayenne

½ to 1 tsp. crushed red pepper flakes

⅛ tsp. salt

1 tsp. whole black peppercorns

1. In a quart jar, layer cucumbers and onions, packing them in as tightly as you can. Top with garlic.

2. In a small saucepan over medium-high heat, whisk together apple cider vinegar, water, unprocessed sugar, mustard seed, turmeric, cayenne, crushed red pepper flakes, salt, and peppercorns. Bring to a boil, and simmer for 5 to 10 minutes or until sugar dissolves.

3. Pour mixture over cucumbers and onions, and let cool for 15 minutes.

4. Cover and seal the jars, and let sit for 15 more minutes. Store in the refrigerator. Pickles will be ready after 24 hours. Store in the refrigerator for up to 3 weeks.

Variation: For **Extra Spicy Pickles,** add fresh hot peppers or dried *chile de árbol* peppers to the cucumbers.

KEEP THE PICKLE JUICE!

When you're out of cucumbers, don't throw out the juice. You can add other veggies or place more cucumbers in the jar. Be sure the cucumbers are fully submerged before refrigerating.

Marinated Olives

I love having a predinner nosh, whether it's before just an intimate dinner for two or a raucous dinner party. These olives are so easy to throw together, and they make a great addition to an antipasto plate.

Yield:	Prep time:	Marinate time:	Serving size:
1½ cups	5 minutes	24 hours	2 or 3 olives

1½ cups green olives	Zest of 1 medium lemon (1 TB.)
3 small sprigs fresh rosemary	1 TB. balsamic vinegar
3 cloves garlic, peeled and smashed	½ cup olive oil

1. If olives are pitted, smash green olives. If olives have pits, cut small slits into olives.

2. In a small, sealable container, combine olives, rosemary, garlic, lemon zest, and balsamic vinegar. Add olive oil, and stir to combine.

3. Cover and marinate in the refrigerator for 24 hours. Store in the refrigerator for up to 2 weeks. The flavor will intensify with time.

Roasted Red Peppers

Roasted red peppers add smoky, sweet sophistication to any dish. Instead of relying on oil-soaked, expensive jarred versions, make your own in your broiler. Stir some in hummus, add them to a salad, or serve on an antipasto platter.

Yield:	Prep time:	Cook time:	Serving size:
1 cup	5 minutes	30 to 40 minutes	2 tablespoons

2 large red bell peppers

1. Set an oven rack close to the broiling element. Preheat the broiler to 500°F. Line a rimmed baking sheet with aluminum foil.

2. Place whole red bell peppers on the baking sheet, and broil for 5 to 10 minutes or until tops of peppers are charred. Flip over peppers as needed until all sides are charred.

3. When peppers are fully charred, place in medium bowl and cover bowl with plastic wrap. Let peppers cool for 15 to 20 minutes or until room temperature.

4. Using a paper towel, rub skins off peppers and remove seeds. Store roasted peppers in an airtight container in the refrigerator for 3 or 4 days.

SIMPLE SKIN REMOVAL

When removing the charred pepper skin, resist the urge to do so under running water. The water will remove a lot of the charred and smoky flavor. Instead, use paper towels to rub off the skin and your fingers to remove the seeds.

Roasted Garlic

Making this understated garlic is as easy as cutting a head of garlic in half. The end result is sweet, buttery garlic at its very best. Spread it on warm Basic Bread, mix it with homemade Mayonnaise (recipe in Chapter 6), mash it in a milder version of homemade hummus (recipes in Chapter 11), or just substitute it in any of your favorite recipes that call for garlic.

Yield:	Prep time:	Cook time:	Serving size:
1 head garlic	5 minutes	30 to 40 minutes	1 or 2 cloves

1 head garlic, split in ½ horizontally	1 TB. olive oil

1. Preheat the oven to 350°F. Make a small nest of aluminum foil within a square baking pan.

2. Place garlic in the aluminum foil, then add the olive oil, and lightly cover garlic with another piece of foil.

3. Broil garlic for 30 to 40 minutes, checking after 20 minutes, or until garlic is light, golden, and soft.

4. Let garlic cool. Store in an airtight container in the refrigerator for up to 1½ weeks.

Plain Yogurt

This yogurt is mild and creamy. Flavor it with homemade preserves (recipes in Chapter 6), honey, or Cinnamon Sugar (recipe in Chapter 7). To make a tangier version, add more of the organic yogurt.

Yield:	Prep time:	Cook time:	Serving size:
½ gallon	5 minutes	10 hours	½ cup

½ gal. organic whole milk   ¼ cup plain, organic yogurt

1. Place a casserole dish on a cooling rack, and set aside.

2. Pour all but ¼ cup whole milk in a heavy-bottomed saucepan over medium-high heat. Heat milk for 10 to 15 minutes or until it reaches 180°F, stirring often with a wooden spoon so it doesn't burn to the bottom of the saucepan.

3. Pour milk into the casserole dish, and let cool for 45 minutes to 1 hour or until it reaches 105°F to 110°F.

4. Meanwhile, in a medium bowl, whisk together yogurt and remaining ¼ cup whole milk.

5. Preheat the oven to 200°F.

6. When milk has cooled, stir in yogurt-milk mixture until well combined.

7. Turn off the oven.

8. Cover the casserole dish and wrap dish in 1 or 2 dishtowels. Place in the warm oven, turn on the oven light, and leave casserole in the oven for 8 or 9 hours. Do not open the oven door during this time.

9. After 8 or 9 hours, check yogurt. It should be thick and creamy with some liquid on top. If it hasn't reached the desired consistency, return it to the oven for 1 more hour.

10. Transfer yogurt to an airtight container, and store in the refrigerator for up to 2 weeks.

FULL-FAT INGREDIENTS

For all my recipes, I encourage you to go full-fat or go home. This may seem counterintuitive for a "healthy" cookbook, but a lot of the lower-fat versions contain added sugars and chemicals. In addition, you'll be more satisfied by eating something with more fat and flavor. When making this yogurt, whole milk results in a creamier and thicker finished product. Look for organic milk if at all possible. Use a high-quality, organic plain yogurt as your starter. After you've made your own yogurt, you can reserve some to use as a starter for your next batch.

Greek Yogurt

Greek yogurt is a thicker, tangier yogurt. It's a great replacement for sour cream in most recipes and is a luxurious dessert, breakfast, or snack.

Yield:	Prep time:	Cook time:	Serving size:
1 quart	5 minutes	3 hours	½ cup

    1 qt. Plain Yogurt (recipe earlier in
       this chapter)

1. Line a fine-mesh strainer with 4 layers of cheesecloth.

2. Place the strainer on top of a bowl, and spoon Plain Yogurt into the strainer.

3. Place the bowl and strainer in the refrigerator for 3 or 4 hours.

4. After 3 or 4 hours, discard liquid in the bowl, and spoon Greek yogurt into an airtight container. Store in the refrigerator for up to 2 weeks.

Yogurt Cheese

Yogurt cheese is a creamier, more decadent version of cream cheese. I suppose I should also mention that it's much healthier, and once you try this recipe, you'll scoff at the idea of ever buying cream cheese in foil-packaged bricks again. This creamy goodness is perfect for spreading on toasted bagels, using to make frosting, or eating straight with a spoon.

Yield:	Prep time:	Cook time:	Serving size:
1 quart	5 minutes	8 to 12 hours	¼ cup

> 1 qt. Plain Yogurt (recipe earlier in this chapter)

1. Line a fine-mesh strainer with 4 layers of cheesecloth.

2. Place the strainer on top of a bowl, and spoon Plain Yogurt into the strainer.

3. Place the bowl and strainer in the refrigerator for 8 to 12 hours. The longer you strain it, the thicker it will be.

4. After 8 to 12 hours, discard liquid in the bowl, and spoon yogurt cheese into an airtight container. Store in the refrigerator for up to 2 weeks.

Tofucotta

When I first started reading about making ricotta cheese from tofu in vegan cookbooks and on vegan blogs, I was excited. Then I realized something. I hate ricotta cheese. It has an okay texture, but it's so boring and tasteless. When I decided to make my own dairy-free ricotta, it was my chance to redo ricotta. This "tofucotta" is packed with flavor. It's perfect on top of a pizza or stuffed into pasta shells. Mix it with some mozzarella cheese, or dare to go dairy free. Either way, this makes a fantastic protein- and flavor-packed topping for your favorite snacks and meals.

Yield:	Prep time:	Serving size:
2½ cups	10 minutes	¼ cup

> 1 (10-oz.) pkg. firm or extra-firm tofu
> Juice of 1 small lemon (2 TB.)
> 1 TB. dried basil
> 1 TB. Italian Seasoning (recipe in Chapter 7)
>
> 1 TB. olive oil
> ¼ cup nutritional yeast flakes
> ¼ tsp. salt
> ¼ tsp. ground black pepper

1. In a large bowl, crumble and mash tofu with your hands or a fork.

2. Add lemon juice, basil, and Italian Seasoning, and mash with your hands or a fork until well combined.

3. Add olive oil, and mash with a fork. (It will start to get too messy at this point to use your hands.)

4. Add nutritional yeast flakes, and mash until well combined. Store in an airtight container in the refrigerator for up to 3 days.

Get a Little Saucy ∞ 4

There's something about making my own sauces that makes me feel very much like a chef. Maybe it's because I usually end up with more sauce on me than in the pan; or maybe it's the smells that emanate from the kitchen as I cook; or maybe it's just the fun of telling someone about making my own hot sauce and watching their eyebrows go up in that "wow-that's-really-cool" and "are-you-sure-you-know-what-you-are-doing?" kind of way.

In addition to having complete control of what goes into your food and, therefore, in your body, you can taste so much more of the actual ingredients in homemade sauces: the spicy kick from the basil in the pesto, the richness of the cheddar cheese in the cheese sauce, the slow burn from the cayenne in the hot sauce, or the sweet tomatoes and sharp garlic in the marinara. It's amazing how much more you taste and notice when you make your own sauce.

Perfect Pesto

When I was in graduate school, I had one foodie friend who was always making drool-worthy dishes. I told her I had some fresh basil to use and asked her how to make pesto. She told me to toss some basil, toasted pine nuts, garlic, and olive oil into a food processor. Being completely clueless, I threw equal parts basil, (burnt) pine nuts, and olive oil with 2 cloves garlic into my food processor. For the record, that doesn't make pesto. It makes green, inedible goo. I couldn't even look at pesto for months after that.

Since then, I've honed my pesto recipes considerably. Pesto is a great way to use up fresh basil (or other herbs), and because it freezes so well, it's also a great way to get the taste of fresh herbs in your meals year-round.

PESTO PAIRINGS

Pesto is often associated with pasta. Don't get me wrong; it's great for tossing with warm pasta, but don't stop there. Make a gourmet grilled cheese by spreading pesto beneath the cheese, or dip your grilled cheese sandwich into it. Use it as a pizza sauce with mozzarella, Tofucotta (Chapter 3), and fresh tomatoes. Mash it into your potatoes. Or use it as a dipping sauce for veggies or Tofu Dippers (Chapter 12).

Tomato-Based Sauces

Let it be known that I do not crave french fries, pasta, or even pizza; I crave the tomato sauces that accompany these foods. Really, I just want a vehicle to get the ketchup, marinara, or pizza sauce into my mouth.

Prior to my clean-eating days, I struggled to find a pasta sauce or ketchup I truly loved. It was like rolling dice trying to pick out one that wouldn't be too sweet or too salty. When I began my whole-food diet, I began to read labels and was shocked at the amount of sugar and high-fructose corn syrup in my beloved sauces.

The sauces in this chapter are all fairly simple to throw together. You'll notice I use a lot of canned tomatoes in the recipes. Watch out for cans that have the white plastic lining; they leach BPA (a potentially harmful chemical) into your food.

Make Your Own Mustard

It never occurred to me to make my own mustard until I was getting ready to write this book. As I began to research the spicy condiment, I discovered one of the best-kept secrets of the cooking world: making mustard is ridiculously easy.

I had to limit myself to three mustards because the more I learned, the more I realized I could easily fill a chapter, if not a whole book, with homemade mustards. Here's the basic equation: soak mustard seeds in equal parts acid (vinegar or lemon juice) and a neutral liquid (water, wine, or beer) and then add spices, sweeteners, and other flavor enhancers. With those variables, the possibilities are endless.

The mustard will peak in terms of the strength of the flavor (or in some cases, the harshness) and then mellow after a few days.

MUSTARD SEEDS AND OTHER INGREDIENTS

I use mustard seeds in all my recipes. You can typically find yellow (or white) mustard seeds at the grocery store, and these have the mildest taste. Brown and black mustard seeds are a little harder to find. Look online or in specialty stores. Start with the Basic Mustard and Cranberry Honey Mustard recipes that both use yellow seeds. If you fall in love with making mustard (like I did), you can move on to the recipes that take more unique ingredients like the brown and black mustard seeds. In terms of other ingredients, have fun! Garlic and horseradish enhance the mustard's spiciness while sweeteners (honey or brown sugar) tone down the flavor.

Hello, Hot Sauce

Spicy is a relative term. My spicy is mild compared to my Texan neighbor, Chris, who eats ghost peppers (the hottest pepper in the world) for fun. My mild is way too hot for my dad, who sweats when he eats ketchup.

Use your judgment when making hot sauce. As a guide, here are some of the most common peppers, listed from mild to hot:

Sweet bell peppers (red, yellow, orange, green): Red and green bell peppers come from the same plant. They begin as green peppers and turn red as they ripen. Red, yellow, and orange peppers are different plants but have a similar, sweet taste. To most people, these add sweetness with no heat. My dad would disagree.

Poblano peppers and ancho chiles: Poblano peppers are either green or red, and the red poblanos pack a little more heat than their green counterpart. Ancho chiles are dried poblano peppers. They're the sweetest of the dried peppers.

Banana peppers: Banana peppers combine sweet and heat in one little yellow package. Banana peppers can vary greatly on their level of heat. When in doubt, remove the ribs and seeds.

Jalapeño peppers: Jalapeños are one of the most popular hot peppers. With ribs and seeds, these peppers pack some serious heat (and should not be given to toddlers, which I learned the hard way …). If you remove the ribs and seeds, these are much milder and add just enough heat to enhance flavor.

Guajillo peppers: Guajillo peppers are dried mirasol peppers. They have a sweet taste with a hot finish. *Guajillo* means "little gourd" because of the sound of its rattling seeds inside.

Serrano peppers: Serrano peppers have a more biting heat than jalapeño peppers. They're slender and small, with colors ranging from green to red to brown, depending on ripeness.

Árbol chiles: The árbol, related to the cayenne pepper, is so named because of its woodlike stem—*árbol* means "treelike." Like many peppers, it starts out green and turns red as it matures.

The dried version retains its bright red color, making it a common choice for decorative wreaths … or hot sauce.

Tabasco peppers: Tabasco peppers are small, slim peppers that begin as a yellowish green and turn red as they ripen. They are used for their namesake hot sauce.

Habanero peppers: Habanero peppers are small, round, powerful peppers. They begin as a yellowish green and turn red as they ripen. If you catch them in that yellowish-green state, you'll find a sweet, hot pepper, perfect for salsas and spicy dishes. Let it ripen, and it'll get hotter.

Ghost peppers: Ghost peppers are rumored to be the world's hottest peppers. They're red and orange in color and appear slightly shriveled.

Because fresh peppers aren't always in season, I've also included two recipes in this chapter that use dried peppers. For a long time, dried peppers intimidated me. I let one package sit in my pantry for more than a year before opening the bag (and yes, they were still good) because I was afraid of them. Dumb move. I can now say with confidence that past me was stupid to do that. Dried peppers are awesome and very easy to use. I include instructions in the later recipes for getting the best flavor from your dried peppers. They're a great and economical way to make a from-scratch hot sauce any time of the year.

Caution! Caution! Caution!

I had read about taking great care when handling hot peppers countless times, and I always shrugged it off as being too cautious.

Then I got burned. Literally.

I was cutting hot peppers for a quick salsa and assumed that because it didn't burn initially, I was fine. An hour later, I felt like my thumb, forefinger, and that fleshy part under my nose were being burned by hot water. As you may have guessed, there was no hot water in sight. I tried running cold water over them, icing them, even sitting on the couch with my fingers in a bowl of ice water while my eyes watered from my burning nose. (If I could have figured out a way to submerge my face for an extended period of time, I would have.) Nothing helped. I couldn't even sleep that night because it burned so badly.

Don't be me. Don't think you're tougher than the pepper. Because I have news for you: you're not. The pepper will win every time.

Buy a package of disposable rubber gloves to keep in your kitchen. Whenever you're going to touch hot peppers, put on the gloves. And don't wipe your nose, face, or any other body part that you don't want to burn while you're wearing them. If you're handling a super-hot pepper like a habanero or ghost pepper, wear two pairs of rubber gloves.

Beware Hot Sauce Fumes

Be careful of hot sauce fumes. I've never sneezed as much—or as violently—as I did when testing the hot sauce recipes. Was I told not to inhale the fumes? Of course. Did I listen? Have you noticed any patterns in my behavior yet?

I paid the price, but you shouldn't have to. Be careful, and keep your kitchen well ventilated. Don't smell the sauce directly. Use your hand to waft the fumes toward you, and even then, don't take a big whiff. And just in case, keep a box of tissues handy.

Classic Pesto

At its most basic, pesto is ground herbs, nuts, cheese, garlic, and oil. My version is a little healthier and more down-to-earth. I swap out some of the olive oil for vegetable broth. In my view, pine nuts are expensive, burn too easily, and go rancid faster than I can use them. Enter the dependable walnut. Toasted or raw, it brings just the right amount of nuttiness to pesto for a fraction of the price.

Yield:	Prep time:	Cook time:	Serving size:
2 cups	5 minutes	5 minutes	¼ cup

2 cups fresh basil

1 clove garlic, peeled

⅓ cup toasted or raw walnuts

¼ cup shredded Parmesan cheese

⅓ cup vegetable broth

Juice of 1 small lemon (1 TB.)

2 to 4 TB. extra-virgin olive oil

Pinch salt

1. In a food processor fitted with a chopping blade, pulse basil, garlic, walnuts, Parmesan cheese, vegetable broth, and lemon juice until combined.

2. Add extra-virgin olive oil by the tablespoon, and pulse until pesto reaches your desired consistency.

3. Add salt, and pulse to combine.

4. Store in an airtight container in the refrigerator for up to 2 weeks, or freeze in ice-cube trays and transfer to zipper-lock freezer bags, and freeze for up to 3 months.

Variations: For **Sun-Dried Tomato Pesto,** add ½ cup sun-dried tomatoes. For a **Mixed-Herb Pesto,** substitute 1 cup arugula, ½ cup cilantro or parsley, and ½ cup baby spinach for the basil. For a milder version, substitute 1 clove Roasted Garlic (recipe in Chapter 3) for the fresh garlic.

Dairy-Free Pesto

Although I love Classic Pesto, I have to admit this dairy-free version is my go-to pesto. The nutritional yeast flakes add the flavor of cheese minus the dairy.

Yield:	Prep time:	Cook time:	Serving size:
2 cups	5 minutes	5 minutes	¼ cup

2 cups fresh basil

1 clove garlic, peeled

⅓ cup toasted or raw walnuts

⅓ cup nutritional yeast flakes

⅓ cup vegetable broth

Juice of 2 small lemons (2 TB.)

1 to 3 TB. extra-virgin olive oil

Pinch salt

1. In a food processor fitted with a chopping blade, pulse basil, garlic, walnuts, nutritional yeast flakes, vegetable broth, and lemon juice until combined.

2. Add extra-virgin olive oil by the tablespoon, and pulse until pesto reaches your desired consistency.

3. Add salt, and pulse to combine.

4. Store in an airtight container in the refrigerator for up to 2 weeks, or freeze in ice-cube trays and transfer to zipper-lock freezer bags, and freeze for up to 3 months.

Nut-Free Pesto

Toasted sunflower seeds offer a nuttiness of their own without all the potential negative side effects nuts might bring. If you can find unsalted sunflower kernels, use them. If not, don't include any additional salt to the pesto.

Yield:	Prep time:	Cook time:	Serving size:
2 cups	5 minutes	5 minutes	¼ cup

2 cups fresh basil

1 clove garlic, peeled

⅓ cup toasted, unsalted sunflower seed kernels

⅓ cup shredded Parmesan cheese

⅓ cup vegetable broth

Juice of 1 small lemon (1 TB.)

1 to 3 TB. extra-virgin olive oil

Pinch salt

1. In a food processor fitted with a chopping blade, pulse basil, garlic, sunflower seed kernels, Parmesan cheese, vegetable broth, and lemon juice until combined.

2. Add extra-virgin olive oil by the tablespoon, and pulse until pesto reaches your desired consistency.

3. Add salt, and pulse to combine.

4. Store in an airtight container in the refrigerator for up to 2 weeks, or freeze in ice-cube trays and transfer to zipper-lock freezer bags, and freeze for up to 3 months.

Marinara Sauce

Marinara was the first sauce we made on our own. Remember the $12 jar of spaghetti sauce? With a can of diced tomatoes or a few cups of fresh tomatoes, you can create a sensational sauce.

Yield:	Prep time:	Cook time:	Serving size:
1 quart	5 minutes	15 minutes	½ cup

¼ cup olive oil

1 medium sweet onion, diced

2 cloves garlic, peeled and minced

1 (28-oz.) can diced tomatoes, with juice

1 TB. Italian Seasoning (recipe in Chapter 7)

¼ tsp. crushed red pepper flakes

⅛ tsp. salt

1. In a Dutch oven or heavy-bottomed pan over medium heat, heat 1 tablespoon olive oil. Add sweet onion, and sauté for 3 to 5 minutes or until softened.

2. Add garlic, and sauté for 1 more minute.

3. Add tomatoes with juice, Italian Seasoning, crushed red pepper flakes, remaining olive oil, and salt, and stir to combine.

4. Bring to a simmer, reduce heat to medium-low, and simmer, stirring occasionally, for 10 more minutes.

5. Serve immediately. Store leftovers in an airtight container in the refrigerator for up to 1 week or in the freezer for up to 3 months.

CANNED TOMATOES

You'd think canned tomatoes would all be clean, right? I wish that were true. Check your tomatoes to be sure no chemicals or mysterious "spices" have been added. Look for organic tomatoes, and if you can find them, opt for San Marzano tomatoes. You can substitute fresh tomatoes if you have them available and have time to chop them up.

Marinara Sauce with Garden Veggies

When we have a summer bounty of produce, we like to jazz up our regular marinara with some extra veggies. As community supported agriculture (CSA) members, we're often overwhelmed with peppers, eggplants, zucchini, and tomatoes. This sauce is always one of our go-to meals during those times. You can substitute other fresh veggies for the ones listed. Maintain the ratios for a colorful, flavorful marinara sauce.

Yield:	Prep time:	Cook time:	Serving size:
6 cups	15 minutes	20 minutes	½ cup

¼ cup plus 2 TB. olive oil

1 medium sweet onion, peeled and diced

2 cups fresh white mushrooms, cleaned and quartered

1 medium red bell pepper, ribs and seeds removed, and diced

2 small eggplants or 3 small zucchini, diced (about 2½ cups)

1 cup carrots, peeled and diced small

3 cloves garlic, peeled and minced

1 (28-oz.) can diced tomatoes, with juice

2 TB. Italian Seasoning (recipe in Chapter 7)

½ tsp. crushed red pepper flakes

⅛ tsp. salt

1. In a Dutch oven or heavy-bottomed pan over medium heat, heat 2 tablespoons olive oil. Add onion, mushrooms, red bell pepper, eggplants, and carrots, and sauté for 5 to 7 minutes or until softened.

2. Add garlic, and sauté for 1 more minute.

3. Add tomatoes with juice, Italian Seasoning, crushed red pepper flakes, remaining ¼ cup olive oil, and salt, and stir to combine.

4. Bring to a simmer, reduce heat to medium-low, and simmer, stirring occasionally, for 15 more minutes.

5. Serve immediately. Store leftovers in an airtight container in the refrigerator for up to 1 week or in the freezer for up to 3 months.

CUTTING VEGETABLES

When cutting vegetables, it's important to have a very sharp chef knife. A cut from a dull knife happens more often and is more painful than a cut from a sharp knife. To cut a pepper, stand the pepper up straight. Starting at the top, cut off the sides of the pepper and then cut off the bottom. You may get a few seeds, but unless you're serving some very picky guests, a few pepper seeds won't hurt anything. To cut an onion, cut off the bottom first. Stand the onion up on the flat bottom, and cut the onion in half lengthwise, so there's part of the root on each side. Lay the onion half-cut side down, and make 6 to 8 lengthwise cuts, not quite cutting to the root. Then, cut horizontally to produce the dice. The number of horizontal cuts will correlate with how fine of a dice you need.

Pizza Sauce

Less is more when it comes to pizza sauce. Take this from the girl who has made every complicated pizza sauce recipe she could find before realizing sometimes the best is the easiest—and the most delicious.

Yield:	Prep time:	Serving size:
2½ cups	5 minutes	¼ to ½ cup

1 (28-oz.) can diced tomatoes, with juice	1 clove garlic, peeled and minced
3 TB. olive oil	1 tsp. crushed red pepper flakes
	½ tsp. salt

1. In a medium bowl, combine tomatoes with juice, olive oil, garlic, crushed red pepper flakes, and salt.

2. Use immediately, or store in an airtight container in the refrigerator for 1 week or in the freezer for up to 3 months.

Ketchup

I love ketchup. I'm someone who plans a meal around the condiment. I order foods at restaurants and make things at home that allow me to consume ketchup in a socially acceptable manner. It's not that I want french fries or a hamburger or even eggs; I want a vehicle for the ketchup. Because of this, it took me a long time to perfect this recipe. We have many containers of "not ketchup" in our freezer. I made some amazing sauces, but with this one, I hit the right balance of flavor and texture.

Yield:	Prep time:	Cook time:	Serving size:
1 quart	15 minutes	1 hour, 15 minutes	2 to 4 tablespoons

1 TB. canola oil

1 medium sweet onion, peeled and chopped

½ medium red bell pepper, ribs and seeds removed, and chopped

¼ cup celery, chopped

2 TB. tomato paste

½ cup apple cider vinegar

1 (28-oz.) can tomato purée

1 tsp. garlic powder

1 tsp. ground mustard

¼ cup agave nectar

½ tsp. salt

1. In a Dutch oven or heavy-bottomed saucepan over medium heat, heat canola oil. Add sweet onion, red bell pepper, and celery, and sauté for 15 minutes until onions are translucent.

2. Add tomato paste, and cook, stirring constantly, for 1 minute.

3. Deglaze the pan with apple cider vinegar and tomato purée. Stir in garlic powder, ground mustard, and agave nectar.

4. Bring to a boil, reduce heat to medium-low to medium, and simmer gently, stirring occasionally, for 45 minutes. Season with salt.

5. Remove from heat, and let cool for 10 to 15 minutes.

6. Pour into a quart glass jar, seal, and store in the refrigerator for 2 or 3 weeks.

BLEND IT SMOOTH

For a smoother ketchup, you can blend the mixture before using. After you remove it from heat, pour half of the mixture into a blender. If you can, remove the stopper from the blender lid, and cover the hole with a towel. Blend on low for 1 minute and then increase to high for 2 minutes. Pour into the glass jar, and repeat with second half.

Basic Mustard

This is a bare-bones, minimalist mustard. Don't get me wrong; it still has a good kick and serves as a great starting point for your mustard adventure. I love the tang of this mustard on sandwiches or as a dip for pretzels and sun-dried tomatoes.

Yield:	Prep time:	Cook time:	Serving size:
1 cup	5 minutes plus 18 to 48 hours	5 minutes	1 or 2 tablespoons

¼ cup yellow mustard seeds

¼ cup cold water

¼ cup apple cider vinegar

Pinch salt

1. In a medium bowl, soak yellow mustard seeds in cold water and apple cider vinegar for 18 to 48 hours at room temperature. Seeds will plump as they soak.

2. When seeds have soaked up the majority (if not all) of liquid, place soaked seeds and remaining liquids in a blender, add salt, and pulse until mustard reaches your desired consistency.

3. Store in an airtight container in the refrigerator for up to 1 week.

Variation: To make **White Wine Mustard,** substitute white wine for the water and white wine vinegar for the apple cider vinegar.

Spicy Mustard

When I eat mustard, I like a condiment that bites back. This recipe does not disappoint. Black and brown mustard seeds come together with bite and are tempered by sweet autumn spices.

Yield:	Prep time:	Cook time:	Serving size:
2 cups	5 minutes plus 18 to 48 hours	5 minutes	1 or 2 tablespoons

½ cup brown mustard seeds
¼ cup black mustard seeds
½ cup water
1 cup white vinegar
¾ tsp. ground turmeric

½ tsp. ground cinnamon
¼ tsp. ground allspice
⅛ tsp. ground ginger
Pinch ground nutmeg
Pinch salt

1. In a medium bowl, soak brown mustard seeds and black mustard seeds in water and white vinegar for 18 to 48 hours at room temperature. Seeds will plump as they soak.

2. When seeds have soaked up the majority (if not all) of liquid, place soaked seeds and remaining liquids in a blender. Add turmeric, cinnamon, allspice, ginger, nutmeg, and salt, and pulse until mustard reaches your desired consistency.

3. Store in an airtight container in the refrigerator for up to 1 week.

Cranberry Honey Mustard

I'm a sucker for anything cranberry, so of course I couldn't resist making my own cranberry mustard. This is sweet, tart, and a perfect addition to your Thanksgiving dinner. Really, it's a perfect addition to *any* meal.

Yield:	Prep time:	Cook time:	Serving size:
1 cup	5 minutes, plus 18 to 48 hours	5 minutes	1 or 2 tablespoons

¼ cup yellow mustard seeds
2 TB. chopped fresh cranberries
¼ cup white wine

¼ cup white vinegar
2 TB. honey
Pinch salt

1. In a medium bowl, soak yellow mustard seeds and cranberries in white wine, white vinegar, and honey for 18 to 48 hours at room temperature. Seeds will plump as they soak.

2. When seeds have soaked up the majority (if not all) of liquid, place soaked seeds, cranberries, and remaining liquids in a blender, add salt, and pulse until mustard reaches your desired consistency.

3. Store in an airtight container in the refrigerator for up to 1 week.

Barbecue Sauce

I loved a certain bottled barbecue sauce until I saw that one of the first ingredients was high-fructose corn syrup (HFCS). I knew the sauce was sweet, but I was shocked to find HFCS was a main ingredient. This recipe yields a sweet and smoky sauce. As it simmers on the stove, your kitchen will be filled with its sultry, tomatoey aroma. Don't be tempted to cut down the simmering time. The sauce will seem done after just a few minutes, but if you wait the full 20 minutes it takes to simmer, you'll be rewarded with a thick, rich, slather-worthy sauce.

Yield:	Prep time:	Cook time:	Serving size:
1 quart	5 minutes	25 minutes	¼ cup

1 (28-oz.) can tomato sauce	1 tsp. garlic powder
¾ cup brown sugar, firmly packed	1 TB. tomato paste
3 TB. Worcestershire sauce	⅛ tsp. salt
¼ cup ground mustard	2 TB. liquid smoke, or 1 TB. smoked paprika

1. In a Dutch oven or heavy-bottomed saucepan over medium-high heat, whisk together tomato sauce, brown sugar, Worcestershire sauce, ground mustard, garlic powder, and tomato paste. Bring to a simmer, and adjust heat to maintain a gentle simmer for 20 minutes, stirring occasionally so sauce doesn't stick to the bottom of the pan.

2. Remove from heat, and stir in salt and liquid smoke.

3. Let cool to room temperature.

4. Store in a glass jar or an airtight container in the refrigerator for up to 3 weeks.

Teriyaki Sauce

This teriyaki sauce is a delicate balance of sweet, salty, and tangy, and is terrific on tofu or grilled meat. Marinate your tofu or meat in the sauce and then broil or grill. You can also use it to make Teriyaki Beef Jerky (recipe in Chapter 12).

Yield:	Prep time:	Cook time:	Serving size:
2 cups	10 minutes	15 minutes	2 to 4 tablespoons

¼ cup cold water

2 TB. cornstarch

1 (1-in.) piece fresh ginger, peeled and minced (1 tsp.)

1 clove garlic, peeled and minced

½ cup soy sauce or tamari sauce

⅓ cup plus 1 TB. sucanat or brown sugar, firmly packed

¼ cup apple cider vinegar

1. In a small bowl, whisk together cold water and cornstarch.

2. In a small saucepan over medium-high heat, whisk together ginger, garlic, soy sauce, sucanat, and apple cider vinegar. Bring to a boil, and reduce heat to medium.

3. Whisk cornstarch mixture into the saucepan, and return to a simmer. Reduce heat to medium-low, and cook, stirring often, for about 5 minutes or until sauce thickens.

4. When sauce has thickened, remove from heat and let cool to room temperature.

5. Store in an airtight container in the refrigerator for up to 2 weeks.

Variation: For **Spicy Teriyaki Sauce,** add 2 tablespoons Hot Sauce (recipe later in this chapter) to the initial soy mixture.

Peanut Sauce

A good peanut sauce can transform a meal. It can take veggies and noodles to another level, serve as a delicious dipping sauce for chicken tenders or Tofu Dippers (recipe in Chapter 12), or jazz up a plain chicken breast. You can vary the thickness of the sauce by changing the amount of water you add. I like my sauces thick, but a thinner sauce is easier to use for pasta salads and with meats. Experiment to see what you like best.

Yield:	Prep time:	Cook time:	Serving size:
2 or 3 cups	10 minutes	15 minutes	2 to 4 tablespoons

1 TB. canola oil

1 (1-in.) piece fresh ginger, peeled and minced (1 TB.)

2 medium cloves garlic, peeled and minced

1 medium jalapeño pepper, seeded and minced

1 cup Creamier Peanut Butter (variation in Chapter 6)

1 or 2 cups water

2 TB. soy sauce or tamari sauce

¼ cup rice vinegar

1 TB. agave nectar

2 tsp. hot sauce (recipes later in this chapter)

¼ tsp. crushed red pepper flakes

¼ tsp. salt

1. In a small skillet over medium heat, heat canola oil. Add ginger, garlic, and jalapeño pepper, and sauté for 2 or 3 minutes or until softened and fragrant.

2. In a medium bowl, whisk together Creamier Peanut Butter, water, soy sauce, rice vinegar, agave nectar, hot sauce, crushed red pepper flakes, and salt. Add garlic mixture, and whisk to combine.

3. Store in an airtight container in the refrigerator for up to 2 weeks.

Fresh Pepper Hot Sauce

This hot sauce has a bright flavor and is a great way to use up the summer's bounty of peppers. Select your peppers using the ranking earlier in this section. I give you a basic outline here, but I encourage you to pick peppers within your spice realm. For example, if Chris, my Texan neighbor, made hot sauce, he would pick mostly hot peppers (serrano, tabasco, habanero, and probably some ghost peppers) with a few jalapeños to tone it down. My dad, the sweating ketchup eater, would want to do 2 or 3 jalapeño peppers and the rest would be sweet red peppers. If you can find red peppers, use them for the most vibrant-looking sauce. If not, make peace with having an orange hot sauce.

Yield:	Prep time:	Cook time:	Serving size:
5 or 6 cups	45 minutes	2 hours (includes cool time)	2 tablespoons

1 TB. canola oil

20 medium to medium-hot jalapeño and/or banana peppers, chopped, seeds and ribs optional (about 6 cups)

30 hot habanero and/or Serrano peppers, seeded and chopped (about 2 or 3 cups)

1 medium sweet onion, peeled and roughly chopped

½ cup celery, chopped

½ tsp. salt

3 cloves garlic, peeled and sliced

1 cup tomato paste

1 cups apple cider vinegar

2 water

¼ cup plus 2 TB. brown sugar

2 tsp. smoked paprika

1. In a Dutch oven or heavy-bottomed saucepan over medium-high heat, heat canola oil. Add jalapeño peppers, habanero peppers (or others), onion, celery, and salt. Cover and cook for 2 or 3 minutes.

2. Uncover and sauté for about 10 minutes or until veggies have softened.

3. Reduce heat to medium, add garlic, and cook for 1 or 2 more minutes or until fragrant.

4. Add tomato paste, and cook, stirring constantly, for 2 to 4 minutes or until tomato paste is brown.

5. Add apple cider vinegar, water, brown sugar, and smoked paprika. Increase heat to medium-high, and bring to a boil. Reduce heat to medium-low, and simmer for 20 minutes, adjusting heat to maintain a gentle simmer.

6. Remove from heat, and let cool for 1 hour.

7. Fill a blender half full of saucepan mixture, and purée until smooth. If mixture is still hot, cover the blender with a dishtowel and remove the stopper in the blender lid. This will keep the blender from exploding on you and your kitchen. (Not that I know this from experience ….)

8. Pour puréed mixture through a fine-mesh strainer to remove any remaining grit, seeds, or ribs.

9. Store in an airtight container in the refrigerator for 2 or 3 weeks or in the freezer for up to 3 months.

HOT STUFF

The heat of the pepper comes mostly from the seeds and ribs. If you remove all the seeds and ribs, your hot sauce will be much less spicy. This is why I almost fainted from my first batch of hot sauce. Fearful of making it too mild, I left most of the seeds and ribs in the hot sauce. It was the first—and hopefully only—time my knees literally buckled because of spice. Use caution and adjust the spice level according to your comfort level. If you do eat something too spicy, have some dairy and bread. These will temper the heat better than water.

Dried Pepper Hot Sauce

I love the combination of hot árbol peppers and smoky, broiled tomatoes. To me, this is the ultimate hot sauce and the sauce I'll be making again and again throughout the winter months. To increase the heat, add more árbol chile peppers and reduce the amount of tomatoes.

Yield:	Prep time:	Cook time:	Serving size:
5 cups	5 minutes	30 minutes	2 tablespoons

5 medium tomatoes, cut in ½	1 clove garlic, peeled
1 medium sweet onion, peeled and quartered	½ cup apple cider vinegar
10 dried árbol chiles	½ tsp. salt
2 cups water	1 TB. agave nectar

1. Preheat the broiler to 500°F. Line a rimmed baking sheet with aluminum foil.

2. Place tomatoes and onion cut side down on the baking sheet, and broil for 5 to 15 minutes until skins are black and blistered.

3. Meanwhile, cut stems off árbol chiles and shake out seeds.

4. Pour water into a medium bowl, and set aside.

5. Heat a medium skillet over medium-high heat. When hot, add chiles and cook for 30 to 40 seconds per side. You don't want to toast chiles, just heat them enough to bring out the flavor. Place cooked chiles in water, and let soak for 15 minutes.

6. In a food processor fitted with a chopping blade, pulse tomatoes, onion, garlic, chiles, soak water, apple cider vinegar, salt, and agave nectar until smooth.

7. Strain mixture through a fine-mesh strainer.

8. Store in glass jars in the refrigerator for 2 or 3 weeks or in the freezer for up to 3 months.

Sweet and Smoky Hot Sauce

This isn't your typical hot sauce. It's thick, rich, sweet, and smoky, and the perfect garnish for grilled meats. Dilute it with water, and use it in any recipe that calls for typical hot sauce. I first learned about this type of sauce from a good friend and local Madison chef, Matt Pace. I use his technique of reheating the sauce to get a shiny finish and concentrated taste.

Yield:	Prep time:	Cook time:	Serving size:
1 cup	10 minutes	1 hour	1 or 2 teaspoons

3 dried ancho chile peppers, ribs and seeds removed

3 dried guajillo peppers, ribs and seeds removed

1 to 1½ cups water

2 cloves garlic, peeled

1 tsp. ground cloves

2 TB. brown sugar

⅛ tsp. salt

4 TB. tomato paste

1. Heat a skillet over medium-high heat. When hot, add ancho chiles and guajillo peppers, and cook for 30 to 45 seconds per side until fragrant.

2. Remove chiles from the skillet and place in a medium saucepan. Cover peppers with water, set saucepan over high heat, and bring to a boil. Remove from heat, cover, and set aside for about 15 minutes or until chiles are plump.

3. In a food processor fitted with a chopping blade, pulse 1 cup water from saucepan, garlic, ground cloves, brown sugar, salt, tomato paste, and chiles until smooth. Add more chile water to get the right consistency, and purée until smooth.

4. Push mixture through a fine-mesh strainer.

5. Heat a medium skillet over medium-high heat. To test when skillet is hot enough, sprinkle some water in it. When you hear the telltale *whoooosshhhhh,* the skillet is ready.

6. Pour sauce into the pan, and bring to a boil. Reduce heat to medium-low and simmer, stirring constantly, for 15 minutes. Sauce will turn deep red-brown and become very shiny.

7. Remove from heat, and let cool.

8. Store in a glass jar in the refrigerator for 2 or 3 weeks.

Cheese Sauce

To the outsider, my dad is the paragon of health. When he turned 70, he went for his physical and his doctor said, "Tom, you are in perfect health for a 40-year-old." He bikes thousands of miles a year, eats fresh produce, juices just about anything he can fit into his juicer, doesn't drink any alcohol, and plays racquetball with the best of them (most of them half his age). But I know his kryptonite: Cheez Whiz. Yes, the paragon of health loves that orange, blobby cheese product. This is why making my own cheese sauce was so critical. I understand the need for drizzling cheesy goodness over veggies or tortilla chips. What I don't understand is why Cheez Whiz is so orange and has a shelf life longer than most small dogs. My cheese sauce is flavored with actual cheese and can be reheated the next day. The white pepper gives it sweetness, the smoked paprika gives it a smoky edge, and the cayenne warms you up after you take your first bite. Drizzle this sauce over some Baked Tortilla Chips (recipe in Chapter 10) for healthy and delicious nachos, or dunk some toasted Basic Bread (recipe in Chapter 3) in it for an informal fondue.

Yield:	Prep time:	Cook time:	Serving size:
1½ cups	5 minutes	5 minutes	¼ cup

1 cup 2 percent or whole milk

2 TB. whole-wheat flour or whole-wheat pastry flour

1 TB. ground mustard

¼ tsp. ground white pepper

¼ to ½ tsp. cayenne

⅛ tsp. salt

¼ tsp. smoked paprika

1½ to 2 cups shredded cheddar cheese

1. In a small saucepan over medium heat, whisk together milk, whole-wheat flour, ground mustard, white pepper, cayenne, salt, and smoked paprika.

2. Add cheddar cheese ½ cup at a time, and stir to combine, letting cheese start to melt before adding the next ½ cup, until sauce reaches your desired cheesiness.

3. Drizzle over veggies or Baked Tortilla Chips, or serve with Basic Bread.

4. Store leftovers in an airtight container in the refrigerator for 1 or 2 days. For best results, reheat gradually in a saucepan or a microwave, stirring often.

Variation: Play with the type of cheese and combination of cheeses to truly make this sauce your own. This would be great with Swiss cheese. Or for an extra kick, try pepper jack.

Dress Up Your Salads

5

Confession: we don't eat very much salad dressing at our house. *But Badger Girl,* you might be thinking, *you said you ate at least one salad every day!* It's true—I do. But here's the thing: 9 times out of 10, our salads are the foundation for the rest of our dinner. Spaghetti? Curry? Tacos? Sloppy joes? All go on top of a bed of greens. If we need a little extra sauce, we add salsa. Incorporating greens this way is so easy, and it ensures that we eat a healthy amount of greens and not just a few spare leaves.

That's not to say I don't love salad dressings. I love them with a passion generally reserved for shoes, chocolate, and wine. Prior to my clean days, you could find dozens of bottled dressings in my fridge. And I can say, without a doubt, this is my favorite chapter in the book.

If you do nothing else to incorporate whole foods into your diet, stop eating bottled dressings. Most dressings contain some chemicals. How else would they have such a long unrefrigerated shelf life? And if they're "organic," how can you trust that the oil hasn't gone rancid?

Before you proceed to this chapter's recipes, I need to warn you about something: you're not going to find frou-frou, foodie-type salad dressings in this chapter. Remember, I was a girl of the 1980s and grew up on French dressing. The only non-French variety I remember was Thousand Island, and that was just for taco salads. We didn't even have ranch dressing. I didn't even know you could put ranch on a salad until I was in high school.

As I got older, my taste horizons expanded. I like a good vinaigrette on occasion. (I've included three of my favorites in this chapter.) My mother, on the other hand, has refused to eat any of my more "foodie" takes on salad dressings. She would try them and then give the fridge a worried look: "You don't have any French, do you? Ranch? Thousand Island?" This chapter is for her. And for you. You'll find all the dressings of your childhood, plus a few more, in these pages.

So if I love dressings so much, why don't I keep more in our fridge? For me, each salad dressing pairs with a certain type of salad. I make salad dressings if I have a particular salad in mind, but to make that kind of a decision on a nightly basis is overwhelming. I am my mother's daughter, and I suddenly understand why French was always a safe choice.

I share some winning pairings for each dressing in the recipes, but trust your tastes. There's no shame in rocking out with that French dressing on any salad you choose.

STORING FRESH DRESSINGS

Dressings that contain mayonnaise will stay good in the refrigerator for 3 or 4 days. Dressings with no mayonnaise will keep in the fridge for up to 2 weeks. If a dressing contains oil, you might want to take it out of the refrigerator 20 to 30 minutes before serving to allow the oil to loosen up a bit.

French Dressing

This is one is for my mom. It's sweet and tangy, and it brings me back to Sunday dinners when we always started our meal of pot roast and potatoes with a small salad of iceberg lettuce, tomatoes, shredded cheese, hard-boiled eggs, croutons, and French dressing.

Yield:	Prep time:	Serving size:
1 cup	10 minutes	2 tablespoons

½ cup Ketchup (recipe in Chapter 4)

½ cup Mayonnaise (recipe in Chapter 6)

2 TB. apple cider vinegar

1 TB. honey

1 TB. tomato paste

½ tsp. ground mustard

1 tsp. Worcestershire sauce

⅛ tsp. salt

1. In a blender, purée Ketchup, Mayonnaise, apple cider vinegar, honey, tomato paste, ground mustard, Worcestershire sauce, and salt until smooth.

2. Store in an airtight container in the refrigerator for up to 4 days.

CLASSIC COMBINATIONS

Try this dressing with a classic iceberg or romaine wedge salad. Top the lettuce with blue cheese crumbles, white onion slivers, tomatoes, and Croutons (recipe in Chapter 3).

Thousand Island Dressing

Growing up, Thousand Island was an exotic treat for me. I could never figure out what was in it, but I knew I loved it. Thousand Island dressing originated in the small Upstate New York town of Clayton, where a local fishing guide served the dressing with his fish dinners. He took visitors on fishing trips to the 1,000 islands, and upon request, his wife gave out the recipe and called it Thousand Island dressing.

Yield:	Prep time:	Serving size:
1½ cups	15 minutes	2 tablespoons

¾ cup Mayonnaise (recipe in Chapter 6)

3 TB. Ketchup (recipe in Chapter 4)

3 TB. chopped Bread-and-Butter Pickles (cucumbers and onions; recipe in Chapter 3)

2 TB. minced white onion

1 TB. minced red bell pepper

1 TB. chopped hard-boiled egg

1 TB. white vinegar

⅛ tsp. salt

⅛ tsp. ground black pepper

1. In a blender, purée Mayonnaise, Ketchup, Bread-and-Butter Pickles, white onion, red bell pepper, egg, white vinegar, salt, and black pepper until smooth.

2. Store in an airtight container in the refrigerator for up to 4 days.

TACO SALAD TOPPER

Try this dressing with a taco salad. You can eat the salad hot, or toss it with the cooked taco meat, tomatoes, lettuce, and shredded cheese, and serve it cold. In both cases, add some Baked Tortilla Chips (recipe in Chapter 10) for crunch.

Ranch Dressing

To me, *ranch dressing* means creamy, herby, tangy, and perfect for dips and indulgent salads. This version does not disappoint. I love the fresh herbs, but if you don't have fresh herbs available, use *half* the amount of dried herbs. If you use fresh herbs, you should know something: this dressing will turn out green. But don't judge it on its color. It's the ranch you grew up loving, just made with all fresh ingredients.

Yield:	Prep time:	Serving size:
1½ cups	1 hour, 20 minutes	2 tablespoons

1 small clove garlic, peeled and chopped

¼ tsp. salt

½ cup Mayonnaise (recipe in Chapter 6)

¼ cup Greek Yogurt (recipe in Chapter 3)

1 tsp. Dijon mustard

Juice of ½ medium lemon (2 TB.)

2 TB. fresh Italian parsley, chopped

½ TB. fresh dill, chopped

1 TB. fresh cilantro, chopped

1 TB. fresh chives, chopped

1 TB. white vinegar

⅛ tsp. hot sauce (recipes in Chapter 4)

1. In a small bowl, place garlic. Pour ⅛ teaspoon salt on top, and using a fork, mash garlic into paste.

2. In a blender, purée Mayonnaise, Greek Yogurt, Dijon mustard, lemon juice, garlic paste, remaining ⅛ teaspoon salt, Italian parsley, dill, cilantro, chives, white vinegar, and hot sauce until smooth.

3. Transfer to an airtight container, and refrigerate for at least 1 hour to allow flavors to meld. Store in the refrigerator for up to 4 days.

RANCH SO RIGHT

I love ranch dressing as a dipping sauce with raw vegetables, Baked French Fries (recipe in Chapter 10), Clean Chicken Nuggets (recipe in Chapter 12), or Baked Potato Chips (recipe in Chapter 10). In terms of salads, try this with a spicy chicken breast salad or any salad that includes Croutons (recipe in Chapter 3).

Dairy-Free Ranch Dressing

This is the classic ranch dressing but dairy-free for those who can't tolerate dairy. I've tried many nondairy milk variations, but I love the richness the coconut milk yields and how the Mayonnaise gives the dressing a little more heft. To make it even thicker, freeze the coconut milk for 2 hours or refrigerate it for 24 to 48 hours before using.

Yield:	Prep time:	Serving size:
1 cup	1 hour, 10 minutes	2 tablespoons

½ cup full-fat coconut milk, shaken

½ cup Mayonnaise (recipe in Chapter 6)

1 tsp. dried chives

½ tsp. dried parsley

½ tsp. dried dill

½ tsp. dried oregano

½ tsp. garlic powder

⅛ tsp. onion powder

1 tsp. Worcestershire sauce

¼ tsp. dried mustard

⅛ tsp. crushed red pepper flakes

1. In a blender, purée coconut milk, Mayonnaise, chives, parsley, dill, oregano, garlic powder, onion powder, Worcestershire sauce, dried mustard, and crushed red pepper flakes until smooth.

2. Transfer to an airtight container, and refrigerate for at least 1 hour to allow flavors to meld. Store in the refrigerator for up to 4 days.

Honey Mustard Dressing

For me, this sweet, tangy, and creamy dressing is the ultimate comfort food. Try it as a salad dressing, but also use it as a dipping sauce for pretzels, a simmering sauce for chicken, or a condiment for your favorite sandwich.

Yield:	Prep time:	Serving size:
1 cup	5 minutes	2 tablespoons

½ cup Mayonnaise (recipe in Chapter 6)

3 TB. Dijon mustard

1 TB. honey

1 TB. apple cider vinegar

1. In a blender, purée Mayonnaise, Dijon mustard, honey, and apple cider vinegar until smooth.

2. Serve immediately, or store in a glass jar or an airtight container in the refrigerator for up to 4 days.

SERVING SUGGESTIONS

Try this dressing with Clean Chicken Nuggets (recipe in Chapter 12) or over mixed greens, shredded carrots, and Croutons (recipe in Chapter 3).

Italian Dressing

I'm leery of all bottled Italian dressings. Why is it so yellow? What are those flecks? And why does the ingredient list contain so many chemicals? This version is all natural and packed with flavor. Plus, it's so easy, you can make it in less than 5 minutes!

Yield:	Prep time:	Serving size:
1½ cups	5 minutes	2 tablespoons

1 cup olive oil

½ cup red wine vinegar

3 TB. Italian Seasoning (recipe in Chapter 7)

1 tsp. unprocessed sugar or sucanat

¼ tsp. ground mustard

1. In a glass jar or an airtight container with a tight-fitting lid, shake to combine olive oil, red wine vinegar, Italian Seasoning, unprocessed sugar, and ground mustard.

2. Serve immediately, or store in the refrigerator. If refrigerated, allow to set at room temperature for 20 minutes before serving.

PERFECT PAIRING

Try this dressing with lots of red, yellow, and green bell peppers; fresh onions; and mixed greens.

Dijon Balsamic Dressing

If you've read my blog (learntocookbadgergirl.com), you might recognize this salad dressing as what I modestly call the "Best Dressing Ever." Along with a bag of mixed greens, this is what I brought to every potluck when I worked as a corporate trainer. When I left that job, my co-workers weren't as interested in where I was going or what I was going to do. No, they were more concerned about this salad dressing. I had to write the recipe for the entire training team before I left. It's so easy to make and so incredibly good. (Funny, I haven't heard from any of them since I gave up the recipe ….)

Yield:	Prep time:	Serving size:
1 cup	5 minutes	2 tablespoons

6 TB. olive oil

¼ cup balsamic vinegar

3 TB. Dijon mustard

2 tsp. honey

⅛ tsp. ground black pepper

1. In a glass jar or an airtight container with a tight-fitting lid, shake to combine olive oil, balsamic vinegar, Dijon mustard, honey, and black pepper.

2. Serve immediately, or store in the refrigerator for up to 2 weeks. If refrigerated, allow to set at room temperature for 20 to 30 minutes before serving.

SENSATIONAL SERVE-WITHS

I love this dressing with spinach, sun-dried tomatoes, and slivers of Vidalia onions. It's also a great dressing for any salad that accompanies Italian food—pizza, spaghetti, lasagna, you name it.

Avocado Dressing

I have a major crush on avocados. I love them. They are my green eggs and ham of produce; I can eat them here or there, I can eat them anywhere. I love any excuse to eat them. This dressing is hearty, spicy, and packed with buttery avocado goodness.

Yield:	Prep time:	Serving size:
2 cups	10 minutes	¼ cup

2 medium avocados, pitted and peeled

1 clove garlic, peeled

2 TB. olive oil

1 TB. Taco Seasoning (recipe in Chapter 7)

1 cup fresh cilantro, chopped

¼ tsp. salt

Juice of 2 small limes (¼ cup)

1 to 1½ cups water

1. In a blender, purée avocadoes, garlic, olive oil, Taco Seasoning, cilantro, salt, lime juice, and ½ cup water until smooth. Add additional water to reach your desired consistency.

2. Serve immediately, or store in an airtight container in the refrigerator for up to 3 days.

AMAZING AVOCADOS

I love this dressing with Summer Quinoa Salad (recipes in Chapter 9) and spinach. It's hearty enough to stand up to the quinoa or any other cooked grain.

Creamy Garlic Dressing

This is my version of the classic Caesar dressing. Or maybe I should say, this is what I like about Caesar dressing: creamy garlic goodness. If you eat this dressing, you might want to offer it to anyone in the near vicinity, too, so they'll be as garlicky as you are.

Yield:	Prep time:	Serving size:
1 cup	10 minutes	2 tablespoons

1 large clove garlic, peeled and chopped

¼ tsp. salt

½ cup Mayonnaise (recipe in Chapter 6)

½ cup Greek Yogurt (recipe in Chapter 3)

1 TB. balsamic vinegar

¼ tsp. garlic powder

1 tsp. Dijon mustard

2 TB. olive oil

½ tsp. ground black pepper

1. In a small bowl, place garlic. Pour ⅛ teaspoon salt on top, and using a fork, mash garlic into paste.

2. In a blender, purée Mayonnaise, Greek Yogurt, balsamic vinegar, garlic paste, garlic powder, Dijon mustard, olive oil, black pepper, and remaining ⅛ teaspoon salt until smooth.

3. Store in an airtight container in the refrigerator for up to 4 days.

GREAT GARLICKY GOODNESS

Use this dressing as you would a Caesar dressing. Serve with grilled chicken breast, Parmesan cheese, Croutons (recipe in Chapter 3), and romaine lettuce.

Lemony Vinaigrette Dressing

This is spring in a jar—crisp lemon with just a subtle sweetness and distinct tang. It's great with any greens; drizzled over grilled fish, chicken, or asparagus; or eaten with a spoon.

Yield:	Prep time:	Serving size:
1 cup	10 minutes	2 tablespoons

⅓ cup olive oil

2 TB. seasoned rice vinegar

1 tsp. lemon zest

Juice of 2 small lemons (3 TB.)

1 tsp. Dijon mustard

½ tsp. fresh thyme, chopped

1 tsp. honey

1. In a medium bowl, whisk together olive oil, seasoned rice vinegar, lemon zest, lemon juice, Dijon mustard, thyme, and honey.

2. Serve immediately, or store in a glass jar or an airtight container in the refrigerator for up to 2 weeks. If refrigerated, allow to set at room temperature for 20 minutes before serving.

SUPER SPRING SALAD

Try this dressing with spinach or spring mix, sliced almonds, and fresh blueberries. Add some crumbled goat cheese or fresh pea shoots if you're feeling extra gourmet.

Curry Vinaigrette Dressing

In my world of salad dressings, this is as frou-frou as I get. I had a curry vinaigrette at a deli one day and fell in love. I love curry, but it never occurred me to make a dressing starring curry. I love the sweet, spicy tang of this dressing. If the French dressing is for my mother, this dressing is dedicated to my mother-in-law, the only woman who loves curry more than I do.

Yield:	Prep time:	Serving size:
1 cup	5 minutes	2 tablespoons

½ cup canola oil

3 TB. apple cider vinegar

2½ TB. curry powder

1 tsp. honey

½ tsp. Dijon mustard

1. In a medium bowl, whisk together canola oil, apple cider vinegar, curry powder, honey, and Dijon mustard.

2. Serve immediately, or store in an airtight container in the refrigerator for up to 2 weeks.

CREATIVE WITH CURRY

This dressing is perfect with mixed greens, dried cranberries, and toasted (or raw) pecans. To give it a little more heft, add cooked quinoa or Israeli couscous.

Super Spreads 6

Whether it's on your morning toast, freshly baked bread, or even apple slices, there's no reason to settle for commercial spreads. When you start reading labels on your favorite store-bought spreads, you're going to be shocked at all the extra ingredients and how many times you find corn in some form. (Since when does corn belong in strawberry preserves?)

A few expensive brands use minimal ingredients, but once you realize how easy it is to make your own clean spreads, you'll be happy to say good-bye to the commercial versions. You'll reduce your grocery bill just as easily as you reduce the number of unclean ingredients.

Better Butters

I grew up in a small town. Our little village wasn't known for fine dining experiences, and we hit the Ritz when we got a breadbasket on our table. After I moved to a bigger city, I judged restaurants not by the breadbasket, but the accompanying butter. Was it spreadable? 3 stars. Flavored? 4 stars. And then I proceeded to judge the rest of the food. Then I realized how easy it was to make "fancy butters." Since then, my standards have gone up considerably.

You can spread flavored butters on your favorite bread or rolls, or use them to jazz up baked potatoes. Try tossing them with hot pasta for an easy, light sauce. You can mash them with boiled potatoes or root vegetables, or use them to add a twist to corn on the cob. The possibilities are somewhat endless.

A NOTE ABOUT SUGAR

For the recipes in this chapter, I reduced the sugar as much as possible. For the preserve recipes, this meant I had to cook the fruit much longer to achieve a thick consistency. Although the cooking times may look like a lot, the result is a rich, naturally sweet, and healthy spread that's well worth the wait.

Peanut Butter

What spinach is to Manatee, peanut butter is to me. I love the stuff. I've tried all the different brands—natural, flavored, chunky, and creamy. As long as it's not packed with hydrogenated corn oil, I don't discriminate. But now that I've tasted homemade, I may never go back. This is seriously too easy and too good *not* to make at home.

Yield:	Prep time:	Serving size:
2 cups	5 minutes	2 tablespoons

2 cups roasted, unsalted peanuts	1 tsp. salt

1. Pour peanuts and salt into a food processor fitted with a chopping blade. Cover the top of the food processor bowl with plastic wrap (to simplify cleanup), and secure the lid on the bowl. Process on high for 5 minutes, stopping occasionally to lift the plastic wrap, scrape down the sides of the bowl, and replace the plastic wrap.

2. Store in an airtight container in the refrigerator for up to 2 weeks. Allow to set at room temperature for 5 to 10 minutes before serving.

Variations: For **Creamier Peanut Butter,** process for 1 or 2 minutes, add ⅓ cup of a neutral-tasting oil such as canola, and finish puréeing. For **Honey Peanut Butter,** add 1 tablespoon honey while adding the peanuts and salt.

Almondtella

My version of the classic chocolate-almond spread is a little grainier than the store-bought version, but it's equally delicious.

Yield:	Prep time:	Cook time:	Serving size:
2 cups	15 minutes	10 minutes	2 tablespoons

1 cup almonds	1½ cups milk chocolate chips
2 TB. canola oil	¼ cup milk or nondairy milk
¼ tsp. salt	

1. Preheat the oven to 350°F.

2. Spread almonds in single layer on a rimmed baking sheet. Bake for 10 to 12 minutes or until dark brown and fragrant. Let cool on the baking sheet for 5 minutes.

3. In a food processor fitted with a chopping blade, pulse together almonds, canola oil, and salt until a paste forms and begins to clump together. (If you stop now, you'll have a delicious almond butter.)

4. Pour chocolate chips into a medium glass bowl. Microwave on high for 30 seconds, and stir chocolate chips. Microwave for 15 more seconds, and stir. Chocolate should start to melt. Repeat microwaving at 8- to 10-second intervals until chocolate is melted and smooth.

5. Pour melted chocolate and milk into the food processor with almonds, and pulse until a paste forms.

6. Transfer to glass jars, and store at room temperature for up to 1 week.

Variation: For **Chocolate Peanut Almondtella,** substitute ¾ cup peanut butter chips for ¾ cup chocolate chips.

Sunflower Seed Butter

Sunflower seeds are packed with vitamin E, and this butter provides a nutritious, nut-free alternative to peanut butter.

Yield:	Prep time:	Cook time:	Serving size:
2 cups	5 minutes	40 minutes	2 cups

2 cups raw sunflower seeds
⅛ tsp. salt
1 TB. honey

3 or 4 TB. canola or another neutral cooking oil

1. In a large frying pan over medium heat, toast 1 cup sunflower seeds, stirring constantly, for 2 to 4 minutes or until seeds are golden color. (This may take up to 20 minutes.) Remove toasted seeds from the pan, and repeat with remaining 1 cup sunflower seeds. The second cup will toast much faster—about 8 to 10 minutes.

2. Let seeds cool for 5 to 10 minutes.

3. Transfer seeds to a food processor fitted with a chopping blade, and add honey and salt. Process for 5 to 10 minutes or until seeds are ground and sticking to the sides of the food processor bowl.

4. Scrape down the sides of the bowl with a spatula, and continue puréeing, adding 3 or 4 tablespoons canola oil, 1 tablespoon at a time, until mixture turns into a paste.

5. Store in an airtight container in the refrigerator for up to 1 week. Allow to set at room temperature for several minutes before serving.

TASTE VERSUS APPEARANCE

If you don't toast the sunflower seeds (or toast them correctly), the finished butter might have a grayish tinge to it. Don't worry. It still has the sweet, nutty taste you'd expect. Toasting the seeds to that light golden color brings out more of the nutty flavor and gives the butter a more attractive look. When you're toasting the seeds, patience will pay off. The more you toast the seeds, the richer the taste of the butter.

Avocado Butter

I'm lactose intolerant, so I'm always looking for alternatives to butter. I'm also always looking for excuses to eat avocados. I love using this avocado butter on toast, English muffins, sandwiches, and most of all, cornbread.

Yield:	Prep time:	Serving size:
¼ to ½ cup	5 minutes	2 tablespoons

½ small to medium avocado   ⅛ tsp. salt

1. In a medium bowl, and using a potato masher, mash avocado until smooth.

2. Stir in salt, and enjoy serve immediately. Enjoy as a spread on your favorite bread.

3. This spread is best served immediately. If you do store it, place plastic wrap directly onto the top to prevent it from turning brown. Eat within 6 hours.

SKIP THE SALT

If you're watching your sodium intake, omit the salt. I add it because it enhances the flavor, but it's not essential.

Lemon Chive Butter

Crisp lemon and spicy chives make this butter taste like spring on whatever you spread it on.

Yield:	Prep time:	Serving size:
½ cup	35 minutes	1 tablespoon

1 stick unsalted butter (½ cup), at room temperature

Zest of 1 small lemon

¼ cup fresh chives, chopped

½ to 1 tsp. garlic powder

1. In a medium bowl, combine unsalted butter, lemon zest, chives, and garlic powder.

2. Using an electric mixer on medium speed, beat, scraping down the sides of the bowl with a spatula, for about 5 minutes or until smooth.

3. Refrigerate for 30 minutes. Allow butter to return to room temperature before serving with bread.

4. Store in an airtight container in the refrigerator for up to 1 week.

Tomato Basil Butter

This butter is particularly good for making garlic bread. Slice a loaf of French or another rustic bread halfway through, and fill the crevices with minced garlic, this butter, and maybe even a little shredded mozzarella cheese. Yum! This is also great for tossing with warm pasta for a very light, tomato-y butter sauce.

Yield:	Prep time:	Serving size:
½ cup	35 minutes	1 tablespoon

1 stick unsalted butter (½ cup), at room temperature	2 TB. Italian Seasoning (recipe in Chapter 7)
1½ TB. tomato paste	

1. In a medium bowl, combine unsalted butter, tomato paste, and Italian Seasoning.

2. Using an electric mixer on medium speed, beat, scraping down the sides of the bowl with a spatula, for about 5 minutes or until smooth.

3. Refrigerate for 30 minutes. Allow butter to return to room temperature before serving with bread.

4. Store in an airtight container in the refrigerator for up to 1 week.

Apple Butter

Names can be deceiving. In my family, butter comes from a cow, and if you spread fruit, it's a jam. When I make this, I just tell them it's applesauce to put on bread. When the eyebrows go up, I simply unscrew the top of the jar. As soon as the smell of warm leaf-pile-days and cool autumn nights hits their noses, they're reaching for their knives.

Yield:	Prep time:	Cook time:	Serving size:
3 cups	10 minutes	1 hour, 30 minutes	2 tablespoons

10 small apples (3 lb.), cored, quartered, and then halved	⅓ cup dark brown sugar, firmly packed
4 cups water	1 tsp. ground cinnamon
3 (2-in.) cinnamon sticks	½ tsp. ground nutmeg
6 whole cloves	Juice of 1 small lemon (1 TB.)

1. In a medium pan over high heat, combine apples, water, cinnamon sticks, and cloves. Cover, bring to a boil, and reduce heat to medium. Cook for 20 to 25 minutes or until you can cut apples in half by pressing to the side of the pan with a wooden spoon. Remove from heat.

2. Strain apples, reserving ½ cup cooking water.

3. Remove cloves and cinnamon sticks.

4. If you have an immersion blender, return apples to the pan and blend until you reach a smooth consistency. If you do not have an immersion blender, purée apples in two batches in a blender. Return apples to the pan.

5. Mix in dark brown sugar, cinnamon, nutmeg, and lemon juice.

6. Bring to a simmer, and reduce heat to medium-low. Simmer, stirring occasionally to prevent mixture from sticking and burning, for 55 to 65 minutes or until mixture has reduced by ⅓ to ¼. Apple butter will turn a dark brown and become very thick.

7. To test for doneness, scoop a portion onto a small plate, and place in the freezer for 10 minutes. When you can run a finger through the middle of mixture and it doesn't come back together, it's done.

8. Remove from heat, and cool to room temperature. Spoon into glass containers, and store in the refrigerator for 2 or 3 weeks.

BLENDING SAFETY

When blending hot liquids, fill the blender only halfway full, and place a towel over the lid when you hold it down. The heat from the liquid can cause the top to fly off and spatter a hot mess all over you and your kitchen. (Not like that's ever happened to me with hot enchilada sauce or anything ….)

Pumpkin Butter

I'm a firm believer in eating all things pumpkin year-round. This jammy pumpkin butter is great to make when you have extra pumpkin purée. It's great on toast and scones, but it's even better with slices of fresh apples and pears. This is chunkier than most pumpkin butters because I add apple pieces instead of cooking it in apple cider. I'd rather use orange juice to bring out the pumpkin flavor because it's more accessible year-round.

Yield:	Prep time:	Cook time:	Serving size:
2½ cups	10 minutes	55 minutes to 1 hour	2 tablespoons

3 cups pure pumpkin purée (1 [14.5-oz.] can plus 1 cup)

1 cup fresh orange juice (4 to 6 medium oranges), or ½ cup water and ½ cup orange juice

Zest of 1 medium orange (2 tsp.)

2 medium apples, peeled, cored, quartered, and then halved

1 TB. pumpkin pie spice

⅓ cup plus 1 TB. brown sugar, firmly packed

1. In medium saucepan over medium heat, combine pumpkin purée, orange juice, orange zest, apples, pumpkin pie spice, and brown sugar. Cover and simmer, stirring occasionally, for 20 to 25 minutes or until apples are tender.

2. When apples are tender, mash with a potato masher.

3. Reduce heat to medium-low, and simmer for 30 to 35 more minutes or until butter is thickened and a deep, dark brown.

4. Store in an airtight container in the refrigerator for 2 or 3 weeks.

FANTASTIC FRUIT BUTTERS

Apple and pumpkin butters have many uses. Spread them on toast, muffins, and scones, or swirl some into oatmeal. You can even use fruit butter to replace oil in cake recipes in a 1:1 ratio.

Mayonnaise

Mayonnaise and I have a long, twisted relationship. For most of my life, I wasn't interested. Then during a cookbook project, I found myself with a vat of mayonnaise in my refrigerator and an expiration date that was rapidly approaching. I mixed it with salsa to make a creamy salad dressing, dunked French fries and roasted vegetables into it, and spread it on toast with avocado. In the meantime, I fell in love with it. After the expiration date, the infatuation grew. I decided that if I really wanted it, I had to make it. But recipe after recipe failed. This recipe, however, became my savior. The Dijon mustard aids in the emulsification while the water (supposedly) helps keep it from breaking.

Yield:	Prep time:	Serving size:
1½ cups	10 minutes	2 tablespoons

2 large egg yolks

¼ tsp. water

2 TB. Dijon mustard

1 cup canola oil

Juice of 1 small lemon (1 TB.)

1. Wrap a damp towel around the base of a medium bowl to secure it in place.

2. In the bowl, whisk together egg yolks, water, and Dijon mustard.

3. Continue whisking with one hand while with the other hand, you very slowly—a few dribbles at a time—pour in canola oil. Do not stop whisking, and do not add more oil until previous drops have been totally absorbed by egg mixture.

4. When you've added more than ½ of canola oil, you can add it a little more quickly, but be very careful to be sure oil is absorbed before adding more.

5. Stir in lemon juice.

6. Serve immediately, or store in an airtight container in the refrigerator for up to 1 week.

Aioli

To me, aioli is dressed-up mayonnaise. This simple recipe makes a great dipping sauce for crispy veggies, a fancy spread for sandwiches, or a great sauce to eat with grilled or baked fish.

Yield:	Prep time:	Serving size:
½ cup	10 minutes	2 tablespoons

1 clove Roasted Garlic (recipe in Chapter 3)

1 TB. olive oil

¾ cup Mayonnaise (recipe earlier in this chapter)

½ to 1 tsp. hot sauce (recipes in Chapter 4)

Juice of 1 small lemon (2 TB.)

1. In a small bowl, and using a fork, mash Roasted Garlic with ½ tablespoon olive oil.

2. In a larger bowl, combine Roasted Garlic paste, remaining ½ tablespoon olive oil, Mayonnaise, hot sauce, and lemon juice.

3. Serve immediately, or store in an airtight container in the refrigerator for up to 1 week.

Strawberry Refrigerator Preserves

When I was growing up, every summer my mother and I went to a you-pick strawberry farm. We'd spend the morning filling flats (and my mouth) with fresh, sweet berries. We'd come home with stained fingers, and my mother would set to work on her strawberry jam. I love the smell of strawberries boiling on the stove. These are the berries of my memory; exaggerated with time, these berries are summer on a spoon.

Yield:	Prep time:	Cook time:	Serving size:
1 pint	15 minutes	45 to 55 minutes	2 tablespoons

5 cups strawberries, washed and hulled

Juice of 1 small lemon (1 TB.)

½ cup evaporated cane juice or unprocessed sugar

1. In a large bowl, and using a potato masher, crush berries until they're your desired consistency. I like to have some small chunks of berry remaining.

2. In a Dutch oven or heavy-bottomed pan over medium heat, combine strawberries, lemon juice, and evaporated cane juice. Bring to a boil, reduce heat to medium-low, and simmer for 45 to 55 minutes, stirring occasionally so fruit doesn't stick to the pan.

3. To test for doneness, scoop a portion onto a small plate, and place in the freezer for 10 minutes. When you can run a finger through the middle of mixture and it doesn't come back together, it's done.

4. Remove from heat, and ladle into a glass jar. Let cool for a few minutes and then seal. Store in the refrigerator for up to 4 weeks.

NOT YOUR TYPICAL JAM

These strawberry preserves and the others in this chapter aren't your typical jams or jellies. You'll notice I don't use pectin, and I use very little sugar. That's why you need to cook the fruit longer, to get the thicker consistency you have in jelly or jam. Essentially, you're reducing the fruit to thicken it. My friend tells me I'm laughing in the face of physics and chemistry, but really I'm just trying to get the essence out of the fruit. I just can't accept that you need to add cup after cup of sugar to fruit that's already naturally sweet.

Grape Preserves

As I researched grape jellies and jams, I kept reading about peeling the grapes. I don't know about you, but I have better things to do than peel a quart of grapes. But I also wasn't ready to give up my dreams of a homemade, low-sugar grape spread. I eventually found success. I guarantee that after you cook down the grapes to their grapey essence, you won't mind a few skins here and there.

Yield:	Prep time:	Cook time:	Serving size:
1 cup	15 minutes	1 hour, 10 minutes	2 tablespoons

4 cups black or concord grapes, stems removed and washed

Juice of ½ small lemon (1 TB.)

¼ cup evaporated cane juice or unprocessed sugar

1. In a Dutch oven or heavy-bottomed pan over medium heat, combine black grapes and lemon juice. Cook, stirring occasionally to prevent grapes from sticking, for about 10 minutes or until grapes have softened.

2. Remove from heat, and using a potato masher, crush grapes until they're your desired consistency.

3. Add evaporated cane juice, and bring to a simmer over medium to medium-low heat. Simmer for 45 to 55 minutes.

4. To test for doneness, scoop a portion onto a small plate, and place in the freezer for 10 minutes. When you can run a finger through the middle of mixture and it doesn't come back together, it's done.

5. Remove from heat, and ladle into a glass jar. Let cool for a few minutes and then seal. Store in the refrigerator for up to 4 weeks. Preserves will thicken overnight.

Blackberry Preserves

In terms of fruit matchmaking, I decided long ago that blackberries and limes are soul mates. Every time I make blackberries, I can't help but reach for a lime, too. These preserves are more tangy than sweet, so if that's not your preference, increase the sugar and add lemon or orange juice for the acidic component.

Yield:	Prep time:	Cook time:	Serving size:
1 pint	5 minutes	55 minutes to 1 hour, 15 minutes	2 tablespoons

5 cups fresh blackberries
Juice of 1 small lime (2 TB.)

⅓ cup evaporated cane juice or unprocessed sugar

1. In a Dutch oven or heavy-bottomed pan over medium-high heat, combine blackberries, lime juice, and evaporated cane juice. Mash with a potato masher until combined.

2. Bring to a boil and then reduce heat to medium. Simmer for 55 minutes to 1 hour, 15 minutes or until mixture reaches your desired consistency.

3. To test for doneness, scoop a portion onto a small plate, and place in the freezer for 10 minutes. When you can run a finger through the middle of mixture and it doesn't come back together, it's done.

4. Remove from heat, and ladle into a glass jar. Let cool for a few minutes and then seal. Store in the refrigerator for up to 4 weeks. Preserves will thicken overnight.

Variation: For **Raspberry Preserves,** replace blackberries with an equal amount of raspberries and swap out the lime juice with lemon juice. Depending on the sweetness of the berries, you may also reduce the evaporated cane juice to ¼ cup.

Spice It Up  7

When I was first learning to cook, I fell in love with spices. Keep in mind, I was raised on the 1980s spice trinity: paprika, oregano, and cinnamon. If you had those, did you really need anything else? How little I knew.

Over the years, I have evolved my spice collection into an overflowing cascade of bottles and jars. As a cooking expert, I tell you that you should only keep what you use. But as a real person, I have far more spices than I care to admit. Also, as someone in the role of cooking expert, I know I should tell you to toast and grind your own spices. I wish I could tell you I toast and grind my own. But I don't.

I happily use a variety of spices. I have my standbys: cayenne, ground cloves, nutmeg, and smoked paprika. I also love a good spice mix, and I've tried many Italian and taco seasonings in my day. After a while, I found I was always adding extra spices to get the exact taste I craved. I did this for longer than I care to admit before realizing the obvious: I could make my own spice mixes that would be exactly what I wanted.

Consider the recipes in this chapter a starting point. Like a lot of cinnamon? Add it. Can't stand fennel (like Manatee)? Take it out. Make these spices work for you.

Store spices in airtight container in a cool, dry place to extend the shelf life and keep the spice tasting fresh.

THE NOSE KNOWS

When combining spices for the first time, I let my nose do most of the work. For spice mixes like Pumpkin Pie Spice, Garam Masala, and Italian Seasoning, I let my nose do the bulk of the work. (I taste-test Cinnamon Sugar and Lemon Pepper.) I smell the spices individually and taste a little of them. As I add them to the recipe, I smell the mix to be sure the spices that are standing out are the ones I want to taste. As I start cooking with the spice blend, I continue making adjustments until I reach the perfect balance.

Cinnamon Sugar

This is so simple and so good. I love sprinkling it on a warm piece of buttered bread or toast. It's equally good combined with cocoa for some Cocoa Roasted Almonds or on popcorn for Dessert Popcorn (recipes in Chapter 10). I like a little more sugar in my cinnamon sugar, but play around with the ratio to suit your tastes.

Yield:	Prep time:	Serving size:
¼ cup plus 1 tablespoon	5 minutes	1 teaspoon

2 TB. ground cinnamon	3 TB. unprocessed sugar or evaporated cane juice

1. In a small bowl, whisk together cinnamon and unprocessed sugar.

2. Store in an airtight container for up to 1 year.

Pumpkin Pie Spice

I can't make anything pumpkin without including some of this spice blend. It contains all my favorite spices combined in the perfect autumn package. For an extra-special treat, use it to sweeten homemade whipping cream and use it to top your pumpkin pie or your morning coffee.

Yield:	Prep time:	Serving size:
¼ cup plus 1 tablespoon	5 minutes	1 teaspoon

2 TB. ground cinnamon	2 tsp. ground allspice
1 TB. ground nutmeg	1 tsp. ground cloves
3 tsp. ground ginger	⅛ tsp. salt

1. In a small bowl, whisk together cinnamon, nutmeg, ginger, allspice, cloves, and salt.

2. Store in an airtight container for up to 1 month.

Italian Seasoning

I had to find a way to make my own Italian blend because I can't keep enough of it in the house. Manatee eats it on everything: eggs, salads, popcorn, hummus, raw mushrooms, and of course, pizza and anything else Italian.

Yield:	Prep time:	Serving size:
¼ cup	5 minutes	1 teaspoon

3 TB. dried oregano

1 TB. dried rosemary, ground

1 TB. dried basil

2 tsp. dried parsley

1 tsp. ground fennel seed

1 tsp. crushed red pepper flakes

1 tsp. dried thyme

1 tsp. onion powder

1 tsp. garlic powder

½ tsp. ground anise

⅛ tsp. salt

⅛ tsp. ground black pepper

1. In a small bowl, whisk together oregano, rosemary, basil, parsley, fennel seed, crushed red pepper flakes, thyme, onion powder, garlic powder, anise, salt, and black pepper.

2. Store in an airtight container for up to 1 month.

GRINDING SPICES

Wait, you told me you don't grind your own spices? Normally, I don't. With fennel seeds and rosemary, however, I find it's so much better to grind them right before using them. Before you picture me toiling away at a mortar and pestle, let me share a secret: the personal-size blender. It's perfect for grinding small batches of spices with the push of a button. And when you're done, you can throw it in the dishwasher. If that's still too much, you can buy ground fennel seed, and whole rosemary is fine in this blend.

Spicy Italian Seasoning

You'd think this version would be a Manatee creation, wouldn't you? *Au contraire.* When it comes to spices, I want the most flavor punch with the least amount of effort. Think Italian Spice exaggerated and with a serious spice kick. This is my answer to jazzing up any Italian sauce or dish.

Yield:	Prep time:	Serving size:
⅓ cup	5 minutes	1 teaspoon

2 TB. dried oregano

1 TB. dried rosemary, ground

2 TB. dried basil

2 tsp. dried parsley

1 tsp. dried thyme

2 tsp. ground fennel seed

1 TB. crushed red pepper flakes

1 tsp. onion powder

1 tsp. garlic powder

½ tsp. ground anise

¼ tsp. cayenne

⅛ tsp. salt

⅛ tsp. ground black pepper

1. In a small bowl, whisk together oregano, rosemary, basil, parsley, thyme, fennel seed, crushed red pepper flakes, onion powder, garlic powder, anise, cayenne, salt, and black pepper.

2. Store in an airtight container for up to 1 month.

HEAT WARNING

If you taste this spice mix on its own, you might get the hiccups from the level of spice (not that I would know from experience).

Taco Seasoning

I'm a huge fan of tacos, and for me, the taco seasoning can make or break the dish. Prior to making my own blend, I was always doctoring the store-bought versions. After a lot of mixing, I found the secret ingredient was corn flour. It complements the cumin without letting the cumin take over the dish. Unlike other recipes in this chapter, this makes a hearty portion. Keep it in an airtight container. You'll go through it faster than you think.

Yield:	Prep time:	Serving size:
⅔ cup	5 minutes	3 tablespoons to ¼ cup

¼ cup corn flour

¼ cup cumin

1 TB. chili powder

1 tsp. crushed red pepper flakes

½ tsp. onion powder

½ tsp. garlic powder

¼ tsp. salt

1. In a small bowl, whisk together corn flour, cumin, chili powder, crushed red pepper flakes, onion powder, garlic powder, and salt.

2. Store in an airtight container for up to 1 month.

RATIOS FOR COOKING

When using this with taco meat or tofu, start with 1 tablespoon per pound and then start tasting. When cooking for my spice-adverse father, I stick to 1 or 2 tablespoons, but when cooking at home, I use about ¼ cup. When making taco meat, I add this with ⅓ to ¼ cup water after I've browned the meat.

Lemon Pepper

Don't let the cook time deceive you. This is *still* an easy recipe. Once you get the zest and the pepper in the oven, the smell emanating from your kitchen will be reason enough to make this. After you zest the lemons, why not make some lemonade (recipes in Chapter 17)?

Yield:	Prep time:	Cook time:	Serving size:
½ cup	20 minutes	45 minutes to 1 hour	2 teaspoons

Zest of 7 small lemons (⅓ cup)   1 tsp. ground coriander
¼ cup ground black pepper

1. Preheat the oven to 200°F. Line a rimmed baking sheet with parchment paper.

2. In a small bowl, whisk together lemon zest, black pepper, and coriander. Spread out spice mixture in a single layer on the baking sheet. Bake for 45 minutes to 1 hour or until zest is completely dry.

3. Let cool on the baking sheet to room temperature.

4. In small blender or a food processor fitted with a chopping blade, pulse spice mixture until well combined, fine, and consistent.

5. Store in an airtight container for up to 1 month.

Spicy Ranch Seasoning

My favorite chips were always Cool Ranch Doritos. But not only do they contain dairy (a big no-no to my lactose-intolerant self), I'm also pretty sure they aren't clean. This flavoring allows me all the flavor with no guilt or upset stomach.

Yield:	Prep time:	Serving size:
¼ cup	5 minutes	2 teaspoons

2 TB. nutritional yeast flakes   ¼ tsp. chili powder
2 tsp. onion powder   1 tsp. ground black pepper
1 tsp. garlic powder   1 tsp. corn flour
1 tsp. cayenne   ½ tsp. cumin
1 tsp. ground mustard

1. In a small bowl, whisk together nutritional yeast flakes, onion powder, garlic powder, cayenne, ground mustard, chili powder, black pepper, corn flour, and cumin.

2. Store in an airtight container for up to 1 month.

Garam Masala

Garam masala is an Indian spice and one of my favorite combinations of sweet and salty. I love adding it to curries and anything involving squash. I like to think of it as Pumpkin Pie Spice's older, more sophisticated sister. It has the sweetness and warmth of Pumpkin Pie Spice, with a salty edge of cumin and coriander.

Yield:	Prep time:	Serving size:
3 tablespoons	5 minutes	1 teaspoon

1½ TB. ground cinnamon

1 TB. ground cumin

1 TB. ground coriander

2 tsp. ground black pepper

2 tsp. ground cloves

1½ tsp. ground nutmeg

½ tsp. ground ginger

1. In a small bowl, whisk together cinnamon, cumin, coriander, black pepper, cloves, nutmeg, and ginger.

2. Store in an airtight container for up to 1 month.

Snacks, Salads, and Mini-Meals  3

Now that we've covered the basics, let's start using these recipes in fun and creative ways.

First, I give you recipes for everything you need in the A.M. Whether you have a sweet tooth in the morning (like me) and are hankering for some homemade toaster pastries or quick breads, or you're more of a health nut who wants to nosh on granola and sip smoothies, I have you covered.

Next I share a collection of the super creative salads, perfect for afternoon snacking or for midday meals. I picked only the coolest salads and slaws for this chapter. Curry Chicken Salad, Summer Quinoa Salad, and Thai Peanutty Coleslaw are just a few of the fun dishes in this chapter.

But that's not all. I also share recipes for tons of terrific snacks. First up are those munchies you can easily eat from hand to mouth, like nuts, chips, crackers, and popcorn—all healthy treats you can enjoy while watching a movie or on the go.

If you linger by the dip at parties, Chapter 11 will make your processed favorites seem as distant and foreign as powder blue leisure suits and poodle skirts. Take your pick of one of six varieties of salsa, three varieties of guacamole, and seven varieties of hummus.

Feeling a little hungrier than usual? Mini-meals to the rescue. From jerky to nachos to quesadilla, who says healthy has to be boring?

Morning Munchies

8

Mornings were tough when I went clean. There's a school of thought that claims you can eat anything in the morning you'd eat for the rest of the day, but I'm not one of those people who can rock leftovers before 11:30 A.M. I need something breakfastlike, preferably sweet, and healthy. And like most people, I don't have a lot of time to prepare snacks in the morning.

I devised the recipes in this chapter with these principles in mind—sweet, healthy, portable. Pair them with a piece of fruit, and you're on your way to a healthy day.

Making Your Own Toaster Pastries

When researching for the toaster pastry recipes in this chapter, I decided to go back to the source. I bought an organic version of a toaster pastry. I have to admit, it didn't taste bad, but within 30 minutes, my stomach was reminding me why I don't eat processed foods. My version solves that problem.

Toaster pastries aren't hard to make, although there is a lot of cooling time involved. I can tell you the results are worth it.

Toaster Pastry Dough

I'm not proud of this, but Pop-Tarts were my saving grace in college. They were my go-to breakfasts and prerunning foods. For whatever reason, these portable pies have been deemed socially acceptable to eat for breakfast. And I love an excuse to eat sweets in the morning. This recipe is for the basic dough. You can make it with your choice of two whole-grain flours: spelt or graham flour. The spelt gives the dough a more nutty taste, while the graham flour gives it more of a graham cracker taste. I use a little more graham flour than spelt because it's not as dry as spelt.

Yield:	Prep time:	Cook time:	Serving size:
8 regular or 16 mini toaster pastries	1 hour, 15 minutes	25 to 30 minutes	1 toaster pastry or 2 mini toaster pastries

1½ cups whole-wheat pastry flour

1 cup spelt flour or 1¼ cups graham flour

2 TB. sucanat or unprocessed sugar

1 tsp. salt

½ cup cold butter, cut into pieces

⅓ cup Yogurt Cheese (recipe in Chapter 3) or cream cheese

1 large egg

2 TB. cold water

1 tsp. apple cider vinegar

1. In a food processor fitted with a chopping blade, pulse together whole-wheat pastry flour, spelt flour, sucanat, and salt.

2. Add butter, and pulse until mixture becomes a coarse meal.

3. Transfer mixture to a large bowl, and stir in Yogurt Cheese.

4. In a small bowl, whisk together egg and water. Add to flour mixture with apple cider vinegar, and stir to combine.

5. Break dough into halves. Form each half into a flat rectangle, and wrap in plastic wrap. Refrigerate for 30 minutes.

6. Prepare a floured workspace, and cover a plate with parchment paper or a silicone mat. Fill a small bowl with water.

7. Remove ½ of dough. Roll out dough to a ⅛-inch thickness.

8. Set a 3×5 note card on dough, and cut around it using a butter knife. To make mini pastries, cut that rectangle in half horizontally. Use your hands to stretch rectangles a little thinner and place on the prepared plate. Repeat with remaining dough.

9. Prick dough rectangles with a fork. This helps steam escape and keeps dough from rising too much.

10. Place ½ to 1 tablespoon filling (depending on if you're doing regular or mini pastries) in the middle of dough.

11. Dip your finger in the bowl of water, and run it around edge of pastry. Place another rectangle on top, and press edges together. Using a fork, press edges to crimp together. Repeat with remaining dough rectangles.

12. Refrigerate pastries for 30 minutes.

13. Meanwhile, form pastries with remaining half of dough. Repeat refrigeration.

14. Preheat the oven to 350°F.

15. Place parchment paper with pastries on a baking sheet, and bake for 25 to 30 minutes or until tops turn golden brown.

16. Cool pastries on a cooling rack until room temperature. At this point, you can add a glaze.

17. Store in an airtight container at room temperature for 3 to 5 days, or in the freezer for up to 2 months. To reheat, toast in a toaster or toaster oven.

PASTRY POINTERS

Work quickly because you don't want the dough to get too warm. And keep rotating—roll out one half of the dough, and while those pastries are chilling, roll out the other half. When it comes to the filling, less is more. If you overfill the pastries, the filling will run out the sides. Keep the filling flat to get a flatter pastry so you can fit them into your toaster.

Berry Toaster Pastries

Before Pop-Tarts got all crazy with flavors like cookie dough and s'mores, there were the classic berry flavors. Check out Chapter 6 for some homemade preserves recipes, or grab your favorite no-sugar-added, organic jam.

Yield:	Prep time:	Cook time:	Serving size:
8 regular or 16 mini toaster pastries	1 hour, 20 minutes	25 to 30 minutes	1 regular toaster pastry or 2 mini toaster pastries

1 batch Toaster Pastry Dough (recipe earlier in this chapter)

5 TB. plus 1 tsp. berry preserves or jam of choice

1 TB. milk or nondairy milk

$^2/_3$ cup confectioners' sugar

1. Prepare and bake Toaster Pastry Dough using 5 tablespoons berry preserves as filling.

2. In a small bowl, whisk together remaining 1 teaspoon berry preserves, milk, and confectioners' sugar. Brush glaze on cooled, baked toaster pastries, and let dry completely.

3. Store in an airtight container for 2 or 3 days or freeze for up to 2 months. Pastries can go directly from the freezer to the toaster.

Peanut Butter and Jelly Toaster Pastries

PB&J meets pie—two classics in one hand. Sounds like a winner to me!

Yield:	Prep time:	Cook time:	Serving size:
8 regular or 16 mini toaster pastries	1 hour, 20 minutes	25 to 30 minutes	1 regular toaster pastry or 2 mini toaster pastries

1 batch Toaster Pastry Dough (recipe earlier in this chapter)

$4^1/_2$ TB. Peanut Butter (recipe in Chapter 6)

2 TB. berry preserves (recipes in Chapter 6)

1 TB. milk or nondairy milk

$^2/_3$ cup confectioners' sugar

1. Prepare and bake Toaster Pastry Dough using 3 tablespoons Peanut Butter and berry preserves as filling.

2. In a small bowl, whisk together remaining 1½ tablespoons Peanut Butter, milk, and confectioners' sugar. Brush glaze on cooled, baked toaster pastries, and let dry completely.

3. Store in an airtight container for 2 or 3 days or freeze for up to 2 months. Pastries can go directly from the freezer to the toaster.

Brown Sugar Toaster Pastries

For some reason, these Pop-Tarts were my go-to nosh before a run. This homemade version does not disappoint. The Yogurt Cheese adds a richness you just can't get with chemical fillers. If you don't have any Yogurt Cheese left from your last batch, you can substitute cream cheese.

Yield:	Prep time:	Cook time:	Serving size:
8 regular or 16 mini toaster pastries	1 hour, 20 minutes	25 to 30 minutes	1 regular toaster pastry or 2 mini toaster pastries

½ cup Yogurt Cheese (recipe in Chapter 3) or cream cheese

3 TB. brown sugar

5 TB. Cinnamon Sugar (recipe in Chapter 7)

1 batch Toaster Pastry Dough (recipe earlier in this chapter)

1 tsp. ground cinnamon

1 TB. milk or nondairy milk

⅔ cup confectioners' sugar

1. In a small bowl, whisk together Yogurt Cheese, brown sugar, and Cinnamon Sugar.

2. Prepare and bake Toaster Pastry Dough using Cinnamon Sugar mixture as filling.

3. In another small bowl, whisk together cinnamon, milk, and confectioners' sugar. Brush glaze on cooled, baked toaster pastries, and let dry completely.

4. Store in an airtight container for 2 or 3 days or freeze for up to 2 months. Pastries can go directly from the freezer to the toaster.

Chocolate Toaster Pastries

Nothing says breakfast treat like chocolate. These toaster pastries are perfect for taming your sweet tooth, whether it's in the morning or a dessert later in the day.

Yield:	Prep time:	Cook time:	Serving size:
8 regular or 16 mini toaster pastries	1 hour, 20 minutes	25 to 30 minutes	1 regular toaster pastry or 2 mini toaster pastries

1 batch Toaster Pastry Dough (recipe earlier in this chapter)

6 TB. Almondtella (recipe in Chapter 6)

2 tsp. cocoa powder

1 TB. milk or nondairy milk

⅔ cup confectioners' sugar

1. Prepare and bake Toaster Pastry Dough using Almondtella as filling.

2. In a small bowl, whisk together cocoa powder, milk, and confectioners' sugar. Brush glaze on cooled, baked toaster pastries, and let dry completely.

3. Store in an airtight container for 2 or 3 days or freeze for up to 2 months. Pastries can go directly from the freezer to the toaster.

Badger Girl Granola 6.0

I have high standards when it comes to granola. I can't stand any of the overly sweet store-bought brands, so I knew I had to make my own. I also can't stand the idea of using mounds of butter and fat to make granola. For five rounds, I battled it out with granola. I ended up with flimsy, burnt, and inedible versions. Manatee ate every single round, and I learned the meaning of unconditional love. Version 6.0 came about when I had given up on granola and decided to make granola bars. Lucky for me, the bars didn't stick. After pouting for 3 days, I finally gave in and had some with a sliced banana. I was shocked; it was amazing. Since then, we always have a batch in our house. Manatee eats his with almond milk as a home-made cereal, and I eat it with my beloved bananas.

Yield:	Prep time:	Cook time:	Serving size:
3 quarts	10 minutes, plus 4 to 8 hours (cooling)	1 hour	⅓ cup

1½ cups rolled oats

½ cup raw pumpkin seeds

½ cup raw sunflower seeds

1½ cups slivered or sliced almonds

½ cup raw quinoa, rinsed

¼ cup flaxseeds

2 TB. coconut oil

⅓ cup agave nectar

½ cup your choice nut butter

¼ cup protein powder

½ cup raisins

¼ cup dried cranberries

¼ cup finely unsweetened shredded coconut or coconut flakes

1. Preheat the oven to 325°F. Grease 2 large rimmed baking sheets.

2. In a large bowl, combine rolled oats, pumpkin seeds, sunflower seeds, almonds, quinoa, and flaxseeds.

3. In a small saucepan over medium heat, heat coconut oil and agave nectar. Stir until coconut oil is melted, and immediately remove from heat.

4. Drizzle coconut oil glaze over oat mixture, and stir, using a wooden spoon, until combined. Spread oat mixture onto the prepared baking sheets, keeping mixture away from the edges of the pan.

5. Bake, stirring occasionally so granola cooks evenly, for 20 to 25 minutes or until golden brown.

6. Meanwhile, in a small bowl, combine nut butter and protein powder.

7. Grease a 9×9 cake pan. Clean out the bowl you used earlier for oat mixture.

8. When oat mixture is done, remove it from the oven and allow it to cool for 10 to 15 minutes.

9. Return oat mixture to the large bowl. Mix in raisins, cranberries, and coconut. Add nut butter mixture, and stir until combined. (I start with a wooden spoon and then use my hands to incorporate nut butter into granola.)

10. Press granola into the prepared cake pan, and cool for 4 to 8 hours. Store in an airtight container for up to 3 weeks.

RIMMED BAKING SHEETS

Use two rimmed baking sheets so you can spread out the oat mixture and none of it has to be close to the edge of the pan. The heat is greater by the edges of the pan, so the food there is more likely to burn. I've tried this on flat cookie sheets, but that usually resulted in a very messy oven.

Fruit and Nut Salad

This is my go-to snack when I have a ton of errands to run and not a lot of time to eat. I love eating this salad with walnuts because of their high omega-3 content. Just ¼ cup walnuts has 2.27 grams omega-3s—compare that to salmon, where 4 ounces nets you only 1.47 grams. And you know the saying: an apple a day ….

Yield:	Prep time:	Serving size:
1 cup	5 minutes	1 cup

1 medium apple, cored and diced

⅓ cup toasted or raw walnuts

¼ cup raisins

1. In a small bowl, combine apple, walnuts, and raisins.
2. Serve immediately. (You could store it for later, but walnuts will lose their crunch and apples might turn brown.)

Variation: Substitute your favorite nuts and dried fruit. I love dried cranberries and almonds. You can also substitute a pear for the apple.

Cran-Blueberry Smoothie

I was very slow to get on the smoothie train. When Manatee and I visited some friends in Chicago, we got smoothies at the Green City Market (a farmers' market near Lincoln Zoo), and I saw another side of this breakfast drink. Made with fresh apple cider, my smoothie was refreshing and full of fall flavors. I couldn't wait to go home and make my own version.

Yield:	Prep time:	Serving size:
2 cups	10 minutes	2 cups

1 cup frozen blueberries

½ cup fresh cranberries

1 cup apple cider

1 TB. protein powder

1 TB. ground flaxseeds (optional)

1. In a blender, combine blueberries and cranberries. Pour in apple cider, add protein powder and ground flaxseed (if using), and purée until smooth.

2. Serve immediately.

Peanut Butter Cup Smoothie

A lot of people are into "green" smoothies. They throw a bunch of kale and spinach in a blender, give it a whirl, and tell everyone how good it is. Yeah, right. You keep your green drinks; I prefer smoothies that taste like chocolate peanut butter cups. And believe it or not, this is not junk food. Frozen blueberries enhance the chocolaty factor while frozen bananas add a creaminess that can't found in salad greens. Throw in some protein powder, chia seeds, and ground flaxseeds, and we'll see whose smoothie is healthier.

Yield:	Prep time:	Serving size:
2 cups	10 minutes	2 cups

1 cup crushed ice

¼ cup frozen blueberries

1 frozen banana, peeled

½ cup water

1 cup milk or unsweetened nondairy milk

1 TB. Hot Cocoa Mix (recipe in Chapter 17)

1 TB. Peanut Butter (recipe in Chapter 6)

1 TB. protein powder (optional)

2 TB. chia seeds (optional)

1 TB. ground flaxseeds (optional)

1. In a blender, combine ice, blueberries, and banana. Pour in water and milk. Add Hot Cocoa Mix and Peanut Butter, followed by protein powder, chia seeds, and ground flaxseeds (if using). Purée until smooth.

2. Serve immediately.

CHEW ON THIS

Chia seeds are a whole protein, contain a ton of calcium and omega-3s, keep you full longer, and aid in digestion. They don't have a taste of their own, but they will intensify other tastes.

Peanut Butter and Banana Quesadillas

I love peanut butter, and I love bananas. I've tried peanut butter and banana on toast, but I feel way too full after. Enter the tortilla, which holds my beloved ingredients together, is portable, and leaves me feeling satisfied and not stuffed. Pair this with an apple, and you have a complete breakfast.

Yield:	Prep time:	Cook time:	Serving size:
3 pieces	5 minutes	3 to 5 minutes	3 pieces

2 TB. Peanut Butter (recipe in Chapter 6)	½ banana, peeled and sliced
1 (8-in.) Wheat Tortilla (recipe in Chapter 3)	

1. Spread Peanut Butter on ½ of Wheat Tortilla. Top Peanut Butter with banana slices and fold tortilla over to cover filling.

2. Place folded tortilla in a toaster oven, and place the baking tray over tortilla to press it down. Or place tortilla in a small skillet over medium heat with a glass bowl on top of it.

3. Heat tortilla for 3 to 5 minutes or until tortilla is starting to brown and filling is warm. Cut into thirds, and serve immediately.

Cranberry and Pumpkin Muffins

These muffins combine the Badger Girl trinity I can't get enough of: cranberry, pumpkin, and orange. The orange brings out the sweetness of the pumpkin and the tartness of the cranberry. I love making a batch of these and throwing them in the freezer. Before I get ready for the day, I pull out a muffin from the freezer, and by the time I'm headed out the door, it's ready to eat.

Yield:	Prep time:	Cook time:	Serving size:
12 muffins	20 minutes	20 to 25 minutes	1 muffin

1¾ cups whole-wheat pastry flour

2 TB. chia seeds (optional)

½ cup sucanat or unprocessed sugar

1 TB. baking powder

½ tsp. baking soda

3 tsp. Pumpkin Pie Spice (recipe in Chapter 7)

¼ tsp. salt

½ cup unsweetened applesauce

1 cup canned pumpkin purée

2 tsp. vanilla extract

Zest of 1 or 2 medium oranges (2 tsp.)

2 large eggs

½ cup milk or nondairy milk

¾ cup dried cranberries

½ cup chopped pecans

1. Preheat the oven to 350°F. Grease and flour a 12-cup muffin pan.

2. In a medium bowl, whisk together whole-wheat pastry flour, chia seeds (if using), sucanat, baking powder, baking soda, Pumpkin Pie Spice, and salt.

3. In a large bowl, and using an electric mixer on medium speed, cream together applesauce, pumpkin purée, and vanilla extract.

4. Add orange zest, eggs, and milk to pumpkin mixture, and blend on medium speed.

5. With the mixer on low speed, slowly add flour mixture.

6. Using a wooden spoon, fold in cranberries and pecans.

7. Pour batter into the prepared muffin pan, filling cups almost to the top. This will cause muffins to puff up and over the pan.

8. Bake for 20 to 25 minutes or until a toothpick inserted in center of cupcakes comes out clean or with 1 or 2 crumbs.

9. Let cool in the muffin pan for 10 to 15 minutes and then invert onto a cooling rack. Store muffins in an airtight container at room temperature for 3 to 5 days or in the freezer for up to 2 months.

Healthy Egg Muffins

I have a confession. Prior to committing to a whole foods diet, I loved a certain egg sandwich from a certain fast-food chain. I worked at a nonprofit for a year that required me to drive an hour each way to work. Thirty minutes into the drive, I would often go through this drive-thru. It might have tasted good, but I never felt good when I got to work. Did that stop me? Not at all. This version tastes far better than its commercially produced brother, and you feel great afterward.

Yield:	Prep time:	Cook time:	Serving size:
1 sandwich	5 minutes	5 minutes	1 sandwich

1 English muffin	⅛ tsp. ground black pepper
3 large egg whites, or 1 large egg and 1 large egg white	2 TB. water
⅛ tsp. garlic powder	½ TB. butter
	1 TB. Ketchup (recipe in Chapter 4)

1. Split English muffin in half, and toast.

2. In a small bowl, whisk together egg whites, garlic powder, black pepper, and water.

3. In a small skillet over medium heat, melt butter. Add egg mixture, and cook, using a spatula to continuously push egg whites around the pan, for 5 to 8 minutes or until egg whites are fully cooked.

4. Spread Ketchup on English muffin halves. Place egg whites on one half, and top with remaining English muffin half to make a sandwich.

5. Serve immediately, or wrap in aluminum foil to eat on the go.

Variations: For a **Fresh Garden Healthy Egg Muffin,** omit the butter, and place 1 tomato slice on each English muffin half. For a **Californian Egg Muffin,** replace the Ketchup with Avocado Butter (recipe in Chapter 6) and add 2 fresh tomato slices. You can also add a slice of cheese or meat to the sandwich.

EATING ON THE GO

To make this a driver-friendly sandwich, wrap it in aluminum foil before you leave home. Just be careful when you eat it because the foil can cut you. Once when I was eating this sandwich on the go and enthusiastically smashing it into my mouth as I drove, I got to work to find hundreds of miniscule cuts on my chin from the foil.

Triple Threat Apple Bread

As an acting major, I yearned to be a triple threat: someone who could act, sing, and dance. I had the acting thing down, and thanks to my years of dance classes, I could do choreography. Singing was my problem. During an audition for a Sondheim musical, I decided to do a song where I could "talk" through it. Let's just say that when I finished, I wanted nothing more than to hide. In my hurry to make my exit, I managed to take the wrong set of stairs and ended up *under* the stage. Good thing I can cook! This bread is a true triple threat: applesauce, apple butter, and fresh apples. It would kick that audition in the butt and then turn down the role for something better. And when you eat this bread, you'll feel like a triple threat: healthy, happy, and satisfied.

Yield:	Prep time:	Cook time:	Serving size:
2 (9×5×3-in.) loaves	20 minutes	40 to 50 minutes	1 slice

2 cups whole-wheat pastry flour

1 cup spelt flour

2 tsp. ground cinnamon

½ tsp. ground nutmeg

1 tsp. baking soda

½ tsp. baking powder

⅛ tsp. salt

3 large eggs, beaten

1½ cups sucanat or unprocessed sugar

½ cup Apple Butter (recipe in Chapter 6)

½ cup unsweetened applesauce

1 tsp. vanilla extract

2 cups diced, skin-on apples

½ cup chopped walnuts

½ cup dried cranberries (optional)

1. Preheat the oven to 350°F. Grease and flour 2 (9×5×3-inch) loaf pans.

2. In a medium bowl, whisk together whole-wheat pastry flour, spelt flour, cinnamon, nutmeg, baking soda, baking powder, and salt.

3. In a large bowl, and using an electric mixer on medium speed, beat eggs, sucanat, Apple Butter, and applesauce. Stir in vanilla extract.

4. Stir in flour mixture until combined. Fold in apples, walnuts, and cranberries, and pour batter into the prepared loaf pans.

5. Bake for 40 to 50 minutes or until a toothpick inserted in center of loaf comes out clean.

6. Let cool in pans on a cooling rack for 15 to 20 minutes. Slide a butter knife around the edges, and invert loaves on the rack to cool completely.

7. Store wrapped in aluminum foil at room temperature for 3 to 5 days or in the freezer for up to 2 months.

Banana Blueberry Bread

This bread combines two of my favorite morning fruits: bananas and blueberries. The blueberries add a flash of color and sweetness and keep the bread moist. This is a great way to jazz up your normal banana bread recipe.

Yield:	Prep time:	Cook time:	Serving size:
1 (9×5×3-inch) loaf	20 minutes	40 to 50 minutes	1 slice

1 cup whole-wheat pastry flour

1½ cups spelt flour

½ tsp. ground cinnamon

1 tsp. baking soda

1 tsp. baking powder

⅛ tsp. salt

½ cup fresh blueberries

3 bananas, peeled and smashed (1¾ cups)

½ cup unsweetened applesauce

½ cup sucanat or unprocessed sugar

1 large egg, beaten

1 tsp. vanilla extract

1. Preheat the oven to 350°F. Grease and flour a 9×5×3-inch loaf pan.

2. In a medium bowl, whisk together whole-wheat pastry flour, spelt flour, cinnamon, baking soda, baking powder, and salt. Fold in blueberries until berries are coated with flour.

3. In a large bowl, mix bananas and applesauce with a wooden spoon. Add sucanat, egg, and vanilla extract, and stir to combine.

4. Stir in flour mixture just until combined. Pour batter into the prepared loaf pan.

5. Bake for 40 to 50 minutes or until a toothpick inserted in center of loaf comes out clean.

6. Let cool in pans on a cooling rack for 15 to 20 minutes. Slide a butter knife around the edges, and invert loaf on the rack to cool completely.

7. Store wrapped in aluminum foil at room temperature for 3 to 5 days or in the freezer for up to 2 months.

Pumpkin and Chocolate Protein Bars

These are not dessert bars; they walk the line between sweet and savory, with the chocolate chips adding the only sweetness. They are a great way to sneak in some more protein and a perfect accompaniment to coffee, tea, or even a glass of red wine.

Yield:	Prep time:	Cook time:	Serving size:
16 bars	20 minutes	20 to 25 minutes	1 bar

1½ cups whole-wheat pastry flour

¼ cup rolled oats, ground

½ cup protein powder

1 TB. Pumpkin Pie Spice (recipe in Chapter 7)

2 tsp. ground cinnamon

1 tsp. ground nutmeg

2 tsp. baking powder

¼ tsp. salt

1 (15.5-oz.) can pumpkin purée

½ cup soft or silken tofu

1 TB. vanilla extract

½ cup mini chocolate chips

1. Preheat the oven to 350°F. Grease a 9×9 pan.

2. In a large bowl, whisk together whole-wheat pastry flour, oats, protein powder, Pumpkin Pie Spice, cinnamon, nutmeg, baking powder, and salt.

3. In a blender, purée pumpkin purée, tofu, and vanilla extract until smooth.

4. Add pumpkin mixture in dry ingredients, and stir until combined. Fold in mini chocolate chips. Batter will be very thick. Pour into the prepared pan.

5. Bake for 20 to 25 minutes or until top is cracked and a toothpick inserted into center of loaf comes out clean.

6. Let bars cool in pan to room temperature before cutting into 16 squares. Store in an airtight container in the refrigerator for up to 2 weeks, or freeze them for up to 2 months.

DON'T BE FOOLED BY THE BATTER

The batter will be thick and taste bitter. Try not to taste it, and if you do, don't judge it. When the bars bake, the sweetness of the chocolate takes over and you'll have some tasty protein bars.

Homemade Cereal Bars

Commercially produced cereal bars contain more than 45 ingredients. My version has 11 ingredients. Which do you think is better? I like making these bars in a muffin pan. They're less messy and easier to store, and you can make multiple flavors at one time.

Yield:	Prep time:	Cook time:	Serving size:
10 to 12 bars	15 minutes	20 to 25 minutes	1 bar

1 cup whole-wheat pastry flour

1 cup spelt flour

1½ cups rolled oats, ground into a coarse meal

1½ tsp. baking soda

1 tsp. ground cinnamon

⅛ tsp. salt

½ cup organic brown sugar, firmly packed

½ cup unsweetened applesauce

½ cup butter, softened

1 tsp. vanilla extract

¾ to 1 cup Strawberry Refrigerator Preserves, Blackberry Preserves, or Grape Preserves (recipes in Chapter 6)

1. Preheat the oven to 350°F. Grease and flour a 12-cup muffin pan.

2. In a medium bowl, whisk together whole-wheat pastry flour, spelt flour, rolled oats, baking soda, cinnamon, and salt.

3. In a large bowl, and using an electric mixer on medium speed, cream together brown sugar, applesauce, butter, and vanilla extract. Reduce speed to low, and add flour mixture.

4. Roll 1 tablespoon dough into a ball, flatten ball, and press it into the muffin pan, pushing dough up the sides of the muffin cup. Spoon ½ tablespoon Strawberry Refrigerator Preserves in middle of dough cup.

5. Roll ½ tablespoon dough into a ball, flatten it, and place it on top of preserves, covering completely.

6. Repeat with remaining dough and preserves.

7. Bake for 20 to 25 minutes or until tops start to crack and turn golden brown.

8. Let cool in the muffin pan for 10 to 15 minutes. Run a knife around edges of each bar. Place a cookie sheet on top of the muffin pan, and invert bars onto the cookie sheet. Continue to cool bars until they're room temperature.

9. Store in an airtight container at room temperature for 3 to 5 days, or store in the freezer for up to 2 months.

Salads and Slaws ❧ 9

Manatee and I eat at least one salad a day. Our typical salad involves dumping whatever I make for dinner—whether it's spaghetti, stir-fry, sloppy joes, or tacos—on top of a bed of lettuce. Even using all my artistic abilities, it's hard to turn that type of salad into a recipe. It might look like this:

1. Make dinner.

2. Dump dinner on a bed of lettuce.

If we're really feeling crazy, we combine different types of lettuce. (And don't think we don't get excited about that. Shredded lettuce is one of my favorite foods, too.)

For this chapter, I wanted to share with you our fun salads, our special-treat-and-vie-for-seconds-and-leftovers salads. They make great light meals or afternoon snacks.

Chicken Salad

Growing up, I think I can count on one hand how many times I ate chicken salad, and all those times, I ate them at parties where I am sure it was a premade salad. This means that chicken salad is a huge treat for me. It's so easy to make, but it reminds me of fancy brunches, luncheons, and party dresses.

I've included three of my favorite recipes in this chapter. All are equally worthy of hoity-toity get-togethers and humble lunches.

COOKING CHICKEN

When making chicken salad—or other dishes that call for chicken—consider poaching. Poaching chicken is a great way to keep it moist for salads or casseroles. You can cook the chicken at the beginning of the week so you have chicken available for making chicken salad or tossing on top of a salad throughout the rest of the week.

Coleslaw

When making coleslaw, it's more cost-effective and healthier to buy heads of cabbage and chop it yourself versus buying bags of coleslaw mix. However, I've had my share of cabbage messes in the kitchen, and bagged coleslaw mix is better than premade coleslaw. Therefore, I've designed all the slaw recipes so you can substitute a 16-ounce bag of coleslaw mix for fresh-cut cabbage. I don't have a great history of cutting carrots, so I do admit to using bagged shredded carrots. This helps my sanity and my marriage (as Manatee often cleans the kitchen after my culinary escapades).

Do you have a mandoline? If you like coleslaw, I recommend you invest in one. No matter how skilled you are with a knife, you'll never get the thin slices you can get with a mandoline. I work part-time at a specialty cooking-supply store, and for months I tried to talk people out of buying mandolines. I equated them with missing fingertips and ER visits. When mandoline-buyers came to my register, I warned them several times to be careful, and if I could, I casually mentioned our excellent knife section. After several persistent friends argued the case for mandolines, I gave in and bought one. Now, I'm completely in love with it. As long as you buy one with a good safety guard and treat it with the respect any sharp object deserves, your fingertips will be safe.

Prepping cabbage takes a few steps. First, remove the outer leaves, cut the cabbage in half, and remove the core with a paring knife. Cut the cabbage into quarters. If you're using a chef's knife, place the cabbage on one of the cut sides, and cut into thin strips. If you're using a mandoline, put your mandoline on its thinnest setting, either $\frac{1}{8}$ or smaller, and slide the cabbage along the mandoline.

A NOTE ON MAYONNAISE

For all the mayonnaise-based recipes, homemade mayonnaise is always best. (I give you a recipe in Chapter 6.) If you do use a store-bought version, read the label carefully. Many times, chemicals are added. You also want to be sure unnecessary sugars aren't included. This happens more often with reduced-fat or no-fat versions. That being said, don't be afraid of using full-fat versions. Nothing satisfies quite like full-fat mayonnaise, and when you're satisfied, you don't need to use as much. Psychologically, you often view it as a treat and, therefore, use it more sparingly. When you eat real-food ingredients, your body knows what to do with them. When you eat chemicals, your body can't fully digest them, so they're more likely to be stored as fat. And they don't taste nearly as good.

Classic Chicken Salad

There are few things I miss from my life as a corporate software trainer. As sad as this is to admit, the corporate deli almost made my 9-to-5 job worth it. All the food was made from scratch to order. This meant two things: I could drag out my lunch hour as long as possible, and I could enjoy their chicken salad on a regular basis. This is my version of their chicken salad. I used onions for flavor, but you could also throw in fresh herbs or bell peppers for another flavor dimension. And feel free to ditch the bread and serve it with leafy greens and freshly cut tomatoes.

Yield:	Prep time:	Cook time:	Serving size:
2½ cups	20 minutes	25 minutes	½ cup

3 (6- to 8-oz.) chicken breasts, or 2 to 2½ cups cooked chicken, diced

2 sweet onions, 1½ onions peeled and quartered and remaining ½ onion diced

½ cup celery, diced

¼ cup pecans, diced

½ cup Mayonnaise (recipe in Chapter 6)

1 tsp. Dijon mustard

¼ tsp. ground black pepper

⅛ tsp. kosher salt

1. If using chicken breasts, place them in a medium saucepan along with quartered onions. (If using cooked chicken, skip to step 3.) Cover with water by 1 inch, set over medium-high heat, and bring to a boil. Reduce heat to medium-low, cover, and cook for 5 minutes.

2. Remove the pan from heat, and let sit for 8 to 12 minutes or until largest piece of chicken reaches an internal temperature of 160°F. Let cool to room temperature, and cut into small pieces.

3. In a medium bowl, combine chicken, remaining diced onion, celery, pecans, Mayonnaise, Dijon mustard, black pepper, and kosher salt.

4. Serve immediately, or store in an airtight container in the refrigerator for 1 day.

Curry Chicken Salad

I associate curry chicken salad with high-end grocery stores and sidewalk cafés. Many markets carry chicken salad, but not *curry* chicken salad. I love eating this wrapped in a leaf of lettuce or scooped with Baked Pita Chips (recipe in Chapter 10).

Yield:	Prep time:	Cook time:	Serving size:
2½ cups	20 minutes	10 minutes	½ cup

3 (6- to 8-oz.) chicken breasts, or 2 to 2½ cups cooked chicken, diced

2 sweet onions, peeled and quartered

¼ cup raisins or golden raisins

¼ cup walnuts, chopped

¼ cup celery, diced

½ cup Mayonnaise (recipe in Chapter 6)

1 TB. curry powder

1. If using chicken breasts, place them in a medium saucepan along with onions. (If using cooked chicken, skip to step 3.) Cover with water by 1 inch, set over medium-high heat, and bring to a boil. Reduce heat to medium-low, cover, and cook for 5 minutes.

2. Remove the pan from heat, and let sit for 8 to 12 minutes or until largest piece of chicken reaches an internal temperature of 160°F. Let cool to room temperature, and cut into small pieces.

3. In medium bowl, combine chicken, raisins, walnuts, celery, Mayonnaise, and curry powder.

4. Serve immediately, or store in an airtight container in the refrigerator for 1 day.

Fruit and Nut Chicken Salad

This chicken salad walks the line between sweet and salty. I love adding fruit to my chicken salad, whether it's grapes or dried cranberries.

Yield:	Prep time:	Cook time:	Serving size:
2½ cups	20 minutes	10 minutes	½ cup

3 (6- to 8-oz.) chicken breasts, or 2 to 2½ cups cooked chicken, diced

2 onions, 1½ onions peeled and quartered and remaining ½ onion diced

¼ cup dried cranberries

¼ cup walnuts, chopped

¼ cup celery, diced

½ cup Mayonnaise (recipe in Chapter 6)

1 tsp. Dijon mustard

¼ tsp. ground black pepper

⅛ tsp. kosher salt

1. If using chicken breasts, place them in a medium saucepan along with quartered onions. (If using cooked chicken, skip to step 3.) Cover with water by 1 inch, set over medium-high heat, and bring to a boil. Reduce heat to medium-low, cover, and cook for 5 minutes.

2. Remove the pan from heat, and let sit for 8 to 12 minutes or until largest piece of chicken reaches an internal temperature of 160°F. Let cool to room temperature, and cut into small pieces.

3. In a medium bowl, combine chicken, remaining diced onion, cranberries, walnuts, celery, Mayonnaise, Dijon mustard, black pepper, and kosher salt.

4. Serve immediately, or store in an airtight container in the refrigerator for up to 1 day.

Variation: Substitute halved red grapes for the dried cranberries for an even sweeter twist to this salad.

EASY LETTUCE WRAPS

I love eating this wrapped in butter lettuce leaves. Butter lettuce (also known as Boston lettuce) is a small, green or red lettuce head with sweet and tender leaves.

Classic Tuna Salad

As a child, I hated caned tuna. I didn't like how it smelled, felt, tasted, or even looked. The easiest way to get me out of the kitchen was to open a can of tuna—and don't think my parents didn't figure that out or use it to their advantage! In college, something changed and I sought out tuna salad. For me, it was never for sandwiches; instead, tuna salad was the perfect spread for crackers or toast. Serve this with something crunchy: celery, cucumbers, or Creamy Wheat Crackers or Baked Pita Chips (recipes in Chapter 10). You will see a new side of tuna salad.

Yield:	Prep time:	Serving size:
1½ cups	5 minutes	½ cup

1 (12-oz.) can tuna packed in water, drained

¼ cup sweet onion, diced

½ cup celery, diced

½ cup Mayonnaise (recipe in Chapter 6)

½ TB. Dijon mustard

⅛ tsp. ground black pepper

⅛ tsp. kosher salt

1. Place tuna in medium bowl, and separate it with a fork.

2. Add onion, celery, Mayonnaise, and Dijon mustard, and stir to combine. Season with black pepper and kosher salt.

3. Serve immediately, or store in an airtight container in the refrigerator for 1 day.

Manatee's Tuna Salad

Manatee and I have very different ideas on tuna salad. You've seen my classic tuna salad, but for him, that's not tuna salad (where are the water chestnuts and artichoke hearts? and no mustard, please), and he was very clear about that when we were first married. We have agreed to disagree about what defines tuna salad. He was very adamant that his tuna salad had equal footing … and even I have to admit that it's pretty darn good.

Yield:	Prep time:	Serving size:
1½ cups	10 minutes	½ cup

1 (12-oz.) can tuna packed in water, drained

¼ cup white onion, diced

½ cup water chestnuts, sliced

¼ cup artichoke hearts, diced

½ cup Mayonnaise (recipe in Chapter 6)

1. Place tuna in a medium bowl, and separate with a fork.

2. Add onion, water chestnuts, artichoke hearts, and Mayonnaise, and stir to combine.

3. Serve immediately, or store in an airtight container in the refrigerator for 1 day.

Classic Egg Salad

Egg salad is a great comfort food. In graduate school, I ate an egg salad sandwich three times a week for an entire semester. On the surface, it was the one sandwich I could get from the deli and know there was no dairy in it, which was a very big deal for a newly diagnosed lactose-intolerant girl. Deep down, when I was struggling with the foreign world of academia, a restrictive diet, and a new town, it was nice to have something familiar.

Yield:	Prep time:	Serving size:
2 cups	15 minutes	½ cup

5 large hard-boiled eggs, peeled and sliced (2 cups)

2 TB. sweet onion, diced

2 TB. celery, diced

¼ cup Mayonnaise (recipe in Chapter 6)

1 tsp. yellow mustard

2 tsp. hot sauce (recipes in Chapter 4)

1. In a medium bowl, mash eggs with a fork.

2. Add onion, celery, Mayonnaise, yellow mustard, and hot sauce, and stir to combine.

3. Serve immediately, or store in an airtight container in the refrigerator for 1 day.

PEELING HARD-BOILED EGGS

Could there be anything more frustrating than peeling a hard-boiled egg? I think not. Here are some tips: be sure the egg is at room temperature. Lightly tap the egg on the counter to create small breaks in the eggshell, and gently roll the egg on the counter to separate the egg from its shell. Peel the egg under running water. This helps you with the peeling and also keeps the egg clean of the shell.

Potato Salad

Potato salad is another one of my guilty pleasures. No cookout is complete without it, and it makes a great afternoon snack. There are tons of different ways to make potato salad, but my favorite is a classic Midwestern standard complete with Mayonnaise, eggs, and mustard.

Yield:	Prep time:	Cook time:	Serving size:
1 quart	15 minutes	1 hour, 15 minutes	¼ cup

4 to 6 medium yellow or red potatoes	1 TB. Dijon mustard
¼ cup celery, diced	½ cup Mayonnaise (recipe in Chapter 6)
¼ cup white onion, diced	1 TB. hot sauce (recipes in Chapter 4)
2 large hard-boiled eggs, peeled and diced (½ cup)	⅛ tsp. salt
Juice of ½ small lemon (1 TB.)	¼ tsp. ground black pepper

1. Clean potatoes and be sure all are a consistent size. If you have some smaller potatoes, cut the others to match the size. If all are consistent, leave them whole.

2. Place potatoes in a large saucepan, cover with at least 1 inch of water, and set over medium-high heat. Cover and bring to a boil. Reduce heat to medium, and simmer for about 15 minutes or until potatoes are tender when you pierce them with a fork.

3. Remove the pan from heat, let cool to room temperature, and cut potatoes in bite-size pieces.

4. In a large bowl, combine potatoes, celery, white onion, and eggs. Add lemon juice, Dijon mustard, Mayonnaise, hot sauce, salt, and black pepper, and stir to combine.

5. Store in an airtight container in the refrigerator for up to 4 days.

POTATO PREFERENCES

I like my potatoes soft. If you like your potatoes *al dente,* or with a little more bite, reduce the cooking time by about 5 minutes.

Creamy Coleslaw

Given our insane love for all things salad, it should be no surprise we love coleslaw so much I have four different slaw recipes to share in this chapter. It also shouldn't be surprising that our favorite way to eat it is—you guessed it—on top of a bed of spinach or leafy greens. Yes, we eat salad on our salads. This is the standard of Midwest coleslaw: creamy, light, and perfect for any barbecue or summer picnic.

Yield:	Prep time:	Serving size:
6 cups	10 minutes, plus 30 minutes marinate time	¼ cup

½ cup Mayonnaise (recipe in Chapter 6)

2 TB. apple cider vinegar

½ TB. unprocessed sugar

1 TB. Dijon mustard

4 cups green cabbage, sliced thin

1 cup red cabbage, sliced thin

1 cup shredded carrots

⅛ tsp. salt

⅛ tsp. ground black pepper

1. In a medium bowl, whisk together Mayonnaise, apple cider vinegar, unprocessed sugar, and Dijon mustard.

2. In a large bowl, combine green cabbage, red cabbage, and carrots. Add mayonnaise mixture, and toss to coat. Season with salt and black pepper.

3. Refrigerate for at least 30 minutes before serving to allow the flavors to meld and the cabbage to soften. (This slaw is even better the next day.)

4. Store in an airtight container in the refrigerator for up to 4 days.

Oil-and-Vinegar Coleslaw

This is another great slaw. It's perfect for a light lunch or alongside some grilled meat or tofu. I love the little bite you get from the dry sherry.

Yield:	Prep time:	Serving size:
6 cups	10 minutes, plus 30 minutes marinate time	¼ cup

¼ cup canola oil

3 TB. white wine vinegar

1 TB. dry sherry

1 tsp. unprocessed sugar

1 TB. Dijon mustard

4 cups green cabbage, sliced thin

1 cup red cabbage, sliced thin

1 cup shredded carrots

¼ tsp. salt

¼ tsp. ground black pepper

1. In a medium bowl, whisk together canola oil, white wine vinegar, dry sherry, unprocessed sugar, and Dijon mustard.

2. In a large bowl, combine green cabbage, red cabbage, and carrots. Add canola oil mixture, and toss to coat. Season with salt and black pepper.

3. Refrigerate for at least 30 minutes to allow the flavors to meld and the cabbage to soften. (This slaw is even better the next day.)

4. Store in an airtight container in the refrigerator for up to 4 days.

Thai Peanutty Coleslaw

I love any excuse to add peanut butter to a recipe. The peanut sauce is light, and this is a great summer salad—refreshing, a little spicy, and perfectly sweet. It's great for a grill-out, or you can toss it with some cooked noodles.

Yield:	Prep time:	Serving size:
6 cups	10 minutes, plus 30 minutes marinate time	¼ cup

2 TB. Creamier Peanut Butter (variation in Chapter 6)

Juice of 1 small lime (2 TB.)

2 TB. canola oil

1 tsp. agave nectar

1 TB. seasoned rice wine vinegar

1 small jalapeño, seeds and ribs removed, and finely diced

4 cups green cabbage, sliced thin

1 cup red cabbage, sliced thin

1 cup shredded carrots

2 TB. green onion, green parts only, sliced

¼ tsp. salt

¼ tsp. ground black pepper

1. In a medium bowl, whisk together Creamier Peanut Butter, lime juice, canola oil, agave nectar, seasoned rice wine vinegar, and jalapeño.

2. In a large bowl, combine green cabbage, red cabbage, carrots, and green onion. Add peanut butter mixture, and toss to coat. Season with salt and pepper.

3. Refrigerate for at least 30 minutes to allow the flavors to meld and the cabbage to soften. (This slaw is even better the next day.)

4. Store in an airtight container in the refrigerator for up to 4 days.

Spicy Slaw

This slaw goes great with tacos. The red cabbage gives the slaw a purple tint, making it a colorful accompaniment to your dinner plate.

Yield:	Prep time:	Serving size:
5 cups	15 minutes, plus 30 min- utes marinate time	⅓ cup

Juice of 2 small limes (¼ cup)

2 TB. hot sauce (recipes in Chapter 4)

2 TB. apple cider vinegar

1 tsp. agave nectar

4 cups green cabbage, sliced thin

1¼ cups red cabbage, sliced thin

1¼ cups shredded carrots

2 TB. green onion, green parts only, sliced

¼ tsp. salt

¼ tsp. ground black pepper

1. In a medium bowl, whisk together lime juice, hot sauce, apple cider vinegar, and agave nectar.

2. In a large bowl, combine green cabbage, red cabbage, carrots, and green onion. Add lime juice mixture, and toss to coat. Season with salt and pepper.

3. Refrigerate for at least 30 minutes to allow the flavors to meld and the cabbage to soften. (This slaw is even better the next day.)

4. Store in an airtight container in the refrigerator for up to 4 days.

Easy-Peasy Caprese

Every year, we get tons of cherry tomatoes. This is one of our go-to summer salads during the height of cherry tomato season. When you cut the tomatoes in half, they soak up more of the vinegar and are so much easier to eat.

Yield:	Prep time:	Serving size:
2 cups	10 minutes	½ cup

2 cups cherry tomatoes, halved

⅓ cup fresh basil, cut or torn into small pieces

2 TB. balsamic vinegar

1 TB. olive oil

¼ cup fresh mozzarella balls, halved (optional)

1. In a medium bowl, combine cherry tomatoes, basil, balsamic vinegar, olive oil, and mozzarella (if using).

2. Serve immediately, or allow salad to sit for 5 to 10 minutes for tomatoes to soak in vinegar.

3. Serve immediately, or store in an airtight container in the refrigerator for 1 day.

Bruschetta Salad

Manatee doesn't like bread, yet I love bruschetta. This salad is our compromise. Bread takes a supporting role to fresh tomatoes, basil, and sweet white onions. I get a taste of my beloved bread, and Manatee gets his salad—everyone's happy.

Yield:	Prep time:	Cook time:	Serving size:
4 cups	20 minutes	6 minutes	½ cup

1½ slices sourdough bread

¼ cup olive oil

½ cup white onion, diced

2 cups cherry tomatoes, halved

1 cup cucumber, seeded and diced

½ cup basil, roughly chopped

2 cloves garlic, peeled and halved

1 TB. balsamic vinegar

1. Heat the grill to high, or preheat the broiler to 500°F.

2. Brush sourdough bread slices with 2 tablespoons olive oil. If using a grill, grill bread for 2 or 3 minutes per side. Bread should be toasted with grill marks but not burned. If using a broiler, place bread on a rack on a cookie sheet, and broil for 2 or 3 minutes per side.

3. Meanwhile, in a large bowl, toss together white onion, cherry tomatoes, cucumber, and basil.

4. When bread is finished, remove from the oven or grill and rub cut end of garlic on both sides of bread. Cut bread into ½-inch cubes, and add to tomato mixture.

5. Add remaining 2 tablespoons olive oil and balsamic vinegar to salad, and toss to combine.

6. Serve immediately, or store in an airtight container in the refrigerator for up to 1 day.

LIGHTER GARLIC BREAD

I love garlic bread, but garlic bread does not love me. By rubbing cut, fresh garlic on warm bread, you get the taste of garlic without it overpowering your meal—or your breath.

Summer Quinoa Salad

We make this quinoa salad at least once a month during the spring and summer. We make it for all our parties; take it to parties we attend; and keep it in the fridge for quick lunches, picnics, and snacks. It's dairy-free, gluten-free, and totally healthy, so we always know we'll have something we can eat. I noticed when I was writing this book that my regular version makes 3 quarts. Realizing that for some people, this could be considered too much, I decided to give you two versions: a party version (or a Badger-Girl-and-Manatee-eat-way-too-much version) and a variation for a regular family–size salad. This recipe is for the larger, party version.

Yield:	Prep time:	Serving size:
3 quarts	25 minutes	½ cup

2 cups quinua, cooked

2 medium red or sweet bell peppers, ribs and seeds removed, and diced (2 cups)

1 medium green bell pepper, ribs and seeds removed, and diced (1 cup)

1 cup green onion, white and green parts, sliced

3 cups cherry tomatoes, halved

1 cup cucumber, seeded and diced

1 cup fresh cilantro, chopped

1 (15.5-oz.) can black beans, rinsed and drained

1 (15.5-oz.) can corn, rinsed and drained

Juice of 2 small limes (¼ cup)

3 TB. seasoned rice vinegar

¼ tsp. salt

¼ tsp. ground black pepper

1. In a large bowl, combine quinoa, red bell peppers, green bell pepper, green onion, cherry tomatoes, cucumber, cilantro, black beans, corn, lime juice, seasoned rice vinegar, salt, and black pepper.

2. Store in an airtight container in the refrigerator for up to 5 days.

Variation: For a family version that makes 1 quart, use only 1 cup cooked quinoa ½ medium red or sweet bell pepper, diced (½ cup), ½ medium green bell pepper, diced (½ cup), ¼ cup sliced green onion, ½ cup halved cherry tomatoes, ½ cup diced cucumber, ¼ cup chopped fresh cilantro, ½ cup canned black beans, ½ cup canned corn, juice of 1 small lime (2 table-spoons), 1 tablespoon seasoned rice vinegar, ¼ teaspoon salt, and ¼ teaspoon ground black pepper.

HOW CAN THEY EAT ALL THAT?

We often treat this like a small meal. Add diced avocado or even some grilled protein, and of course, you can (and should) throw it on top of a bed of spinach or mixed greens. Treat it as a dip, and eat it with Baked Tortilla Chips (recipe in Chapter 10) and a homemade guacamole of your choice (recipes in Chapter 11). This also makes a great picnic food or to-go lunch. In a mason jar, layer 2 tablespoons Avocado Dressing (recipe in Chapter 5), ¼ cup diced sweet peppers or shredded carrots, and ½ cup Summer Quinoa Salad. Fill the rest of the jar with spinach and shredded lettuce. If you're like Manatee and me, you might also want an extra jar of spinach and lettuce. When you're ready to eat it, dump it out on a plate, and enjoy.

Thai Peanut Noodle Salad

I love peanut noodles, and I love them even more when they're left over. It seemed logical to take the next step and make them leftovers on purpose. You can eat this salad warm, but try to wait because it's so much better cold. It's the absolute best when you eat it out of the container with a fork in front of the fridge as you hold open the door.

Yield:	Prep time:	Cook time:	Serving size:
3 cups	5 minutes	8 to 10 minutes, plus 10 minutes cool time	1½ cups

2 cups cooked Basic Whole-Wheat Pasta (recipe in Chapter 3) or 1 cup uncooked store-bought whole-wheat spaghetti or fettuccine

1 medium red bell pepper, ribs and seeds removed, and cut in strips (1 cup)

1 cup broccoli florets

⅓ cup Peanut Sauce (recipe in Chapter 4)

¼ cup shredded carrots

Juice of 1 small lime (2 TB.)

½ cup cooked chicken, beef, or Tofu Dippers (recipe in Chapter 12) (optional)

1 TB. green onions, green parts only, sliced

1. Bring a medium saucepan a little more than half full of water to a rolling boil over medium-high heat. Add Basic Whole-Wheat Pasta, red bell pepper, and broccoli. Reduce heat to medium, and cook for 2 or 3 minutes or until pasta is ready. If using store-bought pasta, cook according to the package directions, and add veggies during the last 2 or 3 minutes of cooking.

2. Drain pasta and veggies.

3. In a medium bowl, toss pasta with Peanut Sauce and carrots. Set salad aside to cool to room temperature.

4. When cool, add lime juice and cooked protein (if using), and stir to combine.

5. Serve topped with green onions, or store in an airtight container in the refrigerator for up to 3 days.

DOUBLE DUTY

I love making my pasta water do extra work for me. Throwing veggies into your pasta water to cook is a great way to make a one-pot meal.

Pesto and Sun-Dried Tomato Pasta Salad

I originally made this pasta salad as a warm dish. One day I couldn't wait to heat up my leftovers and ate it cold. The verdict: it's good either way. I'm a huge advocate for homemade pasta, but if you do decide to use dried pasta, go for penne. The pesto gets caught in the middle and fully coats it in a way you can't get with flat pasta.

Yield:	Prep time:	Cook time:	Serving size:
3 cups	5 minutes	8 to 10 minutes, plus 10 minutes cool time	1½ cups

2 cups cooked Basic Whole-Wheat Pasta (recipe in Chapter 3) or 1 cup store-bought whole-wheat penne pasta

½ cup sun-dried tomatoes, cut in strips

1 cup broccoli florets

⅓ cup pesto (recipes in Chapter 4)

Juice of ½ small lime (1 TB.)

½ cup cooked tofu or chicken

1. Bring a medium saucepan a little more than half full of water to a rolling boil over medium-high heat. Add Basic Whole-Wheat Pasta, sun-dried tomatoes, and broccoli. Reduce heat to medium, and cook for 2 or 3 minutes or until pasta is ready. If using store-bought pasta, cook according to the package directions, and add veggies during the last 2 or 3 minutes of cooking.

2. Drain pasta and veggies.

3. In a medium bowl, toss pasta with pesto. Set salad aside to cool to room temperature.

4. When cool, add lemon juice and cooked protein (if using), and stir to combine.

5. Store in an airtight container in the refrigerator for up to 3 days.

SUN-DRIED TOMATOES

Look for sun-dried tomatoes that are not packed with oil. You can find these packaged in a plastic bag or container in the produce section.

Hand-to-Mouth Snacks  10

I created the recipes in this chapter out of necessity. Some people love chocolate, some love wine, but I love salty and sweet crunchy snacks. When we first decided to come clean, Manatee and I both made an exception. Manatee kept his favorite "healthy" cereal, and I kept crackers and chips. (I got two. What can I say? I'm a better negotiator.) After 6 months of eating clean except for these cheat foods, we both cut the cord and walked away from our vices.

I wish I could tell you it was easy and I never looked back, but that would be a lie. There were times I wanted nothing more than to buy a boxed snack to satisfy my crunchy craving. Instead, I became determined to re-create my favorites. I read recipes and then, in my usual Badger Girl fashion, completely ignored them and did it my own way. Sometimes these experiments resulted in wild successes. But often, I learned all the ways *not* to make something. I share that hard-earned knowledge with you in this chapter.

Flavored Roasted Nuts

I've had to get creative with roasted nuts. Manatee will chow down on raw almonds day after day with no complaints or even a second thought. I like to think I have a more refined palate, but it just might be that I have a harder time adjusting to this whole-foods lifestyle.

Nuts are a great source of protein, fiber, and healthy fats. With a few spices and some time in the oven, they can even start to taste like your favorite junk foods! For a sweet fix, try one of the Cocoa Roasted Almond variations or the indulgent Pumpkin Pie Spiced Pecans. If you want a replacement for croutons, try the Italian Walnuts or the Mexicana Almonds on a taco salad.

VEGAN VERSION

I use egg whites to help bind my seasonings to the nuts. For a vegan option, use 3 tablespoons water instead of the egg white–water mixture called for in the recipe.

Perfect Popcorn

I love snacking on popcorn. I have to admit that in my college days, I would often have a bag of microwave popcorn (movie theater butter flavor, of course) with a can of soda for dinner. I clearly wasn't into healthy eating at the time.

You can make microwave popcorn with regular popcorn. Put ¼ cup popcorn in a brown bag, roll it up, and microwave it for 1½ to 2 minutes. No oil, no chemicals, just fresh-popped popcorn. This is a major go-to snack in our house, and in this chapter, I share three of our favorite toppings.

There's a fine line between good popcorn and burnt popcorn. I prefer to err on the side of having a few unpopped kernels rather than stink up the kitchen with that terrible burnt popcorn smell. Stay close to the microwave the first few times you make it. As soon as the popping starts to slow, remove the bag. After a few times, you'll get an idea of the best timing for your microwave. You might want to try to add more popcorn kernels to the bag, but don't. I can tell you from experience—exploding paper bags, smoke billowing from the microwave, having to air out the entire house for several hours—that ¼ cup is the magic proportion.

Easy Homemade Crackers

Next to chips, crackers were one of the hardest things for me to give up. If only I would have known then how easy it is to make them! I tried one recipe in the early stages of clean eating and it was such a debacle that it was years before I tried again. I share three versions in this chapter. You can mix and match the seasonings for your tastes.

A food processor speeds up the process, but if you don't have one, simply whisk the dry ingredients, cut in the butter, and mix in the milk with a wooden spoon.

CRACKER LIQUIDS

In the cracker recipes in this chapter, I recommend using nondairy, unsweetened almond milk because it makes the crackers more creamy and rich. You could use milk or water instead.

Cocoa Roasted Almonds

These are a great way to satisfy your sweet tooth with little to no guilt. They're not quite as rich as chocolate-covered almonds, but they give you a hint of sweet cocoa goodness.

Yield:	Prep time:	Cook time:	Serving size:
2 cups	5 minutes	12 to 16 minutes	¼ cup

2 TB. cocoa powder

⅛ tsp. salt

1 TB. sugar

1 large egg white

½ TB. water

2 cups raw almonds

1. Preheat the oven to 350°F. Line a baking sheet with parchment paper.

2. In a medium bowl, whisk together cocoa powder, salt, and sugar. Add egg white and water, and whisk to combine. Fold in almonds, and stir until almonds are evenly coated with cocoa mixture. Spread almonds in a single layer on the prepared baking sheet.

3. Bake for 12 to 16 minutes, stirring halfway through the baking time.

4. Let cool to room temperature. Almonds will crisp as they cool.

5. Store in a zipper-lock plastic bag for up to 2 weeks.

Variations: For **Cinnamon Cocoa Roasted Almonds,** replace the sugar with Cinnamon Sugar (recipe in Chapter 7). For **Spicy Cocoa Roasted Almonds,** replace the sugar with Cinnamon Sugar (recipe in Chapter 7) and add ½ teaspoon cayenne.

Mexicana Almonds

One night we were having taco salads and I was out of corn tortillas for Baked Tortilla Chips. I desperately wanted something crunchy. I tried to convince Manatee that I needed corn tortillas and dinner would have to wait, but he suggested I try almonds instead. I grumbled. I scowled. And now I have to thank him. I would have never thought of jazzing up almonds like this. These are one of my favorite salty snacks now. Eat them by the handful, or throw them on a salad. Either way, they're a great way to layer the texture and punch up the flavor.

Yield:	Prep time:	Cook time:	Serving size:
1 cup	2 minutes	7 to 9 minutes	2 tablespoons

1 cup sliced raw almonds
Juice of ½ small lime (1 TB.)

1 tsp. Taco Seasoning (recipe in Chapter 7)

1. Preheat the oven to 350°F. Spray a rimmed baking sheet with oil spray, or line with silicone mat.

2. In a medium bowl, toss almonds with lime juice and Taco Seasoning. Spread almonds in a single layer on the prepared baking sheet.

3. Bake for 7 to 9 minutes, stirring halfway through the baking time, until almonds turn golden brown.

4. Let cool completely. Almonds will continue to crisp as they cool.

5. Store in a zipper-lock plastic bag for up to 2 weeks.

Italian Walnuts

These make a great replacement for salad croutons or a savory snack. Manatee's family is famous for cooking walnuts in butter and salt, but one night I wanted to try to make my own version of the Aime walnuts. These are crisp, salty, and packed with flavor. Who needs butter when you have Italian Seasoning?

Yield:	Prep time:	Cook time:	Serving size:
1½ cups	5 minutes	12 to 15 minutes	¼ cup

1 large egg white
1 TB. water

2 TB. Italian Seasoning (recipe in Chapter 7)
1½ cups raw walnuts

1. Preheat the oven to 350°F. Line a baking sheet with parchment paper.

2. In a medium bowl, whisk together egg white and water. Add Italian Seasoning, and whisk to combine. Add walnuts, and stir until walnuts are evenly coated. Spread walnuts in a single layer on the baking sheet.

3. Bake for 12 to 15 minutes, stirring halfway through, or until walnuts are golden brown.

4. Let cool completely. Walnuts will continue to crisp as they cool.

5. Store in a zipper-lock plastic bag for up to 2 weeks.

Pumpkin Pie Spiced Pecans

Consider this your portable pecan pie. Sweet, crunchy, and rich, it's hard to believe these could be good for you—pecans are packed with vitamin E and have a naturally sweet taste. The brown sugar and pumpkin spice enhance the taste of the pecan without overwhelming it. These are great by the handful, but would also make an outstanding ice cream or cake topper.

Yield:	Prep time:	Cook time:	Serving size:
3 cups	5 minutes	12 to 15 minutes	¼ cup

1½ TB. Pumpkin Pie Spice (recipe in Chapter 7)

2 TB. dark brown sugar

½ tsp. salt

1 large egg white

1 TB. water

3 cups raw pecans

1. Preheat the oven to 350°F. Line a baking sheet with parchment paper.

2. In a medium bowl, whisk together Pumpkin Pie Spice, dark brown sugar, and salt. Add egg white and water, and whisk until combined. Add pecans, and stir until pecans are evenly coated. Spread pecans in a single layer on the baking sheet.

3. Bake for 12 to 15 minutes, stirring halfway through, or until pecans are golden brown

4. Let cool completely. Pecans will continue to crisp as they cool.

5. Store in a zipper-lock plastic bag for up to 1 week.

Trail Mix of the Gods

If I had to pick one treat to eat the rest of my life, this trail mix would be it. Forget about pies, cakes, ice cream, or even cookies. Trail mix has it all: lots of textures, tastes ranging from sweet to salty, and portability. I love making a huge batch and then being able to grab some for road trips, errands, or a salty and sweet dessert.

Yield:	Prep time:	Serving size:
3 quarts plus 1 cup	5 minutes	¼ cup

6 cups mixed roasted, unsalted nuts	1 cup raisins
2 cups dark chocolate chips	1 cup raw pumpkin seeds
3 cups roasted, salted peanuts	1 cup roasted, salted sunflower seeds
1 cup dried cranberries	

1. In a very large bowl, combine roasted nuts, dark chocolate chips, peanuts, cranberries, raisins, pumpkin seeds, and sunflower seeds.

2. Store in an airtight container for up to 1 month.

PARTY MIX

This makes a great to-go treat for summer barbecues or get-togethers. We make a triple batch for our annual Memorial Day weekend party and send everyone home with a little baggie of their own.

Pizza Popcorn

This popcorn contains all the flavors of pizza without any of the grease. I love the added texture it gets from the chewy sun-dried tomatoes.

Yield:	Prep time:	Cook time:	Serving size:
4 or 5 cups	2 minutes	2 minutes	1 or 2 cups

¼ cup popcorn kernels	1 tsp. Italian Seasoning (recipe in Chapter 7)
2 TB. olive oil	¼ cup slivered sun-dried tomatoes
½ TB. nutritional yeast flakes	

1. Pour popcorn into a small brown bag. Fold over bag two or three times. Microwave for 1½ to 2 minutes, stopping as soon as the popping starts to slow down.

2. Remove bag from the microwave, and pour popcorn into a large bowl. Toss popcorn with olive oil. Add nutritional yeast flakes, Italian Seasoning, and sun-dried tomatoes, and toss again.

3. Serve immediately, or store in a zipper-lock plastic bag for 1 day.

THAT "CHEESY POWDER"

I left a cup of nutritional yeast flakes at my parents' house and told my mom it was cheesy powder. If I would have said the word *yeast,* she might have run out the door. A week later, I returned and couldn't find it. Manatee and I love nutritional yeast and go through maybe ¼ to ½ cup a month. So I was convinced my mother—the woman who won't eat anything she hasn't grown up with unless it's covered in chocolate—had thrown it away. When I asked her about it, she said, "Oh that cheesy powder? That was good! I ate it on everything—salads, soup, potatoes. It didn't last very long, though. What was it called again? I want to buy some." If my mom likes it, it's worth trying. Trust me.

Mexicana Popcorn

After such a wild success with the Mexicana Almonds, I had to try it with popcorn. The lime juice made the popcorn a little soggy, so after some substitutions, I found a recipe that could keep the popcorn crisp.

Yield:	Prep time:	Cook time:	Serving size:
4 or 5 cups	2 minutes	2 minutes	1 or 2 cups

¼ cup popcorn kernels

1 TB. canola oil

1½ tsp. Taco Seasoning (recipe in Chapter 7)

¼ tsp. salt

Squeeze fresh lime juice

1. Pour popcorn into a small brown bag. Fold over bag two or three times. Microwave for 1½ to 2 minutes, stopping as soon as the popping starts to slow down.

2. Remove bag from the microwave, and pour popcorn into a large bowl. Toss with canola oil. Add Taco Seasoning and salt, and toss again.

3. Right before serving, squeeze lime juice over popcorn.

4. Store in a zipper-lock plastic bag for 1 day.

Dessert Popcorn

This is a sweet treat for movie nights. Unlike the other two popcorns, this does not store well, so you'll want to eat it immediately. Once you try it, I think you'll agree eating it right away won't be a problem.

Yield:	Prep time:	Cook time:	Serving size:
4 or 5 cups	2 minutes	2 minutes	1 or 2 cups

2 TB. unsalted butter

¼ cup popcorn kernels

½ TB. dark brown sugar

½ TB. Cinnamon Sugar (recipe in Chapter 7)

1. Place butter in a small, microwave-safe bowl, and microwave for 10 to 20 seconds until melted. Set aside.

2. Pour popcorn into a small brown bag. Fold bag over two or three times. Microwave for 1½ to 2 minutes, stopping as soon as the popping starts to slow down.

3. Remove bag from the microwave, and pour popcorn into a large bowl. Pour melted butter over popcorn, and toss to coat. Add dark brown sugar and Cinnamon Sugar, and toss again.

4. Serve immediately.

Creamy Wheat Crackers

These crackers are great to eat with spreads, dips, or a cheese tray. The smoked paprika gives just a hint of smoky aftertaste.

Yield:	Prep time:	Cook time:	Serving size:
60 crackers	20 minutes	8 to 10 minutes	5 crackers

1½ cups whole-wheat pastry flour

½ tsp. salt, plus more for baking

1 tsp. smoked paprika

¼ cup cold unsalted butter, cut into small chunks

½ cup nondairy milk

1. Preheat the oven to 400°F. Line a baking sheet with a silicone mat, or dust with flour and then tap off excess flour.

2. In food processor fitted with a chopping blade, pulse together whole-wheat pastry flour, ½ teaspoon salt, and smoked paprika. Add unsalted butter, and pulse until dough resembles a coarse meal. Add ½ of milk, and pulse until combined. Add remaining milk, and pulse until dough forms.

3. Remove dough from the food processor, and split in ½. Cover one ½ with a slightly damp dishtowel to prevent dough from drying out.

4. Dust a work area with flour, and cover a rolling pin with flour. Place ½ of dough on the work area. If dough is sticky, sprinkle a little flour on top.

5. Roll out dough to approximately ⅛ inch thick. Cut dough into 2½×1-inch rectangles. Carefully place rectangles on the prepared baking sheet, and sprinkle with a little more salt.

6. Bake for 8 to 10 minutes.

7. Meanwhile, roll out, cut, and sprinkle second ½ of dough with a little more salt. Bake as directed with first ½.

8. Cool crackers on a cooling rack. Serve immediately, or store in an airtight container for 3 to 5 days.

Rosemary and Olive Oil Crackers

To me, the combination of rosemary and olive oil seems very grown-up and screams "foodie food!" Maybe because it was a foodie who kindly told me you weren't supposed to eat the rosemary *stems,* or maybe it was because Simon and Garfunkel sang about it. But most likely it was because we never had dried rosemary in our spice rack when I was growing up. It was something I discovered as a grown-up. I love how the earthy rosemary pairs with olive oil in these crackers. They're perfect with wine and designer cheeses … or when you need to feel like an adult.

Yield:	Prep time:	Cook time:	Serving size:
60 crackers	20 minutes	8 to 10 minutes	5 crackers

1½ cups whole-wheat pastry flour
½ tsp. salt, plus more for baking
3 tsp. dried rosemary

¼ cup plus 2 TB. olive oil
½ cup nondairy milk

1. Preheat the oven to 400°F. Line a baking sheet with a silicone mat, or dust with flour and then tap off excess flour.

2. In food processor fitted with a chopping blade, pulse together whole-wheat pastry flour, ½ teaspoon salt, and rosemary. Add ¼ cup olive oil, and pulse until dough resembles a coarse meal. Add ½ of milk, and pulse until combined. Add remaining milk, and pulse until dough forms.

3. Remove dough from the food processor, and split in ½. Cover one ½ with a slightly damp dishtowel to prevent dough from drying out.

4. Dust a work area with flour, and cover a rolling pin with flour. Place ½ of dough on the work area. If dough is sticky, sprinkle a little flour on top.

5. Roll out dough to approximately ⅛ inch thick. Cut dough into 2½×1-inch rectangles. Carefully place rectangles on the prepared baking sheet. Brush with 1 tablespoon olive oil, and sprinkle with a little more salt.

6. Bake for 8 to 10 minutes.

7. Meanwhile, roll out, cut, and brush second ½ of the dough with remaining 1 tablespoon olive oil and sprinkle with a little more salt. Bake as directed.

8. Cool crackers on a cooling rack. Serve immediately, or store in an airtight container for 3 to 5 days.

Gluten-Free Garlic and Herb Crackers

The herb blend in this recipe is modeled after one of my favorite preclean crackers. They're a little strong, so tone down the spices if you want to have any close, intimate conversations after you eat them. The dough will be much wetter than the other cracker recipes in this chapter, but I found that adding flour to it as I was rolling it out worked the best.

Yield:	Prep time:	Cook time:	Serving size:
60 crackers	20 minutes	8 to 10 minutes	5 crackers

1½ cups gluten-free flour mix

½ tsp. salt

½ tsp. garlic powder

½ tsp. Italian Seasoning (recipe in Chapter 7)

¼ cup cold, unsalted butter, cut into small chunks

⅓ cup nondairy milk

1. Preheat the oven to 400°F. Line a baking sheet with a silicone mat, or dust with flour and then tap off excess flour.

2. In food processor fitted with a chopping blade, pulse together gluten-free flour mix, ½ teaspoon salt, garlic powder, and Italian Seasoning. Add unsalted butter, and pulse until dough resembles a coarse meal. Add ½ of milk and pulse until combined. Add remaining milk, and pulse until dough forms.

3. Remove dough from the food processor, and split in ½. Cover one ½ with a slightly damp dishtowel to prevent dough from drying out.

4. Dust a work area with flour, and cover a rolling pin with flour. Place ½ of dough on the work area. If dough is sticky, sprinkle a little flour on top.

5. Roll out dough to approximately ⅛ inch thick. Cut dough into 2½×1-inch rectangles. Carefully place rectangles on the prepared baking sheet. Sprinkle with a little more salt.

6. Bake for 8 to 10 minutes.

7. Meanwhile, roll out, cut, and sprinkle second ½ of dough with a little more salt. Bake as directed with first ½.

8. Cool crackers on a cooling rack. Serve immediately, or store in an airtight container for 3 to 5 days.

GLUTEN-FREE FLOURS

Gluten-free baking is tough, and I have to admit that making these crackers gluten free took a few unsuccessful attempts. I finally found a premixed gluten-free flour blend that did the trick. Find a blend that has no chemicals, like Bob's Red Mill. Stay away from chickpea flour. You won't be able to eat hummus or chickpeas for days. Trust me on this.

Baked Tortilla Chips

I'm not sure if I should admit how often I make these chips. They come together so fast, I can whip up a batch when I'm making dinner or lunch without missing a beat. They stay crispy for at least 3 days. But to be honest, they've never lasted longer than that.

Yield:	Prep time:	Cook time:	Serving size:
16 chips	5 minutes	12 to 15 minutes	8 chips

4 (6-in.) store-bought corn tortillas   ⅛ tsp. salt
Oil spray

1. Preheat the oven to 350°F. Spray baking sheet with oil spray, or line with a silicone mat.

2. Cut corn tortillas into quarters, and place in a single layer on the prepared baking sheet. Spray tortilla chips generously with oil spray, and sprinkle with salt.

3. Bake for 12 to 15 minutes, checking often after 12 minutes. There's a fine line between crisp and burnt.

4. Cool chips on the baking sheet for 5 to 10 minutes.

5. Store in an airtight container for up to 3 days.

Variations: For **Spicy Ranch Tortilla Chips,** sprinkle with 1 tablespoon Spicy Ranch Seasoning (recipe in Chapter 7) instead of salt. For **Lime Baked Tortilla Chips,** squeeze ½ small lime over the chips after spraying them with oil and then sprinkle with salt. For **Baked Spicy Lime Tortilla Chips,** brush on ½ tablespoon hot sauce (recipes in Chapter 4) after spraying chips with oil and then squeeze ½ small lime over the chips.

KEEP IT SIMPLE

I spent years working on this recipe. Like my epic journey with guacamole, I made it much harder than it needed to be. Simplicity is key. Invest in an oil mister that delivers a fine mist of your favorite type of oil. A few sprays and a sprinkle of salt give you a crispy chip you'd never find in a bag. Use only storebought corn tortillas for this recipe. You can find them made without chemicals—be sure to read the label. The Corn Tortillas recipe in this book makes a tortilla that's a little too hardy to make into chips, and the Wheat Tortillas won't crisp in the oven. Don't dunk the poor tortillas into strange concoctions of spices and juices, ramp up your oven heat, or bathe the tortillas in oil. You'll get soggy, burnt, and greasy chips.

Baked Pita Chips

Whenever I serve these chips at parties, I'm always surprised at how impressed people are with them. They're incredibly easy to make and taste so much better than what you can buy at the store. I love them with baba ghanoush or any one of the hummus recipes in Chapter 11.

Yield:	Prep time:	Cook time:	Serving size:
16 chips	5 minutes	12 to 15 minutes	4 chips

2 pita pockets	Juice of ½ small lemon (1 TB.)
Oil spray	¼ tsp. salt

1. Preheat the oven to 350°F. Spray baking sheet with oil spray, or place a silicone baking mat on the pan.

2. Cut pita pockets into quarters, split each quarter in 2, and place in a single layer on the prepared baking sheet. Spray pita chips generously with oil spray, squeeze ½ lemon over chips, and sprinkle with salt.

3. Bake for 12 to 15 minutes, checking often after 12 minutes. There's a fine line between crisp and burnt. Cool on the baking sheet for 5 to 10 minutes.

4. Store in an airtight container for up to 3 days.

Variation: For **Spicy Pita Chips,** brush with ½ tablespoon hot sauce (recipes in Chapter 4) after spraying chips with oil and then squeeze ½ small lemon over the chips before sprinkling with salt.

Baked Potato Chips

Baking your own potato chips is going to teach you a lot about yourself and your oven. Do you have the patience to try to get every slice consistent? Will you give in and buy a mandoline? How determined are you to have crispy chips? How much willpower do you have? How many chips will pass your taste tests? Where are your hot spots in the oven? Here are my stats: no, yes, not determined enough, not much, not many, and all freaking over. For a consistent success rate, I recommend ¼-inch-thick slices. This results in a crisp and chewy texture, the perfect compromise between fries and potato chips. See the variations if you dare to go thinner.

Yield:	Prep time:	Cook time:	Serving size:
25 to 30 chips	10 to 20 minutes	30 to 35 minutes	8 chips

4 medium russet potatoes, washed   ¼ tsp. salt
½ TB. canola or grapeseed oil

1. Preheat the oven to 400°F. Line a baking sheet with a silicone mat, or spray with oil.

2. Cut russet potatoes into ¼-inch-thick slices. Be as consistent as possible. A mandoline helps the process go much more smoothly.

3. Rinse potatoes with hot water to remove excess starch.

4. In a large bowl, toss potato slices with canola oil and salt. Spread potatoes in a single layer on the baking sheet.

5. Bake for 15 minutes, and flip over slices. Bake for 15 to 20 more minutes, checking more often as time goes by.

6. Serve immediately with Ketchup (recipe in Chapter 4) or Aioli (recipe in Chapter 6).

Variations: For **Extra-Crispy Chips,** slice potatoes into ⅛-inch-thick slices. With a mandoline, you can get even thinner slices. As the slice gets thinner, reduce the heat and stick close to your oven. For ⅛ inch, go down to 375°F. For thinner, go to 350°F. You'll need to keep an eye on them, rotate the pan as needed, and accept that there may be casualties. The good news is that the casualties are usually edible. For **Salt and Pepper Chips,** toss potatoes with ¼ teaspoon ground black pepper after you take them out of the oven. If you add it before you put them in the oven, the pepper might burn. For **Sweet Potato Chips** or **Parsnip Chips,** replace potatoes with sweet potatoes or parsnips, and reduce the temperature to 375°F and the baking time to 25 to 30 minutes.

CHIP SEASONINGS

Check out the spice collection in Chapter 7 to have some fun with your chips. Cool Ranch and even Garam Masala (especially with sweet potato chips!) are both great ways to spice up your chips. For a cheesy chip, add nutritional yeast. For barbecue flavor, try smoked paprika. For a foodie chip, try dried rosemary, minced garlic, or fresh chives. Because you're making your own, the possibilities are endless!

Baked French Fries

I crave french fries. It's my go-to reward food after a half-marathon or triathlon or even a challenging workout. Okay, let's be honest. It's my reward food for any kind of challenge, a rough day of work, a long checkout line, or a cloudy day. It's my biggest guilty pleasure. I used to go out for french fries, but restaurant fries no longer do it for me. Not when I can make a better version at home that is always hot and ready to go.

Yield:	Prep time:	Cook time:	Serving size:
20 to 25 fries	15 minutes	45 minutes	8 to 10 fries

2 medium russet potatoes, washed	1 tsp. salt
1 TB. canola or grapeseed oil	½ tsp. ground black pepper

1. Preheat the oven to 450°F. Line a baking sheet with a silicone mat, or spray with oil.

2. Cut russet potatoes into ½- to ¼-inch-thick strips. Thinner strips mean crispier fries. Be as consistent as possible. A mandoline with a julienne setting helps the process go more smoothly.

3. Rinse potatoes with hot water to remove excess starch.

4. In a large bowl, toss potato strips with canola oil and salt. Spread potatoes in a single layer on the baking sheet.

5. Bake for 20 minutes. Check frequently, and toss fries so they cook evenly.

6. Bake for 25 more minutes or until fries reach your desired crispiness.

7. While fries are still warm, toss with ground black pepper or sprinkle with pepper right after you remove them from the oven.

8. Serve immediately with Ketchup (recipe in Chapter 4) or Aioli (recipe in Chapter 6).

Baked Squash Fries

We take part in community supported agriculture (CSA), and as anyone else in a CSA knows, you sometimes get a lot of one type of produce at one time. For us, it's usually squash, so I'm always on the lookout for squash recipes. You can try this with butternut squash, but I have to admit, I've fallen in love with delicata squash. It's shaped like a zucchini but has green and gold stripes. It has the taste of butternut squash with a slightly softer texture. Because of the green and gold stripes, Manatee calls it the Green Bay Packers squash.

Yield:	Prep time:	Cook time:	Serving size:
20 fries	15 minutes	45 to 55 minutes	10 fries

2 medium delicata squash, or 1 medium butternut squash	½ TB. canola or grapeseed oil
	¼ tsp. salt

1. Preheat the oven to 450°F. Line a baking sheet with a silicone mat, or spray with oil.

2. Peel squash with a vegetable peeler. Cut in ½, remove seeds, and cut squash into ½-inch-thick strips.

3. In a large bowl, toss squash strips with canola oil and salt. Spread in a single layer on the baking sheet.

4. Bake for 30 minutes. Check frequently, and toss fries so they cook evenly.

5. Bake for 15 to 25 more minutes or until fries reach your desired crispiness.

6. Serve immediately with Ketchup (recipe in Chapter 4) or Aioli (recipe in Chapter 6).

EASIER CUTTING

I don't know about you, but I was always terrified to cut butternut squash until I learned this tip: remove the ends of the squash first and then cut the squash in ½. You aren't sacrificing much squash, and you aren't risking your fingers to get to its sweet, nutty flesh.

Just Dip It  11

Dips are an easy sell when it comes to clean eating. Once you taste these homemade salsas, hummus, and guacamole, you won't look at twice at those packaged versions on grocery shelves. Fresh tomatoes, creamy avocados, sweet beets, tangy lime juice—you'll be amazed how easy and delicious these recipes are.

The Power of Labels

My husband and I do a lot of entertaining for large groups of people. These people aren't always interested in healthy eating or whole-food recipes. In our tenure of hosting, I admit I rotate certain dishes, and I'm always amazed at how powerful a name can be.

For example, put the word *hummus* on a label, and some people will avoid it like the plague. I've served the same Buffalo BBQ Hummus at multiple soirées, and when I label it Buffalo BBQ Dip, the bowl is scraped clean. You can imagine my amazement the first time I put *hummus* on the label and watched person after person walk by my beloved dip.

Know your audience. Do they like hummus or pesto? Do they even know what these are? Get creative when labeling your dishes, and you might be surprised at how unpicky people can be.

Sensational Salsa

Manatee has three power foods: spinach, frozen blueberries, and salsa. If we're out of any of these items, we have no food in our house and must go to the store. We could have an overflowing pantry and refrigerator, but if we're lacking in any of these items, it means we must stop everything and go directly to the grocery store.

Unlike most people, Manatee couldn't care less whether or not we have tortilla chips. To him, they're a waste of salsa. Salsa is added to every salad—which in our house, means it's added to every meal. He can't eat spinach without salsa, eggs without salsa, or tofu without salsa. If I would develop a salsa smoothie, he would be in heaven.

Great Guacamole

Some people go on spiritual journeys; some spend years searching for their souls; and some are in pursuit of the answers to life, the universe, and everything. In my twenty-fifth year of life, I had my own personal quest: to create the perfect guacamole.

I was living in California, and I was determined to crack the Californian code of condiments. I asked friends, colleagues, waitresses, and strangers on the street how they made their guacamole. Everyone had an opinion. Red onion, garlic powder, olive oil, crushed red pepper flakes, oregano— I could go on and on. I tried every combination, but it wasn't until I returned to Wisconsin that I was able to narrow it down. The three recipes in this chapter represent my favorites.

Roasted Tomato Salsa

This could also be called "The Easiest Salsa *Ever*." There's barely any cutting involved and only 5 minutes prep. Throw it in the broiler and then directly into the food processor it goes. Done, done, and done! This is a salsa to use when making enchiladas, as a sauce for tofu or meat, or for a different kind of dipping salsa.

Yield:	Prep time:	Cook time:	Serving size:
1 quart	5 minutes	15 minutes	¼ cup

5 medium roma tomatoes, halved

1 medium banana pepper, stem removed

2 medium jalapeños, stem removed

2 cloves garlic, peeled

1 medium white onion, peeled, halved, and ends removed

1 cup fresh cilantro, chopped

1 canned chipotle pepper in adobe sauce

1 TB. adobe sauce

Juice of 1 small lime (2 TB.)

½ tsp. salt

1. Preheat the broiler to 500°F. Line a baking sheet with aluminum foil.

2. Place roma tomatoes, banana pepper, jalapeños, garlic, and white onion on the baking sheet, cut side down for onion and tomato halves. Broil for 10 to 15 minutes or until skins are charred. Turn over peppers halfway through the cook time to evenly char.

3. In a food processor fitted with a chopping blade, pulse together broiled vegetables, cilantro, chipotle pepper, and adobe sauce until all ingredients are chopped evenly into small pieces and before smooth. Stir in lime juice and salt.

4. Let cool to room temperature.

5. Store in an airtight container in the refrigerator for 3 to 5 days.

Pico de Gallo

The key for making pico de gallo is a sharp knife. I tried making this at my parents' with one of their not-so-sharp knives, and I'm pretty sure I would have had better luck using a butter knife—the tomatoes were smashed, and I couldn't get the onions finely diced. This recipe takes a little more prep time, but it's definitely worth it. This is a perfect light version of salsa, great for dipping and as an accompaniment to grilled meats and fish.

Yield:	Prep time:	Serving size:
1 quart	15 minutes	¼ cup

4 medium roma tomatoes, diced

½ medium white onion, finely diced

1 jalapeño, seeds and ribs removed, and finely chopped

⅓ cup fresh cilantro, finely chopped

Juice of 1 small lime (2 TB.)

⅛ tsp. salt

1. In a medium bowl, combine roma tomatoes, white onion, jalapeño, cilantro, lime juice, and salt.

2. Serve immediately, or store in an airtight container in the refrigerator for up to 1 day.

Stewed Tomato Salsa with Black Beans and Corn (Mild)

There are two different approaches to this salsa, and each result in a very different salsa experience. I like a salsa I can chew, so I get everything cooking and then reduce it until it meets my chunky standards. This takes patience, but the concentrated flavors and incredibly robust texture makes it worthwhile. If you prefer a more saucelike salsa, simmer it for 10 to 15 minutes, and call it a day. I have made it both ways and devoured it both ways. Let your taste and level of patience be your guides.

Yield:	Prep time:	Cook time:	Serving size:
3 quarts	20 minutes	30 minutes to 1 hour	⅓ cup

2 TB. grapeseed or canola oil

2 cups yellow onion, finely diced

3 cups green peppers, finely diced

½ cup hot peppers, seeds and ribs removed, and finely diced

1½ tsp. minced garlic

4 cups fresh tomatoes, diced

1 (28-oz.) can diced tomatoes, with juice

1 (14.5-oz.) can corn, drained and rinsed

1 (14.5-oz.) can black beans, drained and rinsed

1 cup fresh cilantro, chopped

Juice of 2 small limes (¼ cup)

1½ tsp. salt

1 TB. apple cider vinegar

1. In a Dutch oven or heavy-bottomed pan over medium-high heat, heat grapeseed oil. Add yellow onion and green peppers, and cook for about 5 minutes or until onions and peppers are softened.

2. Add hot peppers, and cook for 1 minute. Add garlic, and cook for 1 more minute.

3. Reduce heat to medium, and add fresh tomatoes, canned tomatoes with juice, corn, and black beans. Simmer for 10 minutes to 1 hour or until mixture reaches your desired consistency.

4. Remove from heat. Stir in cilantro, lime juice, salt, and apple cider vinegar.

5. Serve immediately, or store in an airtight container in the refrigerator for up to 2 weeks.

Variation: For **Spicy Stewed Tomato Salsa with Black Beans and Corn,** replace 1 cup green bell peppers with 1 cup jalapeño peppers. If you want it really spicy, leave the ribs and seeds in the jalapeños. For medium-spicy salsa, remove the ribs and seeds from the jalapeños.

TURN UP THE HEAT

My father sweats when he eats ketchup—*that's* how spice-adverse our family was. The original version of this salsa is so mild Dad could eat it with a spoon. To increase heat, first swap out some of the sweet peppers for hot peppers. For more heat, leave in all the hot pepper seeds and ribs. I don't think poor old Dad could even smell that version without going through a few sweatbands. Keep in mind that the spice level of peppers can vary greatly depending on the type, size, and growing conditions. Proceed with caution or abandon, depending on where you fall on the spice spectrum.

Roasted Salsa Verde

This is the green version of "The Easiest Salsa *Ever*." It's perfect for making enchiladas and as a chip dip. The tomatillos and lime juice make this a tart salsa, so I usually add a ½ tablespoon sugar. If you don't want to add the sugar, omit the lime juice.

Yield:	Prep time:	Cook time:	Serving size:
1 pint	5 minutes	15 minutes	¼ cup

2 cups tomatillos, husks removed and cleaned

2 medium jalapeños, stems removed

2 cloves garlic, peeled

1 medium white onion, peeled, halved, and ends removed

1 cup fresh cilantro, chopped

Juice of 2 small limes (2 TB.)

½ TB. sugar

1. Preheat the broiler to 500°F. Line a baking sheet with aluminum foil.

2. Place tomatillos, jalapeños, garlic, and white onion on the baking sheet, cut side down for onion halves. Broil for 10 to 15 minutes or until skins are charred. Turn over jalapeños halfway through the cook time to evenly char.

3. In a food processor fitted with a chopping blade, pulse together broiled vegetables and cilantro until ingredients are chopped evenly into small pieces and before smooth. Stir in lime juice and sugar.

4. Let cool to room temperature.

5. Store in an airtight container in the refrigerator for 3 to 5 days.

PREPPING TOMATILLOS

To prep the tomatillos, remove the husk and twist off the connecting end. Rinse the tomatillo thoroughly to remove the sticky substance on the exterior before using.

Stewed Salsa Verde

This is a great salsa for cooking as well as dipping. I use it to make enchiladas, and I simmer tofu in it for a vegetarian taco filling. It's also a great alternative to your typical tomato salsa paired with chips.

Yield:	Prep time:	Cook time:	Serving size:
1 quart	15 minutes	30 minutes to 1 hour	⅓ cup

4 cups tomatillos, husked and halved

2 cups jalapeños, sliced in 1-in. slices and stems removed

1½ TB. canola or grapeseed oil

1 cup yellow onion, diced

2 cups sweet green and yellow peppers, diced

1 (4.5-oz.) can chopped green chiles, drained

1 tsp. minced garlic

1 TB. apple cider vinegar

1 cup fresh cilantro, chopped

1 tsp. salt

1. Place tomatillos and jalapeños in medium saucepan. Cover with water by 1 inch, set over medium-high heat, and bring to a boil. Reduce heat to medium, and simmer for 10 minutes or until tomatillos and jalapeños are soft.

2. Meanwhile, in heavy-bottomed pan over medium heat, heat canola oil. Add yellow onion and sweet green and yellow peppers, and cook for about 6 to 8 minutes or until softened. Add green chiles and garlic.

3. Strain tomatillos and jalapeños, remove the pan from heat, and return tomatillos and jalapeños to the pan. Using a potato masher, mash tomatillos and jalapeños until big chunks have been removed. Add tomatillos and jalapeños to onion mixture, and simmer for 5 to 10 minutes or until well combined and heated through.

4. Remove from heat, and stir in apple cider vinegar, cilantro, and salt.

5. Pour into 1-quart mason jar, let cool for 10 to 15 minutes, and seal.

6. Store in the refrigerator for up to 2 weeks.

TART TOMATILLOS

You can eat tomatillos raw, but they're very tart and very firm. When you cook them, the flavor mellows out and the texture resembles that of a cooked tomato.

Salsa Verde with Tomatoes, Black Beans, and Corn

This is the grand finale of salsas. It has it all: tomatoes, black beans, corn, tomatillos, garlic, cilantro, peppers—the list goes on and on. This is a salsa to impress, a salsa that tells your guest you're pulling all the stops. This is a salsa worthy of a celebration. Most importantly, this is a salsa you can eat with a fork. By reducing it for 50 minutes, you get a concentrated flavor and thick consistency that can't be beat.

Yield:	Prep time:	Cook time:	Serving size:
3 quarts	30 minutes	1 hour	⅓ cup

4 cups tomatillos, husked and halved

2 cups jalapeños, sliced in 1-in. slices and stems removed

1½ TB. grapeseed or canola oil

2 cups yellow onion, diced

3 cups sweet green and yellow peppers, diced

1 (4.5-oz.) can chopped green chiles, drained

2 tsp. minced garlic

2 cups fresh tomatoes, diced

1 (14.5-oz.) can black beans, drained and rinsed

1 (14.5-oz.) can corn, drained and rinsed

2 TB. apple cider vinegar

1 cup fresh cilantro, chopped

1 tsp. salt

1. Place tomatillos and jalapeños in medium saucepan. Cover with water by 1 inch, set over medium-high heat, and bring to a boil. Reduce heat to medium, and simmer for 10 minutes or until tomatillos and jalapeños are soft.

2. Meanwhile, in heavy-bottomed pan over medium heat, heat grapeseed oil. Add yellow onion and sweet green and yellow peppers, and cook for about 6 to 8 minutes or until softened. Add green chiles, garlic, tomatoes, black beans, and corn.

3. Strain tomatillos and jalapeños, remove the pan from heat, and return tomatillos and jalapeños to the pan. Using a potato masher, mash tomatillos and jalapeños until big chunks have been removed. Add tomatillos and jalapeños to onion mixture. Salsa will be watery at first. Simmer and reduce for 45 to 50 minutes or until salsa reaches your desired consistency.

4. Remove from heat, and stir in apple cider vinegar, cilantro, and salt.

5. Pour into 1-quart mason jar, let cool for 10 to 15 minutes, and seal.

6. Store in the refrigerator for up to 2 weeks.

Super-Fast Guacamole

One night, Manatee and I were both craving guacamole. We had the avocado but didn't have any peppers, tomatoes, garlic, or red onion. Manatee pulled out a jar of his favorite salsa and thrust it at me. "Salsa has peppers, right?" I had to agree. "Onions? Tomatoes?" He continued. A new recipe was born. This is our go-to guacamole recipe.

Yield:	Prep time:	Serving size:
1 cup	5 minutes	¼ cup

1 medium avocado, pitted	Juice of 1 small lime (2 TB.)
3 TB. salsa	⅛ tsp. salt

1. In a small bowl, mash avocado with a fork or potato masher. Stir in salsa, lime juice, and salt.

2. Serve immediately.

KEEP IT GREEN

Guacamole is best when served immediately. If you do make it ahead, press some plastic wrap tight against the top to prevent it from turning brown. You might be able to eat it the next day, but throw it out after more than 1 day. I once made my nephews guacamole 2 days ahead of time, and it was khaki colored by the time I served it. Their parents made them try it, and 5 years later they still won't touch guacamole. Nothing like scarring some kids with your cooking, eh?

Italian Guacamole

Italian Guacamole? How can that it be? In my quest for guacamole, I ran into many who swore by Italian ingredients like olive oil, dried oregano, and red wine vinegar. It's different. Manatee thinks he died and went to heaven: all his favorite Mexican ingredients pared with his favorite Italian ingredients are here. I think it's great for surprising people. Trust me, this is not your average guacamole.

Yield:	Prep time:	Serving size:
2 cups	15 minutes	¼ cup

2 medium avocados, pitted

2 TB. olive oil

3 TB. red onion, diced

2 medium roma tomatoes, diced

1 tsp. dried oregano

1 TB. crushed red pepper flakes

1 tsp. red wine vinegar

¼ tsp. salt

Juice of 1 small lime (2 TB.)

1. In a medium bowl, mash avocados with a fork or potato masher. Stir in olive oil, red onion, roma tomatoes, oregano, crushed red pepper flakes, red wine vinegar, salt, and lime juice.

2. Serve immediately.

Classic Guacamole

This guacamole contains all the most popular guacamole ingredients—at least according to my year-long research project. If you like a chunkier version, increase the amount of tomatoes, onions, peppers, and cilantro.

Yield:	Prep time:	Serving size:
2 cups	15 minutes	¼ cup

2 medium avocados, pitted

2 medium roma tomatoes, diced

2 TB. jalapeños, finely diced

3 TB. fresh cilantro, chopped

¼ tsp. salt

Juice of 1 small lime (2 TB.)

1. In a medium bowl, mash avocados with a fork or potato masher. Stir in roma tomatoes, jalapeños, cilantro, salt, and lime juice.

2. Serve immediately.

Badger Girl Caviar

This is my version of Texas caviar, or poor man's caviar, or whatever-you-call-it-that's-really-not-caviar-and-you-eat-with-chips. I love serving this at parties or picnics because it's easy to throw together and tastes so good with chips or on a salad.

Yield:	Prep time:	Serving size:
1 quart	10 minutes, plus 1 hour marinate time	¼ cup

1 (14.5-oz.) can black beans, rinsed and drained

1 (14.5-oz.) can pinto beans, rinsed and drained

1 (14.5-oz.) can corn, rinsed and drained, or 2 cups cooked fresh corn off the cob

½ cup green onions, green and white parts, sliced

1½ medium red or yellow bell peppers, ribs and seeds removed, and diced

2 TB. canola oil

1 TB. apple cider vinegar

Juice of 2 small limes (¼ cup)

½ tsp. salt

1. In a medium bowl, combine black beans, pinto beans, corn, green onions, red bell peppers, canola oil, apple cider vinegar, lime juice, and salt.

2. Place in an airtight container and refrigerate for 1 hour to allow flavors to meld.

3. Store in the refrigerator for up to 4 days.

Plain Hummus

This is a great base for making flavored hummus, using as a sandwich spread, or eating on its own. I use Roasted Garlic because it has mellower taste. If you love garlic and want a more garlicky flavor, use fresh instead.

Yield:	Prep time:	Serving size:
2 cups	10 minutes	¼ cup

1 clove Roasted Garlic (recipe in Chapter 3)

1 TB. olive oil

1½ cups canned chickpeas, rinsed and drained

Juice of 2 small lemons (2 TB.)

1 TB. tahini paste

½ cup vegetable broth

½ tsp. salt

½ tsp. smoked paprika

1. In a small bowl, combine Roasted Garlic and olive oil. Mash garlic with a fork to form paste with olive oil.

2. In a food processor fitted with a chopping blade, place garlic paste, chickpeas, lemon juice, tahini paste, vegetable broth, salt, and smoked paprika. Cover the top of the food processor bowl with plastic wrap, attach the lid, and process until smooth, stopping occasionally to scrape down sides.

3. Store in an airtight container in the refrigerator for 7 days.

CLEANUP TIP

Covering the top of your food processor bowl with plastic wrap helps speed cleanup.

Buffalo BBQ Hummus

Are you nervous about coming clean on your diet? Worried that eating healthy means pretending you don't crave junk food? Afraid you'll have to live like a martyr while your friends gorge themselves on Doritos and chicken wings? This dip will be your gateway. Don't let the word *hummus* get in your way; this is junk food flavor at its best. Be forewarned, though: this dip will bite you back. It's hot, it's spicy, and it tastes far better than a greasy chicken wing. For a true buffalo wing experience, serve it with celery sticks and crumbled blue cheese.

Yield:	Prep time:	Serving size:
2 cups	10 minutes	¼ cup

1 clove Roasted Garlic (recipe in Chapter 3)	½ cup vegetable broth
1 TB. olive oil	½ TB. white vinegar
1½ cups canned chickpeas, rinsed and drained	1½ tsp. smoked paprika
Juice of 2 small lemons (2 TB.)	2 or 3 TB. hot sauce (recipes in Chapter 4)
2 TB. tahini paste	1 tsp. celery salt

1. In a small bowl, combine Roasted Garlic and olive oil. Mash garlic with a fork to form paste with olive oil.

2. In a food processor fitted with a chopping blade, place garlic paste, chickpeas, lemon juice, tahini paste, vegetable broth, white vinegar, smoked paprika, hot sauce, and celery salt. Cover the top of the food processor bowl with plastic wrap, attach the lid, and process until smooth, stopping occasionally to scrape down sides.

3. Store in an airtight container in the refrigerator for 7 days.

Variation: If you don't have any Roasted Garlic (or don't want to make it), you can substitute 1 fresh clove garlic instead. Before mixing it with olive oil to make a paste, sprinkle with kosher salt, and mash with a fork. This will break down the garlic into a paste. Then proceed with recipe by mixing it with the olive oil.

Beet Hummus

This hot pink dip is worth making just to see the shocked faces of your guests. We had this as an appetizer at one of our favorite restaurants, and it was love at first taste. Top with crumbled goat cheese, and serve with Baked Pita Chips (recipe in Chapter 10).

Yield:	Prep time:	Serving size:
2 cups	10 minutes	¼ cup

1 clove Roasted Garlic (recipe in Chapter 3)

1 TB. olive oil

1½ cups canned chickpeas, rinsed and drained

Juice of 2 small lemons (2 TB.)

½ cup organic vegetable broth, homemade or store-bought

½ cup cooked beets, quartered

1 TB. Dijon mustard

½ tsp. salt

1. In a small bowl, combine Roasted Garlic and olive oil. Mash garlic with a fork to form paste with olive oil.

2. In a food processor fitted with a chopping blade, place garlic paste, chickpeas, lemon juice, vegetable broth, beets, Dijon mustard, and salt. Cover the top of the food processor bowl with plastic wrap, attach the lid, and process until smooth, stopping occasionally to scrape down sides.

3. Store in an airtight container in the refrigerator for 7 days.

COOKING BEETS

The easiest way to cook beets is to boil them. Trim the ends off the beets and place the beets in a large saucepan. Cover with water and juice from ½ lemon (to prevent them from bleeding). Bring to a boil over medium-high heat, reduce heat to medium-low to medium, and maintain a gentle simmer for 30 to 45 minutes or until beets are tender when pierced with a fork. Use a paper towel to dry the beets, and remove the skin.

Roasted Red Pepper Hummus

I will always be searching for a perfect roasted red pepper hummus. This is my current favorite. I blend fresh peppers with smoky Roasted Red Peppers to make a sweeter hummus with a bright red color.

Yield:	Prep time:	Serving size:
2 cups	10 minutes	¼ cup

1 clove Roasted Garlic (recipe in Chapter 3)

1 TB. olive oil

½ cup Roasted Red Peppers (recipe in Chapter 3)

½ medium red bell pepper, ribs and seeds removed, and diced (¼ cup)

1½ cups canned chickpeas, rinsed and drained

Juice of 2 small lemons (2 TB.)

1 TB. tahini paste

½ cup organic vegetable broth, homemade or store-bought

½ tsp. salt

½ tsp. smoked paprika

1. In a small bowl, combine Roasted Garlic and olive oil. Mash garlic with a fork to form paste with olive oil.

2. In a food processor fitted with a chopping blade, place garlic paste, Roasted Red Peppers, red bell pepper, chickpeas, lemon juice, tahini paste, vegetable broth, salt, and smoked paprika. Cover the top of the food processor bowl with plastic wrap, attach the lid, and process until smooth, stopping occasionally to scrape down sides.

3. Store in an airtight container in the refrigerator for 7 days.

Pesto Hummus

This is two great dips in one bowl—fresh basil pesto with creamy hummus. This is great with veggies, Baked Pita Chips, as a sandwich spread, or even tossed with cooked pasta.

Yield:	Prep time:	Serving size:
2 cups	10 minutes	¼ cup

1½ cups canned chickpeas, rinsed and drained

Juice of 2 small lemons (2 TB.)

½ cup vegetable broth

½ cup Classic Pesto (recipe in Chapter 4)

½ tsp. salt

1. In a food processor fitted with a chopping blade, place chickpeas, lemon juice, vegetable broth, Classic Pesto, and salt. Cover the top of the food processor bowl with plastic wrap, attach the lid, and process until smooth, stopping occasionally to scrape down the sides.

2. Store in an airtight container in the refrigerator for 7 days.

Seven-Layer Hummus

This is the Mediterranean response to taco dip. Imagine a classic Mediterranean plate piled together in layers. This is all my favorite tastes in one bite.

Yield:	Prep time:	Serving size:
6 cups	25 minutes	¼ cup hummus plus ⅓ cup toppings

2 cups Plain Hummus (recipe earlier in this chapter)

1 cup Roasted Red Peppers (recipe in Chapter 3)

½ cup kalamata olives, pitted and sliced

½ cup green onions, green and white parts, sliced

1½ cups shredded iceberg lettuce

1 cup fresh tomatoes, diced

½ cup crumbled feta cheese

1. Spread Plain Hummus across a large platter. Top with Roasted Red Peppers, kalamata olives, green onions, lettuce, tomatoes, and feta cheese.

2. Serve with Baked Pita Chips (recipe in Chapter 10).

Dairy-Free Taco Dip

I've always loved taco dip, but the taco dip of yore always had a sour cream and taco seasoning mix at its base. Being lactose intolerant, I thought I could never have it again. It took years for me to realize I could change the base. This taco dip begins with kidney beans mashed with green chiles and never looks back.

Yield:	Prep time:	Serving size:
5 cups	25 minutes	$\frac{1}{2}$ cup

1 (14.5-oz.) can pinto beans, rinsed and drained

1 (4.5-oz.) can chopped chiles

2 batches Super-Fast Guacamole (2 cups; recipe earlier in this chapter)

1 cup salsa (recipes earlier in this chapter)

3 cups shredded iceberg lettuce

1 cup green onions, green and white parts, sliced

1 (4.5-oz.) can sliced black olives, drained

1½ cups fresh tomatoes, diced

1. In a medium bowl, mash pinto beans with chiles using a fork or potato masher.

2. In a large rectangle cake pan, layer bean and chile paste, Super-Fast Guacamole, salsa, lettuce, green onions, black olives, and tomatoes.

3. Serve with Baked Tortilla Chips (recipe in Chapter 10).

White Bean and Sun-Dried Tomato Dip

This makes a great sandwich spread as well as a great alternative to hummus.

Yield:	Prep time:	Serving size:
1½ cups	5 minutes	¼ cup

1 cup canned white beans, rinsed and drained	1 clove garlic, peeled
¼ cup sun-dried tomatoes	Juice of ½ small lemon (2 TB.)

1. In a food processor fitted with a chopping blade, place white beans, sun-dried tomatoes, garlic, and lemon juice. Cover the top of the food processor bowl with plastic wrap, attach the lid, and process until smooth, stopping occasionally to scrape down the sides.

2. Serve with fresh vegetables, Baked Pita Chips, or spread it on a sandwich.

Baba Ghanoush

How can you not love a dip called *baba ghanoush?* Maybe I just like saying it. If Manatee ever (seriously) revolts against his given pseudonym, I might have to start calling him *Baba Ghanoush*. Back to the dip, this is comfort food at its best. It's creamy, salty, rich, and healthy. Serve it with Baked Pita Chips (recipe in Chapter 10) and Roasted Red Peppers (recipe in Chapter 3).

Yield:	Prep time:	Cook time:	Serving size:
1¼ cups	5 minutes, plus 30 minutes cool time	15 to 20 minutes	¼ cup

1 medium eggplant	½ TB. olive oil
1 TB. tahini paste	Juice of 1 small lemon (2 TB.)
1 clove Roasted Garlic (recipe in Chapter 3)	½ tsp. salt

1. Preheat the oven to 450°F. Line a baking sheet with aluminum foil.

2. Prick eggplant all over with a fork. Place on the baking sheet, and broil for 15 to 20 minutes or until eggplant is soft. Rotate eggplant halfway through the cook time.

3. Split eggplant in ½, and let cool for 30 minutes or until room temperature.

4. Scoop out eggplant flesh into a food processor fitted with a chopping blade. Add tahini paste, Roasted Garlic, olive oil, lemon juice, and salt. Cover the top of the food processor bowl with plastic wrap, attach the lid, and process until smooth, stopping occasionally to scrape down the sides.

5. Serve immediately, or store in an airtight container in the refrigerator for up to 3 days.

Marvelous Mini-Meals

 12

One of the tricks of eating clean is to be sure you never get too hungry or too full. When you're too hungry, you'll be more likely to give in to a craving or make a poor food choice. Suddenly, it won't seem like a big deal to buy a bag of chips or snack on some packaged treat. Equally bad, when you're too full, you're not in tune with your body.

The mini-meals in this chapter are a great way to keep your hunger in check when you need a snack in the afternoon, want to make a light dinner or lunch, or want to have some protein-packed snacks when you're on the go.

Focus on What *Can* You Eat

When you make the decision to cut processed foods from your diet, it's all too easy to focus on everything you *can't* eat. No soda, no potato chips, no packaged chocolate-chip cookies—the list goes on and on.

This chapter contains one of my favorite sets of recipes. With them, you'll find that you can eat a ton of stuff by using fresh, real ingredients. Plus, you won't even miss your old processed versions. Nachos take on a new dimension when you start using real cheese and homemade chips. Beef jerky has so much more flavor when it's not saturated in chemicals. When you make your own chicken nuggets, you know exactly what part of the chicken makes up the nugget. And who knew tofu could be so good?

Think of these recipes as a starting point. I've offered some variations, but don't feel limited by them. I encourage you to customize these recipes and make them your own. Do you like pineapple on your pizza? By all means, add it to the tortilla pizza recipe. Do you prefer pepper jack cheese to cheddar? Swap it. Have fun with these recipes!

Teriyaki Beef Jerky

Beef jerky is a great snack to keep in your car or bag for on-the-go munchies. It's low in fat and packed with protein, but the commercial varieties are also packed with chemicals. If you're a big jerky fan, it's worth investing in a dehydrator. In the long run, you'll save money and have complete control of your ingredients. How can you beat that?

Yield:	Prep time:	Cook time:	Serving size:
25 to 35 pieces	25 minutes, plus 8 to 12 hours marinate time	8 to 10 hours	4 to 6 pieces

1 (2- or 3-lb.) top round beef roast or another beef roast

1 cup Teriyaki Sauce (recipe in Chapter 4)

¼ cup liquid smoke

1 cup soy sauce

½ tsp. ground ginger or 1 (1-in.) piece peeled and minced fresh ginger (1 tsp.)

¼ cup hot sauce (recipes in Chapter 4)

¼ cup apple cider vinegar

1. Place top round beef roast in the freezer while you prepare marinade.

2. In a small bowl, whisk together Teriyaki Sauce, liquid smoke, soy sauce, ginger, hot sauce, and apple cider vinegar.

3. Remove beef from the freezer, and slice into slices ¼ inch to ⅛ inch thick. Use a clean dishtowel to help you hold beef in place.

4. Place beef slices in a gallon zipper-lock plastic bag, squeeze out the air, and seal the bag. Place the bag in a second gallon zipper-lock plastic bag, squeeze out the air, and seal it. (You can also use an airtight container for marinating.) Marinate in the refrigerator for 8 to 12 hours.

5. Remove beef slices from marinade, discard marinade, and place beef on the dehydrator racks. Dehydrate on medium for 8 to 10 hours or at 155°F for 2 to 4 hours. Use your dehydrator's manufacturer's instructions as a guide.

Variation: For **Teriyaki Turkey Jerky,** use 1 (1½- to 2-pound) skinless, boneless turkey breast.

LIQUID SMOKE

Liquid smoke is condensed smoke that's been collected in a tube placed above burning certain types of wood chips, such as hickory. The condensed smoke is filtered, and many brands do not contain any added chemicals. I think it's a great way to add the smokiness of a barbecue without using actual barbecue sauce. When buying liquid smoke, be sure to read the list of ingredients. Some liquid smokes include a lot of unnecessary chemicals or even high-fructose corn syrup. I prefer using Colgin Liquid Smoke. If you can't find liquid smoke or are uncomfortable using it, use 2 tablespoons smoked paprika or adobe sauce instead.

Sweet-and-Spicy Turkey Jerky

Packed with citrus and spice with a fair balance of sweet and salty, this summertime jerky is a great go-to snack when you're running errands and on busy days. It's packed with protein and no chemicals in sight, so it's also a snack you can feel good about eating.

Yield:	Prep time:	Cook time:	Serving size:
25 to 35 pieces	45 minutes, plus 8 to 12 hours marinate time	8 to 10 hours	4 to 6 pieces

1½ to 2 lb. boneless turkey breasts, skin removed

1 cup soy sauce or tamari sauce

½ cup seasoned rice vinegar

1 tsp. liquid smoke

¼ cup hot sauce (recipes in Chapter 4)

½ cup sucanat or organic brown sugar, firmly packed

Juice of 2 small limes (¼ cup)

1. Place turkey breast in the freezer while you prepare marinade.

2. In a small saucepan over medium-high heat, whisk together soy sauce, seasoned rice vinegar, liquid smoke, hot sauce, and sucanat. Bring to a boil, and cook until sucanat has dissolved. Remove from heat, and stir in lime juice. Allow to cool to room temperature.

3. Remove turkey breast from marinade, and slice into slices ¼ inch to ⅛ inch thick. Use a clean dishtowel to hold turkey in place.

4. Place turkey slices in a gallon zipper-lock plastic bag, squeeze out the air, and seal the bag. Place the bag in a second gallon zipper-lock plastic bag, squeeze out the air, and seal it. (You can also use an airtight container for marinating.) Marinate in the refrigerator for 8 to 12 hours.

5. Remove turkey slices from marinade, discard marinade, and place turkey on the dehydrator racks. Dehydrate on medium for 8 to 10 hours or at 155°F for 2 to 4 hours. Use your dehydrator's manufacturer's instructions as a guide.

Variation: For **Sweet and Spicy Beef Jerky,** substitute 1 (2- to 3-pound) lean beef roast for the turkey.

CUTTING TIP

You can place the turkey (or any meat) in the freezer for up to 2 hours before you're ready to use. The longer you keep it in the freezer, the easier it will be to cut into razor-thin slices. If you're around while the meat's dehydrating, rotate the racks from top to bottom and flip the slices halfway through the dehydrating time.

Mini Classic Pizzas

English muffin pizzas were the first "meal" I could make for myself, and I felt so cool that I could make my own pizza whenever I wanted. Consider this the grown-up version of this childhood classic. When you toast or broil the tortilla, you end up with a personal-size thin crust pizza.

Yield:	Prep time:	Cook time:	Serving size:
1 pizza	5 minutes	12 to 15 minutes	1 pizza

1 (8-in.) Wheat Tortilla (recipe in Chapter 3)

¼ cup Marinara Sauce (recipe in Chapter 4)

⅓ cup shredded mozzarella cheese

¼ tsp. Italian Seasoning (recipe in Chapter 7)

1. Preheat the broiler to 500°F.

2. Place Wheat Tortilla on a work surface, and spread Marinara Sauce on top, working sauce out toward edges of tortilla. Sprinkle on mozzarella cheese and Italian Seasoning.

3. Place pizza on baking sheet, and bake for 12 to 15 minutes or until cheese is melted and slightly browned. Serve immediately.

Variations: For **Gluten-Free Pizzas,** use 6-inch corn tortillas. Reduce the cheese to 3 tablespoons, reduce the sauce to 2 tablespoons, and reduce the Italian Seasoning to $\frac{1}{8}$ teaspoon. For **Vegan Pizzas,** substitute Tofucotta (recipe in Chapter 3) for the mozzarella cheese.

CRISPY AND DELICIOUS

For a crispier crust, place the pizza on a cooking rack on top of the baking sheet or use a pizza stone.

Classic Nachos

Growing up, nachos were the ultimate snack at athletic events. I lapped up that orange, chemical-laden cheese sauce like it was my last meal. Now I cringe just thinking about what I was putting into my body. Believe it or not, nachos can be a healthy treat. Homemade baked chips, real cheese, and homemade salsa: what's unhealthy about that? Make it deluxe with shredded lettuce and diced veggies, and this "junk food" could almost be a salad.

Yield:	Prep time:	Cook time:	Serving size:
3 or 4 cups	5 minutes	8 to 10 minutes	4 or 5 chips plus $\frac{1}{4}$ cup toppings

16 to 20 Baked Tortilla Chips (recipe in Chapter 10)

$\frac{1}{3}$ cup Stewed Tomato Salsa with Black Beans and Corn (recipe in Chapter 11)

$\frac{1}{3}$ cup shredded cheddar cheese

1. Preheat the oven to 350°F. Line a baking sheet with aluminum foil.

2. Arrange Baked Tortilla Chips in a single layer on the baking sheet. Spoon Stewed Tomato Salsa with Black Beans and Corn over chips, and top with cheddar cheese.

3. Bake for 8 to 10 minutes or until all cheese is melted. Serve immediately.

Variations: For **Nachos Deluxe,** add ⅓ cup shredded lettuce, 3 tablespoons diced fresh tomatoes, 1 tablespoon sliced black olives, and 2 tablespoons sliced jalapeño peppers or diced sweet peppers to the nachos after they come out of the oven. For **Roasted Tomato or Roasted Salsa Verde Nachos,** substitute Roasted Tomato Salsa (recipe in Chapter 11) or Roasted Salsa Verde (recipe in Chapter 11) for the Stewed Tomato Salsa with Black Beans and Corn. For **Nachos Verde,** substitute Stewed Salsa Verde (recipe in Chapter 11) or with Salsa Verde with Tomatoes, Black Beans, and Corn (recipe in Chapter 11) for the Stewed Tomato Salsa with Black Beans and Corn. For **Nachos Fresco,** substitute Pico de Gallo (recipe in Chapter 11) for the Stewed Tomato Salsa with Black Beans and Corn.

Mediterranean-Style Nachos

In graduate school, I became a nachos connoisseur. One of my favorite bars served a nachos deluxe appetizer that changed how I looked at the nachos of my childhood. I'm pretty sure this bar dumped on whatever ingredients they had on hand: diced apples, red onions, hummus, salsa, and every kind of cheese you could possibly imagine—except that orange cheese sauce that generally comes with nachos. Two ingredients always stood out for me: hummus and feta cheese.

Yield:	Prep time:	Cook time:	Serving size:
3 or 4 cups	5 minutes	8 to 10 minutes	4 or 5 chips and ¼ cup topping

16 to 20 Baked Tortilla Chips (recipe in Chapter 10)	3 TB. diced Roasted Red Peppers (recipe in Chapter 3)
1½ TB. Plain Hummus (recipe in Chapter 11)	3 TB. shredded mozzarella cheese
	1 TB. crumbled feta cheese

1. Preheat the oven to 350°F. Line a baking sheet with aluminum foil.

2. Arrange Baked Tortilla Chips in a single layer on the baking sheet. Spoon Plain Hummus over chips, and top with Roasted Red Peppers, mozzarella cheese, and feta cheese.

3. Bake for 8 to 10 minutes until all cheese is melted. Serve immediately.

Variation: For **Mediterranean Pita Nachos,** replace the Baked Tortilla Chips with Baked Pita Chips (recipe in Chapter 10).

Clean Taco Filling

Healthy tacos? Is that an oxymoron? Not at all! Choose lean meat and pump up the veggies to make a healthier version of a junk-food favorite. I usually double the recipe because this is a great meal for leftovers and it freezes well. The only problem you might run into is lack of space in your average frying pan. My solution: an electric frying pan. It's big, you can control the temperature to the degree, and you can fit a ton of veggies into it. Otherwise, cook the doubled filling in two large frying pans.

Yield:	Prep time:	Cook time:	Serving size:
6 to 6½ cups	25 minutes	35 minutes	1 cup

½ medium yellow onion, diced (1 cup)

½ medium green bell pepper, ribs and seeds removed, and diced (½ cup)

½ medium red or yellow bell pepper, ribs and seeds removed, and diced (½ cup)

½ medium zucchini or summer squash, diced (½ cup)

1 medium stalk celery, diced (¼ cup)

1 TB. canola or grapeseed oil

1 medium carrot, peeled and diced (⅓ cup)

1 cup fresh white button mushrooms, quartered

1 lb. ground beef, turkey, or chicken

¼ cup Taco Seasoning (recipe in Chapter 7)

⅓ cup water

1. In a large frying pan over medium heat, heat canola oil. Add yellow onion, green bell pepper, red bell pepper, zucchini, celery, carrot, and white button mushrooms. Cover and cook for 8 to 10 minutes or until veggies are softened.

2. Add ground beef to the frying pan, and break up large chunks using a spatula. Cook for about 5 minutes or until beef is browned.

3. Add Taco Seasoning and water, stir, and simmer for 10 minutes. Serve immediately, using a slotted spoon.

Variations: For **Spicy Taco Filling,** replace the green bell pepper with 2 small jalapeño peppers. For extra spice, don't remove the seeds. For **Vegan Taco Filling,** replace the ground beef with 1 (14.5-ounce) can black beans and 1 (8-ounce) can corn, both rinsed and drained. Reduce the water to ¼ cup, and increase the Taco Seasoning by 1 tablespoon.

MAKE A TACO BAR!

Taco bars can be as simple or elaborate as you like. At the most basic, set out some shredded lettuce, taco filling, chopped tomatoes, and tortillas. That's a great starting point, but I challenge you to take it to the next step. Add some different types of salsas, olives, guacamole, shredded cheese, and sour cream to make taco night into a taco party! Manatee, my lettuce-loving husband, loves to use butter lettuce leaves as his taco shell. The sweet lettuce is a great compliment to the spicy taco fillings, and the leaves are the perfect size and shape for big and little hands alike.

Tofu Dippers

The first time I served these at a party, I had very low expectations about their reception. Manatee and I love them, so I figured we'd be the only ones who ate them. How wrong I was! People crowded around them. At that party and every party since then, Tofu Dippers are the first appetizer to go. I've had grown men come up to me like guilty little boys and confess that they didn't even think they liked tofu but couldn't stop eating them. I can't explain it, but I suppose when you fry something and serve it with a dipping sauce, you can't go wrong.

Yield:	Prep time:	Cook time:	Serving size:
24 dippers	5 minutes	12 to 15 minutes	4 dippers

1 (10-oz.) pkg. firm or extra-firm tofu

2 TB. canola or grapeseed oil

¼ tsp. crushed red pepper flakes

1. Wrap tofu in paper towels, and press out excess liquid. Cut tofu into ⅛-inch slices. Cut each slice again into 3 (1-inch) rectangles.

2. In a large frying pan over medium heat, heat canola oil. Add tofu, sprinkle ⅛ teaspoon crushed red pepper flakes on top, and cook for 6 or 7 minutes or until one side of tofu is golden brown and crispy. Flip over tofu, and sprinkle with remaining ⅛ teaspoon crushed red pepper flakes. Cook for 6 to 8 more minutes or until both sides are golden and crispy.

3. Serve warm or at room temperature with your favorite dipping sauce, such as Peanut Sauce (recipe in Chapter 4).

Variation: For **Cheesy Tofu Bites,** add 1 tablespoon nutritional yeast with the crushed red pepper flakes.

TYPES OF TOFU

Manatee and I agree to disagree on the type of tofu for this recipe. I prefer extra firm because it's firmer to the touch and a little easier to handle. Manatee prefers firm because the tofu has more of a spongy texture to it. He likes it crisp on the outside and soft on the inside. If you're new to tofu, go for the extra firm because it will be easier to use. After you get used to cooking with it, try the firm and see how you like the texture.

Sweet-and-Spicy Tofu Bites

This is a tofu for the meat-eating crowd. The flavor is a balance of sweet and spicy, tangy, and salty, while the texture is chewy and dense. This was the first tofu I made for Manatee and converted him to the "soy side." The broil-and-baste technique requires little hands-on work but comes together fast. You can eat it warm, cold, or at room temperature. Keep it in the fridge for a protein-packed snack throughout the day, throw it in a lunch box with some dipping sauce, or serve it with steamed veggies and brown rice for a healthy dinner.

Yield:	Prep time:	Cook time:	Serving size:
24 bites	5 minutes	15 minutes	4 bites

1 (10-oz.) pkg. extra-firm tofu	Juice of 1 small lime (2 TB.)
¼ cup soy sauce or tamari sauce	2 TB. agave nectar or maple syrup
2 TB. hot sauce (recipes in Chapter 4)	

1. Wrap tofu in paper towels, and press out excess liquid. Cut tofu into $\frac{1}{8}$-inch slices. Cut each slice again into 3 (1-inch) rectangles. Place tofu in a medium sealable container.

2. In a small bowl, whisk together soy sauce, hot sauce, lime juice, and agave nectar. Pour marinade over tofu, seal the container, shake to distribute marinade, and marinate for at least 1 hour in the refrigerator.

3. Preheat the oven to 500°F, or preheat the broiler. Line a rimmed baking sheet with aluminum foil.

4. Place tofu rectangles in a single layer on the baking sheet. Using a pastry brush or basting brush, brush marinade over tofu. Broil for 7 minutes.

5. Remove tofu from the oven, and brush with another coat of marinade. Broil for 4 more minutes.

6. Remove tofu from the oven, and brush on a third coat of marinade. Broil for 4 more minutes. Serve immediately.

Variation: For a more kid-friendly version, reduce the hot sauce to 1 tablespoon or omit it completely.

REAL MAPLE SYRUP

If you opt for maple syrup in this recipe, use *real* maple syrup. Light or artificial maple syrup will affect the taste and texture of the tofu.

Clean Chicken Nuggets

You don't need a deep fryer to make these juicy chicken bites. The breadcrumbs crisp in the oven so you get all the flavor with none of the guilt. If you think you don't have time to make your own breadcrumbs, think again. They're so fast and easy to make, but I understand if you want to streamline the process. You can use store-bought panko breadcrumbs in a pinch.

Yield:	Prep time:	Cook time:	Serving size:
8 chicken strips or 16 chicken bites	15 minutes	15 to 25 minutes	2 strips or 4 bites

1 lb. skinless, boneless chicken breasts or chicken breast tenders

2 large egg whites

1 TB. olive oil

1½ cups Breadcrumbs (recipe in Chapter 3)

2 TB. Italian Seasoning (recipe in Chapter 7)

1. Preheat the oven to 425°F. Grease a cooking rack with canola oil, and place it on a rimmed baking sheet.

2. If using chicken breasts, cut into 2 strips, lengthwise. For smaller bites, cut each strip horizontally into 2 pieces.

3. In a medium shallow bowl, combine egg whites and olive oil.

4. Place Breadcrumbs in a separate medium shallow bowl to the right of egg whites–olive oil bowl.

5. Place the baking sheet with the rack to the right of the breadcrumbs bowl.

6. Using your left hand, pick up 1 chicken breast strip and dip it into egg whites–olive oil mixture. Transfer chicken to your right hand, and place it in breadcrumbs. Press breadcrumbs onto chicken, and rotate chicken so breadcrumbs completely coat. Place coated chicken on the rack on the baking sheet. Repeat with remaining chicken.

7. Bake for 15 to 25 minutes or until the internal temperature of your largest piece of chicken reaches 165°F on an instant-read thermometer.

8. Remove chicken from the oven, and let sit for 5 minutes before serving with your favorite dipping sauce such as Marinara Sauce (recipe in Chapter 4).

Variation: To make **Dijon Chicken Nuggets,** substitute ½ cup Dijon mustard for the egg whites–olive oil mixture.

Classic Quesadilla

This is a great afternoon snack or predinner nosh. Creamy, real cheese mixed with a little salsa packs a lot of flavor without a lot of effort. In less than 10 minutes, you can have this restaurant menu staple on your own kitchen table.

Yield:	Prep time:	Cook time:	Serving size:
4 slices	5 minutes	6 to 8 minutes	4 slices

¼ cup shredded cheddar cheese

1 TB. Stewed Tomato Salsa with Black Beans and Corn (recipe in Chapter 11)

1 (8-in.) Wheat Tortilla (recipe in Chapter 3)

1. Heat a frying pan over medium heat.

2. In a small bowl, combine cheddar cheese and Stewed Tomato Salsa with Black Beans and Corn. Spread cheese-salsa mixture on ½ of Wheat Tortilla, and fold tortilla over to cover filling.

3. Place tortilla in the frying pan, and heat for 30 seconds. Flip over tortilla, and heat for 1 more minute. Flip over again, and heat for 30 more seconds. If tortilla isn't golden brown, continue heating and flipping every 30 seconds until it is.

4. Remove tortilla from heat, and let sit for 5 minutes to allow cheese to set. Slice pizza-style, and serve.

Variations: For a **Deluxe Quesadilla,** serve with shredded lettuce, sour cream, and/or guacamole. For a **Pizza Quesadilla,** substitute an equal amount of shredded mozzarella cheese for the cheddar cheese and use 1 tablespoon canned tomatoes for the Stewed Tomato Salsa with Black Beans and Corn. Add ½ teaspoon oregano to the cheese and tomato mixture before spreading it on the tortilla. For a **Gluten-Free Classic Quesadilla,** replace the Wheat Tortilla with a Corn Tortilla (recipe in Chapter 3) and reduce the cheese to 2 or 3 tablespoons and the salsa to 1 or 2 tablespoons.

Mediterranean Quesadilla

This is the grown-up version of the classic quesadilla. Hot, creamy hummus is accentuated by the sharp flavors of feta and sweet notes of Roasted Red Peppers, all packaged neatly in a golden brown tortilla. This quesadilla is worthy of dinner parties, fine wine, and good conversation.

Yield:	Prep time:	Cook time:	Serving size:
4 slices	5 minutes	6 to 8 minutes	4 slices

¼ cup shredded mozzarella cheese

1 TB. crumbled feta cheese

1 TB. Plain Hummus (recipe in Chapter 10)

1 TB. Roasted Red Peppers, diced (recipe in Chapter 3)

1 (8-in.) Wheat Tortilla (recipe in Chapter 3)

1. Heat a frying pan over medium heat.

2. In a small bowl, combine mozzarella cheese, feta cheese, Plain Hummus, and Roasted Red Peppers. Spread cheese and hummus mixture on ½ of Wheat Tortilla, and fold tortilla over to cover filling.

3. Place tortilla in the frying pan, and heat for 30 seconds. Flip over tortilla, and heat for 1 more minute. Flip over again, and heat for 30 more seconds. If tortilla isn't golden brown, continue heating and flipping every 30 seconds until it is.

4. Remove tortilla from heat, and let sit for 5 minutes to allow cheese to set. Slice pizza-style, and serve.

Variation: For a **Gluten Free Mediterranean Quesadilla,** replace the Wheat Tortilla with a Corn Tortilla (recipe in Chapter 3), and reduce the other ingredients by half.

Sweet Treats and Beverages 4

I bet you thought that if you started eating healthy, you'd have to give up all your favorite sweets and desserts. Wrong! You can still enjoy tons of healthy sweet treats on your clean-eating diet.

The first chapter in Part 4 is a showcase of desserts as Mother Nature intended, with fruit as the star. These recipes show you how to make the most of fruit, whether it's baking apples, chewy fruit leathers, or warm handheld pies.

Next I share some secrets for incorporating whole grains into your favorite baked goodies, with recipes ranging from chocolate-chip cookies to homemade graham crackers.

If cake's more your thing, you also learn how to make your cake—and you get to eat it, too. I go over the basic cakes—chocolate, vanilla, and angel food—as well as some fun variations like Pumpkin Chocolate.

Chapter 16 contains some of my go-to dairy-free ice creams and homemade ice pops. Get ready to fall in love with clean versions of your favorite icebox goodies!

Finally, I give you some of my favorite beverages for all ages and occasions. Hot ciders, homemade sodas, and some deceptively easy infusions will keep you stocked for everyday drinks and party showstoppers.

Fruity Treats ⟨⟩ 13

My sister always told me your 20s are for experimentation, and in your 30s, you finally accept who you are. When I turned 32, I had to accept an essential truth about myself: I love desserts. For a long time, I tried to limit them to dinner parties and special events, but each night I was poking around for something sweet after dinner. Finally, I decided to just face the facts and planned to have dessert every night.

Manatee, on the other hand, has no need for sweetness. As he likes to say, he's sweet enough (and yes, I rolled my eyes, too).

The fruity treats in this chapter are a great way to get a little sweetness without venturing off the healthy track. By utilizing the natural sweetness in these fruits, you don't have to add additional sugar and fat.

These are great desserts for weeknights because they only need a little prep before you throw them in the oven or the fridge. I like to do my prep right before I sit down to dinner and then the sweet treat is ready when I'm craving my sweet treat for the night.

Making Your Own Fruit Leather

Growing up, fruit rollups were a special treat in my house. As an adult, I'm shocked at the amount of chemicals in the store-bought versions—and the amount of sugar in many of the homemade ones! For the fruit leather recipes later in this chapter, fruit is the star, with very little added sweetness from the low-glycemic super star, agave nectar, or the all-natural leading lady, honey.

Patience is paramount when making fruit leathers. You want to dehydrate the leather until the fruit mixture is totally dry to the touch. The good news is that the actually prep time is only 20 minutes, so when you get that done, it's just a matter of waiting for the mixture to dry. If you can't be home for 6 to 8 hours and don't feel comfortable leaving the oven on, turn the oven off, leave the mixture in the oven, and turn it back on when you get home.

It might seem odd to use plastic wrap to cover the pan, but at such a low oven temperature, it won't melt. The fruit mixture peels off easily when it's done.

TO STRAIN OR NOT TO STRAIN?

I go back and forth on the topic of straining. On one hand, I love the strained texture of smooth fruit leather, but it does require more work, and you know how I feel about more work. If you have a finicky audience, you might want to start with straining the fruit. But if you want to revel in the homemade fruitiness of the leather, make it seeds and all.

Blackberry Fruit Leather

This super-dark fruit leather is the perfect way to use blackberries in their prime. Sweet and tangy, rich and chewy—you can't buy these flavors at the store.

Yield:	Prep time:	Cook time:	Serving size:
8 (1-inch) strips	20 minutes	6 to 8 hours	1 strip

4 cups fresh blackberries, if straining, or 2 cups fresh blackberries, if not straining

½ cup unsweetened applesauce

Juice of 1 small lime (2 TB.)

½ to 1½ TB. agave nectar

1. Preheat the oven to 175°F. Line a rimmed baking jelly roll pan with plastic wrap. You might want to use masking or freezer tape to tape the wrap to the sides of the pan.

2. In a blender, purée blackberries, applesauce, and lime juice until smooth.

3. For the smoothest texture, strain berry mixture through a fine-mesh strainer into a large bowl. If you would prefer a meatier, more natural texture, skip this step.

4. Add agave nectar ½ tablespoon at a time, and stir to combine.

5. Pour mixture onto the prepared pan, and use a spatula to smooth out mixture into a very thin (⅛ inch or thinner), even layer.

6. Bake for 6 to 8 hours or until leather is dry to the touch. Test the middle as well as the sides.

7. Remove from the oven, and cool completely. Using a pizza cutter, cut leather into 1-inch strips. Wrap in waxed paper or parchment paper, and store in a zipper-lock plastic bag for up to 2 weeks.

SWEET STUFF

The amount of agave nectar you add depends on the sweetness of berries you're using, so add a little at a time to avoid oversweetening. And as the fruit leather dries, the sweetness intensifies, so keep that in mind as you're adding the agave nectar.

Raspberry Fruit Leather

You can't help but fall in love with this fruit leather. I'm not even a fan of raspberries, but once you dry them, you get the best of the berry: sweet, tangy, and a deep shade of pink.

Yield:	Prep time:	Cook time:	Serving size:
8 (1-inch) strips	20 minutes	6 to 8 hours	1 strip

4 cups fresh raspberries, if straining, or 2 cups fresh raspberries, if not straining

½ cup unsweetened applesauce

4 to 6 TB. honey

1. Preheat the oven to 175°F. Line a rimmed jelly roll pan with plastic wrap. You might want to use masking or freezer tape to tape the wrap to the sides of the pan.

2. In a blender, purée raspberries and applesauce until smooth.

3. For the smoothest texture, strain berry mixture through a fine-mesh strainer into a large bowl. If you would prefer a meatier, more natural texture, skip this step.

4. Add honey 1 tablespoon at a time, and stir to combine.

5. Pour mixture onto the prepared pan, and use a spatula to smooth out mixture into a very thin (⅛ inch or thinner), even layer.

6. Bake for 6 to 8 hours or until leather is dry to the touch. Test the middle as well as the sides.

7. Remove from the oven, and cool completely. Using a pizza cutter, cut leather into 1-inch strips. Wrap in waxed paper or parchment paper, and store in a zipper-lock plastic bag for up to 2 weeks.

Strawberry Fruit Leather

Don't let the dark red-brown color fool you; this is one tasty fruit treat. It's also a great way to use strawberries that are on the verge of spoiling. And hey, if the dark color means you don't have to share it with as many people, we can keep the sweet berry taste our little secret. My lips are sealed ….

Yield:	Prep time:	Cook time:	Serving size:
8 (1-inch) strips	20 minutes	6 to 8 hours	1 strip

4 cups fresh strawberries, if straining, or 2 cups fresh strawberries, if not straining

Juice of 1 small lemon (2 TB.)

½ cup unsweetened applesauce

2 to 4 TB. honey

1. Preheat the oven to 175°F. Line a rimmed jelly roll pan with plastic wrap. You might want to use masking or freezer tape to tape the wrap to the sides of the pan.

2. In a blender, purée strawberries, lemon juice, and applesauce until smooth.

3. For the smoothest texture, strain berry mixture through a fine-mesh strainer into a large bowl. If you would prefer a meatier, more natural texture, skip this step.

4. Add honey 1 tablespoon at a time, and stir to combine.

5. Pour mixture onto the prepared pan, and use a spatula to smooth out mixture into a very thin (⅛ inch or thinner), even layer.

6. Bake for 6 to 8 hours or until leather is dry to the touch. Test the middle as well as the sides.

7. Remove from the oven, and cool completely. Using a pizza cutter, cut leather into 1-inch strips. Wrap in waxed paper or parchment paper, and store in a zipper-lock plastic bag for up to 2 weeks.

HOW SWEET IT IS

Again, add the honey judiciously. With sweet strawberries you might not need very much at all.

Baked Apples

To me, this is everything that is good about apple pie in a single serving—warm, buttery apples mixed with sugar, nuts, and dried fruit. Let me rephrase my earlier statement: this is way better than apple pie. I'm not picky about what kind of apples I use for this recipe. My motto is to stick to what you like. Do know that the type of apple will affect the baking time. Softer apples like Golden Delicious bake in less time, while heartier apples like Granny Smith take a little longer. Keep an eye on the apples as they bake, and pull them out when your desired softness has been reached.

Yield:	Prep time:	Cook time:	Serving size:
3 small or 2 large apples	10 minutes	30 to 50 minutes	1 apple

3 small apples or 2 large apples	½ tsp. ground cinnamon
2 TB. dried cranberries or raisins	2 TB. pecans, chopped
1 TB. organic brown sugar	2 TB. butter or coconut oil
1 TB. rolled oats	¼ to ½ cup water

1. Preheat the oven to 350°F.

2. Core apples, and slice off top.

3. In a medium bowl, whisk together cranberries, brown sugar, rolled oats, cinnamon, and pecans.

4. Cut butter into thin slices, and cut slices in ½. Using a fork, mash butter into oat mixture until well combined.

5. Place apples in a 8×8- or 9×9-inch square baking dish. Press oat mixture into apple cores, pressing it down as you go.

6. Pour 6 tablespoons water into the pan. Set remaining water aside.

7. Bake for 30 to 50 minutes or until apples are tender but not mushy. Add more water to the pan if it evaporates to keep apples from drying out.

8. Let apples cool on cooling rack, and serve warm with Yogurt Cheese (recipe in Chapter 3) or Dairy-Free Cinnamon Ice Cream (recipe in Chapter 16).

Variation: Substitute your favorite dried fruit, like dried apricots or figs, for the dried cranberries, and use your favorite type of nut, such as slivered almonds or chopped walnuts for the pecans.

Caramelized Grapefruit

Caramelizing grapefruit brings out its inherent sweetness. This is a great twist on your typical grapefruit with sugar, and it's quite a refreshing way to end your meal. You can use a sugar of your choice; all types result in a sweet and tangy dessert. You can save any leftovers for a sweet breakfast treat the next day.

Yield:	Prep time:	Cook time:	Serving size:
2 grapefruit halves	5 minutes	5 to 8 minutes	½ grapefruit

1 grapefruit, cut in ½   1 TB. unprocessed sugar

1. Place the oven rack 5 or 6 inches away from the heating element if possible, and preheat the broiler to 500°F.

2. Place grapefruit halves in 8×8- or 9×9-inch square baking pan. If you don't have a grapefruit spoon, use a paring knife to separate grapefruit flesh from skin, and cut into segments. If you have a grapefruit spoon (a serrated spoon), you don't need to precut grapefruit.

3. Sprinkle unprocessed sugar on top of grapefruit halves.

4. Broil for 5 to 8 minutes or until top is starting to crystallize.

5. Let cool for 1 or 2 minutes before serving.

Deconstructed Fruit Cake

This is one of my favorite treats to serve at holiday parties. It always gets a laugh, and it's usually gone by the end of the night. Light angel food cake and fresh fruit are a great balance to the otherwise heavy holiday dishes. This recipe also works great in the summer time with fresh berries.

Yield:	Prep time:	Serving size:
3 cups	15 minutes	¼ cup

1 Angel Food Cake (recipe in Chapter 15), cut into cubes

1 lb. pkg. strawberries, cleaned and hulled

1 pineapple, peeled, cored, and diced

1 cup pecans

1. In 4 separate bowls, place Angel Food Cake cubes, strawberries, pineapple, and pecans.

2. Place skewers, small bowls, or small plates next to the bowls so guests can assemble their own "fruit cakes."

Variation: You can add Fruit Dip (recipe follows) to the raw ingredients for an extra sweet treat. Feel free to substitute other fruits and nuts, too.

Fruit Dip

This sweet and healthy dip is a great way to "trick" your kids into gobbling up some fruit. Don't stop there; this dip would also be great with Clean Graham Crackers (recipe in Chapter 14) or with the earlier Deconstructed Fruit Cake recipe. Instead of highly processed marshmallow cream, this dip gets it sweetness from maple syrup (or honey). If you don't have Yogurt Cheese available, use 1 part cream cheese mixed with 1 part Greek yogurt instead. But let's be honest, you really should have some Yogurt Cheese because it is just so good to have around.

Yield:	Prep time:	Serving size:
1 cup	5 minutes	2 tablespoons

1 cup Yogurt Cheese (recipe in Chapter 3)

1 TB. maple syrup or honey

½ TB. organic brown sugar

1 tsp. Cinnamon Sugar (recipe in Chapter 7)

1. In a medium bowl, mix together Yogurt Cheese, maple syrup, brown sugar, and Cinnamon Sugar.

2. Serve immediately, or store in an airtight container in the refrigerator for up to 5 days.

Chocolate Fruit and Nut Bark

I hate to admit how easy this is to make for fear my guests won't be as impressed with me, but here's the deal: this is just about the simplest dessert to make and gives you the ability to totally customize the chocolate bars. I prefer melting my chocolate in the microwave. I have a double boiler, and I should probably use it, but that would involve cleaning two dishes. With a recipe this easy, it seems silly to make the cleanup any more difficult than it has to be. Rock out the double boiler if you must, but I'll be standing guard at the microwave.

Yield:	Prep time:	Cook time:	Serving size:
½ cup	5 minutes	5 minutes, plus 1 hour cooling time	2 tablespoons

3 TB. dried cranberries	½ cup dark chocolate, chopped, or ½ cup dark chocolate chips
2 TB. sliced almonds	Pinch kosher salt

1. Line a plate or baking pan (whatever will fit in your refrigerator) with a piece of parchment paper. Spread cranberries and almonds on the parchment paper.

2. Place dark chocolate in a large glass bowl, and microwave on high for 30 seconds. Stir, and microwave for 10 to 15 more seconds, and stir again. Repeat until chocolate is melted and smooth.

3. Pour chocolate over cranberries and sliced almonds, and use a spatula to spread chocolate over it. It's okay if some cranberries or almonds are sticking out on the ends. Sprinkle with kosher salt.

4. Refrigerate for 1 hour or until chocolate is set.

5. Break into pieces, and store in an airtight container in a cool, dry place.

Variation: For **White Chocolate Fruit Bark,** substitute 1 tablespoon chopped dried apricots for 1 tablespoon dried cranberries. Substitute chopped walnuts or pistachios for the almonds and white chocolate for the dark chocolate. Stir in ¼ teaspoon vanilla with the white chocolate for some added sweetness.

THE SKY'S THE LIMIT

I love making this bark because essentially I get to play Willy Wonka and create my own candy bars. Check out your grocery store's fancy chocolate section for inspiration. Like spicy stuff? Sprinkle some cayenne and cinnamon in with the melted chocolate. Love s'mores? Add some crushed Clean Graham Crackers (recipe in Chapter 14) to some melted milk chocolate. Have fun with these! A note about cleanup: wash the bowl (or double boiler) while the chocolate is still melted with warm or hot water. The sooner you clean up, the easier it will be.

Fruit Pizzas

Remember when I told you that when you clean up your diet, foods start tasting overly sweet? This recipe is a perfect example. The fruit pizzas of my youth began with a sugar cookie crust topped with marshmallow cream and cream cheese frosting, with sweet berries and fruit on top of that. My mouth hurts just thinking about it. This cleaned-up version has the tang of the cream cheese, the sweet fruit, and a crispy thin crust. It's a pizza you can't feel bad about eating as a snack in the afternoon—or be shy about serving at your next party.

Yield:	Prep time:	Cook time:	Serving size:
1 (8-inch) pizza	5 minutes	5 to 8 minutes	4 slices

1 (8-in.) Wheat Tortilla (recipe in Chapter 3)

Oil spray

¼ tsp. Cinnamon Sugar (recipe in Chapter 7)

1½ TB. Yogurt Cheese (recipe in Chapter 3)

½ cup fresh berries, sliced

1. Preheat the oven to 350°F.

2. Spray Wheat Tortilla with oil spray, and sprinkle Cinnamon Sugar evenly over top.

3. Place tortilla directly on the oven rack, and bake for 5 to 8 minutes or until sides are crispy.

4. Remove tortilla from the oven, and set on a plate. Spread Yogurt Cheese evenly over tortilla, place berries on top, and cut into quarters.

5. Serve immediately.

Basic Piecrust

This isn't your typical piecrust. Set aside thoughts of buttery, flaky, dry piecrusts of yore. This crust is chewy, nutty, and moist. I should also mention this is quick and foolproof. No more chilling your dough, freezing your butter, or having to wait hours for your pie. Within an hour, you can decide you want pie, make it, bake it, and have it cooling on your counter.

Yield:	Prep time:	Serving size:
1 piecrust	10 minutes	1 piece of pie

4 or 5 ice cubes

3 or 4 TB. ice cold water

1 cup spelt flour

1½ cups whole-wheat pastry flour

¼ tsp. salt

1 tsp. Cinnamon Sugar (recipe in Chapter 7)

½ tsp. ground nutmeg

¼ cup unsweetened applesauce

¼ cup canola oil

¼ cup milk or nondairy milk

1 TB. apple cider vinegar

1. Place ice cubes in a small bowl, and add water. This will keep the water cold for later.

2. In a large bowl, whisk together spelt flour, whole-wheat pastry flour, salt, Cinnamon Sugar, and nutmeg.

3. Make a well in middle of flour mixture, and pour in applesauce, canola oil, milk, and apple cider vinegar. Using a wooden spoon, stir to combine.

4. Add water 1 tablespoon at a time until dough forms. I usually start by using the spoon to combine and then switch to my hands. If you add too much water, you can add more flour when you roll it out.

5. Form dough into a ball, and place on floured workspace. Flatten into a disc, and roll out to a ¼- to ⅛-inch thickness.

6. Fill and bake according to your recipe.

Individual Blueberry Pies

In my mind, Fourth of July requires blueberry pie. There's something about the sweet blueberry that just screams independence and summer barbecues. These handheld versions are a perfect way to keep your servings in check and prevent the classic cut-while-it's-still-warm-berry-waterfall that always seems to happen at our house. Don't be a slave to making sure each slice of dough is perfect. This is supposed to be easy, remember? Be sure they're all roughly the same shape, but embrace the irregularities.

Yield:	Prep time:	Cook time:	Serving size:
8 (4×6-inch) pies	25 minutes	30 to 45 minutes	1 pie

2 cups fresh or frozen blueberries	½ TB. unprocessed sugar
1 large egg, beaten	1 TB. fresh lemon zest
1 TB. whole-wheat pastry flour	1 Basic Piecrust (recipe earlier in this chapter)

1. Preheat the oven to 350°F. Line a baking sheet with parchment paper or a silicone mat.

2. In a medium bowl, toss together blueberries, 1 tablespoon beaten egg, whole-wheat pastry flour, unprocessed sugar, and lemon zest.

3. Roll out Basic Piecrust to ¼- to ⅛-inch thickness. Use a knife to cut out 4×6-inch rectangles.

4. Place rectangles on the prepared pan. Pour berry mixture on ½ of rectangle, leaving a ¼-inch border around the edges. Fold over dough, press ends together, and use a fork to crimp ends together. Repeat with remaining rectangles.

5. Using a pastry brush, glaze pies with remaining beaten egg. Use a paring knife to cut slits in top of pies so steam can release.

6. Bake for 30 to 45 minutes or until tops are golden brown and fruit mixture is bubbling.

7. Let cool for 10 to 15 minutes before serving.

8. Store in an airtight container for 2 or 3 days.

Variation: For a whole **Blueberry Pie,** roll the Basic Piecrust into a circular crust, double the filling ingredients, and sprinkle Basic Crumble Topping (recipe later in this chapter) on top. Bake for 40 to 50 minutes, and let cool for 3 or 4 hours before cutting.

Individual Apple Rhubarb Oatmeal Pies

This is a pie for all the (rhubarb) haters. More apple than rhubarb, it gives the pie a tang without overpowering it. A lot of times, I don't tell people there's rhubarb in it—until the compliments start to roll in and then no one can believe it.

Yield:	Prep time:	Cook time:	Serving size:
8 (4×6-inch) pies	30 minutes	30 to 45 minutes	1 pie

2 medium sweet apples, cored and chopped

1 TB. rolled oats

3 TB. brown sugar

½ cup fresh or thawed rhubarb

1. Preheat the oven to 350°F. Line a baking sheet with parchment paper or a silicone mat.

2. In a medium bowl, toss together apples, rolled oats, brown sugar, and rhubarb.

3. Roll out Basic Piecrust to ¼- to ⅛-inch thickness. Use a knife to cut out 4×6-inch rectangles.

4. Place rectangles on the prepared pan. Pour apple mixture on ½ of rectangle, leaving a ¼-inch border around the edges. Fold over dough, press ends together, and use a fork to crimp ends together. Repeat with remaining rectangles.

5. Using a pastry brush, glaze pies with remaining beaten egg. Use a paring knife to cut slits in tops of pies so steam can release.

6. Bake for 30 to 45 minutes or until tops are golden brown and fruit mixture is bubbling.

7. Let cool for 10 to 15 minutes before serving.

8. Store in an airtight container for 2 or 3 days.

Variation: For a whole **Apple Rhubarb Pie,** roll the Basic Piecrust into a circular crust, double the filling ingredients, and add sprinkle Basic Crumble Topping (recipe later in this chapter) on top. Bake for 40 to 50 minutes, and let cool for 3 or 4 hours before cutting.

FREEZING RHUBARB

I'm always overwhelmed with rhubarb in the early spring. Fortunately, I'm sucker for this sour spring treat. Even better, rhubarb is easy to freeze. Wash it, dry it, cut into 1-inch cubes, date it, and toss it in the freezer. I like to store it in 1- or 2-cup servings so I can take out the whole bag when I'm ready to use it. To thaw it, leave it on the counter for 2 to 4 hours, or place it in a colander and run cool water over it until it thaws. Squeeze out the excess moisture, and proceed with your recipe. Oh, and when you're handling rhubarb, remember that the leaves are toxic if eaten.

Basic Crumble Topping

You could really eat this topping as a dessert. Let me clarify, I *have* eaten this crumb topping as dessert, and it was awesome. You can also use this to top any crisp, crumble, or pie with something sweet and crunchy. I have a crush on pecans when it comes to baking. For me, pecans add a rich sweetness you just can't find in other nuts. Substitute any other nut of choice if you don't feel the same way.

Yield:	Prep time:	Serving size:
1 cup	5 minutes	1 tablespoon

⅓ cup rolled oats

⅓ cup pecans

⅓ cup slivered or sliced almonds

1 tsp. salt

1 to 3 TB. organic brown sugar

3 TB. unsalted butter or coconut oil

1. In a medium bowl, whisk together rolled oats, pecans, almonds, salt, and brown sugar.

2. Cut unsalted butter into slices, and use a fork to mash butter into oats mixture. You might want to use your hands to mix it into a coarse meal.

3. Use crumble mixture to top your crisp, crumble, pie, or other recipe.

HOW MUCH SUGAR?

The amount of brown sugar you use depends on how the crumble will be used. If you're making the Tropical Rhubarb Crumble (recipe follows), you only need 1 tablespoon because the sweetness of the pineapple is going to carry you through the dessert. If you're making a tart crumble like the Cran Apple Berry Crumble (recipe later in this chapter), you might want to add additional sugar to balance out the tartness of the cranberries. The sweeter the fruit in the crumble or pie, the less sugar you need in this recipe.

Tropical Rhubarb Crisp

So many recipes that involve rhubarb rely on cup after cup of sugar to sweeten this tart spring treat. In this recipe, pineapple and strawberries add enough sweetness to counteract the sour rhubarb.

Yield:	Prep time:	Cook time:	Serving size:
4 cups	5 minutes	30 to 40 minutes	½ cup

1½ cups fresh or frozen rhubarb, thawed and drained if frozen

1 (8-oz.) can crushed pineapple (½ cup), drained

1 cup fresh strawberries, quartered

1 TB. rolled oats

1 batch Basic Crumble Topping (recipe earlier in this chapter)

1. Preheat the oven to 350°F. Grease a pie pan.

2. In a medium bowl, toss together rhubarb, pineapple, strawberries, and rolled oats. Pour mixture into the prepared pie pan, and cover evenly with Basic Crumble Topping.

3. Bake for 30 to 40 minutes or until top is browned and filling is bubbling. Let cool for 5 to 10 minutes before serving.

4. Store leftovers in the refrigerator for up to 4 days.

Cran Apple Berry Crisp

This is all my favorite things in one pan: apples, blueberries, cranberries, and Basic Crumble Topping. The tang of the cranberry balances the sweetness of the blueberry. The apples can go either way; for a tangier crumble, go for Granny Smith, or if you're like me, stick to the sweeter varieties like McIntosh or Honey Crisp. Serve this with Yogurt Cheese (recipe in Chapter 3) or Dairy-Free Cinnamon Ice Cream (recipe in Chapter 16).

Yield:	Prep time:	Cook time:	Serving size:
4 cups	20 minutes	45 minutes to 1 hour	½ cup

1 TB. fresh orange zest

2 cups fresh or frozen cranberries

1 cup fresh or frozen blueberries

2 TB. organic brown sugar

3 medium apples, cored and cut into ¼-in. slices (3 cups)

1 batch Basic Crumble Topping (recipe earlier in this chapter)

1. Preheat the oven to 350°F. Grease a pie dish or 8×8- or 9×9-inch square baking pan.

2. In a large bowl, combine orange zest, cranberries, blueberries, and brown sugar.

3. Place one layer of apple slices in the prepared pie pan. Top with ½ of berry mixture. Cover with another layer of apple slices and then rest of berry mixture. Top with Basic Crumble Topping.

4. Bake for 45 minutes to 1 hour or until top is golden brown, berries are bubbling, and apples are tender. Let cool 10 to 15 minutes before serving.

5. Store leftovers in the refrigerator for up to 4 days.

GREASING YOUR PAN

What should you use to grease your pan? Really it's personal preference. I usually use butter or coconut oil, but you can use whatever neutral oil you have around.

A Clean Cookie Jar  14

I grew up in a house where the cookie jar was always full of homemade cookies. Early on, my mother and I struck a deal: I would mix the cookies, and she would clean up. She got her home-made cookies without having to make them, and I got to make a big mess and not clean it up. Win-win situation, right?

My mother always told me to follow the recipe exactly, and like any good daughter, I ignored her. I play fast and loose with baking. This isn't something I recommend, but I have to admit it has helped a lot in my ability to adapt recipes for allergy needs and cut out the not-so-clean ingredients in some recipes.

Cleaning Up Your Favorite Cookie Recipes

In addition to the clean cookie recipes in this chapter, you can convert your favorite cookie recipes to clean versions. It just takes some swapping out of ingredients.

Throw out your all-purpose flour—you can thank me later. White flour spikes blood sugar because of how quickly it metabolizes. Replace your all-purpose flour with whole-grain flours like whole-wheat pastry flour, oat flour, and spelt flour.

Next, get rid of that overly processed white sugar. Trade it for evaporate cane juice, sucanat, organic cane sugar, agave nectar, organic dark brown sugar, and honey.

THE SKINNY ON SUGARS

When I refer to *unprocessed sugar* in the recipes, this refers to evaporate cane juice or organic sugar. You can use white sugar in its place, but eating clean means limiting your amounts of processed foods as much as possible. Use up the white sugar you have and then look for an unprocessed version.

Grab some applesauce to replace that high-fat canola oil, and start playing with dried cranberries and raisins. They can add sweetness and fiber to many baked goods.

Finally, treat yourself to some high-quality chocolate. Look for high percentages of cacao, and you'll get a richer chocolate experience.

Cranberry Pumpkin Cookies

Even though my parents are empty nesters, the cookie-baking continues. My mother loves trying new recipes, but whenever Manatee and I come for a visit, she has a fresh batch of pumpkin cookies waiting for me. These are my rendition of her pumpkin cookies. Lots of orange zest; Pumpkin Pie Spice; and tart, fresh cranberries.

Yield:	Prep time:	Cook time:	Serving size:
44 cookies	40 minutes	12 to 16 minutes	1 cookie

½ cup raisins

1½ cups whole-wheat pastry flour

½ cup rolled oats

2 tsp. baking powder

½ tsp. baking soda

3 tsp. Pumpkin Pie Spice (recipe in Chapter 7)

¼ tsp. salt

½ cup unsalted butter, at room temperature

⅓ cup sucanat or organic dark brown sugar, firmly packed

1 cup pure pumpkin purée

1 large egg

Juice of 2 medium oranges (¼ cup)

1 tsp. vanilla extract

1 cup fresh cranberries, halved and at room temperature

½ cup chopped walnuts

1. Preheat the oven to 375°F.

2. Place raisins in a small bowl, and cover with hot water. Set aside raisins to soak.

3. In a medium bowl, whisk together whole-wheat pastry flour, rolled oats, baking powder, baking soda, Pumpkin Pie Spice, and salt.

4. In a large bowl, and using an electric mixer on medium-high speed, cream unsalted butter and sucanat for about 2 minutes or until light and fluffy. Stir in pumpkin purée, egg, orange juice, and vanilla extract until well combined. Slowly stir in flour mixture.

5. Drain soaked raisins. Fold raisins, cranberries, and walnuts into batter.

6. Scoop cookies by the ½ tablespoon on 2 baking sheets. (Cookies won't spread out very much so you can place them close together.) Bake for 12 to 16 minutes or until cookies are set.

7. Remove cookies from the oven, and cool on the baking sheets for 5 to 10 minutes. Transfer cookies to racks to cool completely.

8. Store in airtight container in the refrigerator for up to 5 days.

RAISINS AND CRANBERRIES

Soaking the raisins makes them more plump and juicy. Fresh cranberries are often frozen. It's fine to use frozen cranberries, but be sure to thaw them completely, to room temperature, before using. If they're still frozen when you make the cookies, the taste and texture of the cookie will be affected.

Trail Mix Cookies

I have tendency to go a little overboard on cookie ingredients. My mother used to plead with me to just follow the directions on her favorite cookie recipe, and I tried—I really did. But then my eyes would be drawn to something in the cupboard: marshmallows, candy bars, raisins, nuts, graham crackers. Surely, she meant for these to go into the cookies, too! Some experiments were more successful than others. You can add almost anything to a cookie as long as you watch your ratios. So if the original recipe calls for 1½ cups chocolate chips, don't replace them with 4 cups add-ins. Keep it close if not equal to the original measurements. Consider these cookies a handful of your favorite trail mix. Keep the add-ins to 1 cup, and you'll be golden.

Yield:	Prep time:	Cook time:	Serving size:
28 cookies	15 minutes	10 to 12 minutes	1 cookie

1 cup whole-wheat pastry flour	½ tsp. vanilla extract
½ cup rolled oats	½ cup milk or nondairy milk
2 tsp. baking powder	¼ cup mini chocolate chips
½ tsp. salt	¼ cup raisins or dried cranberries
½ cup unsalted butter, at room temperature	¼ cup chopped nuts (pecans, walnuts, peanuts, or almonds)
⅓ cup sucanat or organic dark brown sugar, firmly packed	¼ cup unsweetened coconut flakes

1. Preheat the oven to 350°F.

2. In a medium bowl, whisk together whole-wheat pastry flour, rolled oats, baking powder, and salt. Set aside.

3. In a large bowl, and using an electric mixer on medium-high speed, cream unsalted butter and sucanat for about 2 minutes or until light and fluffy. Add vanilla extract, and beat to combine.

4. Add flour mixture and milk to butter mixture, and stir with a wooden spoon. When dough is well combined, fold in mini chocolate chips, raisins, nuts, and coconut flakes.

5. Scoop cookies by the ½ tablespoon onto 2 baking sheets. (Cookies won't spread out very much so you can place them close together.) Bake for 10 to 12 minutes or until cookies are light golden brown and set.

6. Remove cookies from the oven, and cool on the baking sheets for 5 minutes. Transfer cookies to racks to cool completely.

7. Store in airtight container at room temperature or in the refrigerator for up to 5 days.

MINI CHOCOLATE CHIPS

I love using mini chocolate chips because they increase the likelihood of getting a bit of chocolate in every bite. Bonus points if you can combine mini chocolate chips and regular chocolate chips.

Chocolate-Chip Cookies

I'm not a sweets person. I like sweets but in very small amounts but very often. Most processed sweets are too much for me, but these cookies are just right. I reduced the sugar as far as I dared and increased the amount of salt. The result is a light, cakey cookie with the perfect balance of sweet and salty.

Yield:	Prep time:	Cook time:	Serving size:
28 cookies	15 minutes	10 to 12 minutes	1 cookie

1½ cups whole-wheat pastry flour

2 tsp. baking powder

½ tsp. salt

½ cup unsalted butter, at room temperature

3 TB. sucanat or organic dark brown sugar, firmly packed

½ tsp. vanilla extract

½ cup milk or nondairy milk

1 cup dark chocolate chips, or ½ cup dark chocolate chips and ½ cup white chocolate chips

1. Preheat the oven to 350°F.

2. In a medium bowl, whisk together whole-wheat pastry flour, baking powder, and salt. Set aside.

3. In a large bowl, and using an electric mixer on medium-high speed, cream unsalted butter and sucanat for about 2 minutes or until light and fluffy. Add vanilla extract, and beat to combine.

4. Add flour mixture and milk to butter mixture, and stir with a wooden spoon. You might also need to use your hands to combine. Initially, dough will be crumbly. When dough is well combined, fold in chocolate chips.

5. Scoop cookies by the ½ tablespoon onto baking sheets. (Cookies won't spread out very much so you can place them close together.) Bake for 10 to 12 minutes or until cookies are light golden brown and set.

6. Remove cookies from the oven, and cool on the baking sheets for 5 minutes. Transfer cookies to racks to cool completely.

7. Store in airtight container at room temperature or in the refrigerator for up to 5 days.

FREEZING COOKIES

Manatee isn't a sweets person, so I'm often left with entire batches of cookies all to myself. After letting them cool, I freeze most of the cookies in an airtight container and take them out as need. The cookies will stay good for up to 2 months in the freezer. To thaw, simply take a cookie out and let it sit at room temperature for 10 to 15 minutes.

Gluten-Free Chocolate-Chip Cookies

These cookies are a great way to get your chocolate fix without having to worry about wheat. More and more people are finding they're sensitive to gluten, including Manatee. These cookies are light, fluffy, and chewy. Check out the Gluten-Free Coconut Double Chocolate-Chip Cookies variation for a special treat.

Yield:	Prep time:	Cook time:	Serving size:
25 to 28 cookies	10 minutes	12 to 15 minutes	1 cookie

1½ cups ground rolled oats

½ cup rolled oats

3 tsp. baking powder

½ tsp. salt

½ cup unsweetened applesauce

½ cup sucanat or dark brown sugar, firmly packed

½ tsp. vanilla extract

½ cup unsweetened nondairy milk (almond or soy)

¾ cup chocolate chips

1. Preheat the oven to 350°F. Spray a baking sheet with cooking spray, or line with silicone baking mats.

2. In a medium bowl, whisk together ground rolled oats, rolled oats, baking powder, and ¼ teaspoon salt.

3. In a large bowl, whisk together applesauce, sucanat, vanilla extract, and nondairy milk. Add oats mixture, and stir to combine. Fold in chocolate chips.

4. Scoop cookies by the ½ tablespoon onto the prepared pans, and sprinkle with remaining ¼ teaspoon salt. Bake for 12 to 15 minutes or until edges are browned and middles are set.

5. Remove cookies from the oven, cool on racks for 5 to 10 minutes, and remove from racks to cool completely. Store cookies in an airtight container in the refrigerator for up to 5 days.

Variation: For **Gluten-Free Coconut Double Chocolate-Chip Cookies,** replace ½ cup chocolate chips with ¼ cup white chocolate chips and ¼ cup unsweetened coconut flakes.

MAKE YOUR OWN OAT FLOUR

When I first started investigating gluten-free baking, I kept hearing about oat flour. My lack of flour knowledge became evident. What on earth was it, and were would I find it? After further reading, I realized that oat flour is simply ground oats. Grab your rolled or old-fashioned oats (from the freezer, where they'll stay fresher), throw them in a blender, and blend until you have a powder. It takes all of 2 minutes, and it's so much easier than finding it in a store. Also, when buying oats, read the label carefully. Not all oats are processed in facilities that are completely gluten-free. Depending on the severity of your sensitivity, you might want to avoid oats that weren't processed in gluten-free facilities.

Clean Cocoa Crispy Bars

These bars prove that just because you're eating clean, whole foods doesn't mean you don't get a treat every once in a while. With puffed brown rice cereal, rolled oats, coconut oil, homemade peanut butter, and all-natural honey, you can feel good about serving these bars. And if that weren't enough, there's even chocolate!

Yield:	Prep time:	Cook time:	Serving size:
16 bars	5 minutes	15 minutes, plus 1 hour for cooling	1 bar

1½ cups puffed brown rice cereal
¼ cup rolled oats
¼ cup sliced almonds
¼ cup mini chocolate chips

½ cup honey
¼ cup coconut oil
2 TB. Peanut Butter (recipe in Chapter 6)

1. Grease an 8×8-inch cake pan.

2. In a large bowl, mix together puffed brown rice cereal, rolled oats, almonds, and chocolate chips.

3. In a small saucepan over medium heat, combine honey, coconut oil, and Peanut Butter. Bring to a simmer, stirring constantly.

4. When Peanut Butter and coconut oil have melted and incorporated with the honey (approximately 6 to 8 minutes), remove from heat and immediately pour over rice cereal mixture and stir to combine.

5. Pour mixture into the prepared cake pan, and use a spatula to smooth into an even layer. Refrigerate to cool for at least an hour.

6. Store in the refrigerator for up to 5 days. Depending on how cold your fridge gets, you might need to remove bars 5 to 10 minutes before cutting.

Pumpkin Oat Bars

I need to warn you: these bars are dangerous. Yes, they're healthier than most pumpkin bars or pumpkin breads. And yes, they have very little sugar and are packed with fiber from the whole-wheat pastry flour and rolled oats. But all this good stuff goes out the window if you eat the entire pan. Trust me on this. Make these for company, co-workers, family, or neighbors—just be sure you have someone else in mind or you just might eat the whole pan. Not that I would know from personal experience or anything ….

Yield:	Prep time:	Cook time:	Serving Size:
28 bars	15 minutes	25 to 30 minutes	1 bar

½ cup unsalted butter, at room temperature

1 cup organic dark brown sugar

1 (14.5-oz.) can pure pumpkin purée

3 large eggs

Zest of 3 or 4 medium oranges (¼ cup)

2 cups whole-wheat pastry flour

1 cup rolled oats

2½ tsp. baking soda

1 TB. Pumpkin Pie Spice (recipe in Chapter 7)

½ tsp. ground cinnamon

¼ tsp. salt

1. Preheat the oven to 350°F. Grease a 10×15-inch cake pan.

2. In a large bowl, and using an electric mixer on medium-high speed, cream unsalted butter and brown sugar for about 2 minutes or until light and creamy. Add pumpkin purée, eggs, and orange zest, and beat on low speed for 1 or 2 minutes or until well combined.

3. In a medium bowl, whisk together whole-wheat pastry flour, rolled oats, baking soda, Pumpkin Pie Spice, cinnamon, and salt. Add ½ of flour mixture to pumpkin mixture, and stir until just combined. Repeat with remaining flour mixture.

4. Pour mixture into the prepared cake pan, and bake for 25 to 30 minutes or until a toothpick inserted in the middle comes out with 1 or 2 crumbs on it. Cake will continue baking as it cools, so try not to wait until the toothpick comes out clean.

5. Cool cake completely in the cake pan.

6. Store in airtight container in the refrigerator for up to 1 week.

I TOLD YOU THESE BARS ARE DANGEROUS

The texture of this bar is closer to a quick bread. Feel free to spread some butter on your bar or heat it for 10 to 20 seconds in the microwave. This bar also pairs well with coffee, tea, milk, or Hot Cocoa Mix (recipe in Chapter 17). The oats give it a chewy texture, but for a smoother texture, throw the oats in a blender and pulse for up to 1 minute.

Clean Graham Crackers

In elementary school, we were all required to bring graham crackers for our mid-morning snack. I remember sitting at my third-grade desk and seeing the shelves full of graham cracker boxes. As the boxes disappeared, the countdown to summer began. I still love graham crackers. By tweaking the baking time for this recipe, you can make the cracker more of a cookie. I like to split within the batch. The spelt flour gives it a rich, nutty taste, and the honey flavor is far more pronounced than in any cracker you can buy at the store.

Yield:	Prep time:	Cook time:	Serving Size:
60 crackers	25 minutes, plus 4 to 6 hours to set dough	12 to 15 minutes	2 or 3 crackers

1½ cups whole-wheat pastry flour

1 cup spelt flour

½ cup organic dark brown sugar, firmly packed

¾ tsp. salt

2 tsp. ground cinnamon

½ cup unsalted butter, cold

¼ cup honey

½ cup milk or nondairy milk

1 tsp. vanilla extract

1. In a food processor fitted with a chopping blade, pulse together whole-wheat pastry flour, spelt flour, brown sugar, salt, and cinnamon. Add unsalted butter, and pulse until you create a coarse meal. Add honey, milk, and vanilla extract, and pulse until dough is formed.

2. Separate dough in quarters. Between 2 sheets of plastic wrap, roll out each quarter of dough into a ½-inch-thick disc. Refrigerate wrapped discs for 4 to 6 hours.

3. Preheat the oven to 350°F. Line 2 baking sheets with silicone mats or dust with flour and tap off excess.

4. Clean a work area or put down a silicone mat. Dust with flour. Remove 1 dough disc from the refrigerator, remove the plastic wrap, and place dough on your floured work surface. Cover top of dough with another sheet of plastic wrap. Roll out dough as thin as you can, approximately ⅛ inch. Cut dough into 2×2½-inch rectangles, and carefully remove rectangles from your work area and place them on the prepared baking sheets.

5. Bake for 12 to 15 minutes or until lightly browned around the edges. The longer dough bakes, the more crackerlike end result will be. Let set on baking sheet for 2 or 3 minutes and then transfer to a rack. Let the baking sheets cool a bit for the next batch. Repeat with remaining dough discs.

6. Store in an airtight container for up to 1 week.

Variation: For **Cinnamon Graham Crackers,** dust crackers with Cinnamon Sugar (recipe in Chapter 7) before baking.

Cakes and Cupcakes

 **15**

I've never understood the draw of cake mixes. You still need additional ingredients, and you still end up with dirty dishes. Is it really that much harder to make your own cake from scratch? I hope that after you read this chapter, you answer that question with a resounding "No!"

The recipes in this chapter are a mix of my favorite cakes (carrot cake!) and a few good standards to have on hand.

For the best results, be sure your ingredients (specifically your butter, milk, and eggs) are room temperature. If you forget to set them out, warm the eggs by placing them in room temperature water for 5 to 10 minutes. Warm yogurt, milk, or butter for 10 seconds in microwave. Repeat until they reach room temperature.

The Case for Cupcakes

You'll notice that for every recipe, I've included instructions for cupcakes. Nine times out of ten, I make cupcakes. At all our birthday parties, we have cupcakes. At all our cocktail parties, we have cupcakes. At all our barbecues, we have cupcakes (and usually a cupcake bar!). Have you noticed the trend?

Cupcakes are so much less fuss than cutting a cake, and people are more likely to take a cupcake than a hunk of cake. Another bonus? You can freeze cupcakes and just take out one (or three …) when the mood strikes.

You can have your cake and eat it too, but as for me, I want a cupcake.

TO FROST OR NOT TO FROST?

With very few exceptions, I'm not a frosting person. I love cake for its own cakey self, and besides, it's so much easier to freeze (as cupcakes) with no frosting. However, I'm in the minority. For each cake recipe, I suggest a frosting and at least one nonfrosting topping to pair with it.

Creating a Cupcake Bar

Every year, Manatee and I run a half-marathon on the Sunday morning of Memorial Day weekend and then throw a party that afternoon. Three years ago, I had the grand idea that I would recover from the run, shower, get ready, put out all the food, and make fancy little individual-size strawberry shortcakes. All of this I planned to do in the hour and a half we had between getting home from the race and the party.

Needless to say, that did not happen.

With 10 minutes left for the cupcakes and my stress levels escalating, Manatee talked me out of my grand plan and into a cupcake bar. We set out frosting, fresh berries, and naked cupcakes. Manatee made a quick sign with instructions, and our guests arrived.

We thought the kids would get a kick out it—and they did—but it was the adults who couldn't get over it. Grown men were showing off their cupcake masterpieces. This might have had something to do with the Pineapple-Infused Vodka (recipe in Chapter 17) we served, but I also like to think people of all ages get excited about cupcakes and do-it-yourself desserts.

To set up a successful cupcake bar, have several types of cupcakes available. I like to do one chocolate, one vanilla, and one special type (like pumpkin chocolate or blueberry). You can bake the cupcakes up to a week ahead of time and freeze them. The day of the party, take them out of the freezer about an hour or two before you plan on serving them.

Also, have several types of frosting available. I recommend Peanut Butter Frosting, Chocolate Cheese Frosting, and one of the coconut cream frostings in this chapter. You might want to set the frostings in a bowl of ice water. Place the Peanut Butter Frosting in a zipper-lock plastic bag so you can decorate the cupcakes like a pro (see that recipe). Keep extra frosting in the fridge.

Be sure to have a variety of mini chocolate chips, cherries, and other fresh fruit nearby, too.

Finally, make a big deal when someone decorates a cupcake. I love taking pictures of people with their finished cupcakes.

Decorate Like a Pro

It's easy to decorate cupcakes (or cakes) like a pro, even if you don't have all the fancy equipment the pros have.

Simply grab the bottom of a quart zipper-lock plastic bag in one hand and fold the top of the bag over your hand. Use a spoon to fill the bag half full with frosting. Twist the top half of the bag together to form a pastry bag, and push the frosting to one corner of the bottom of the bag. Make a ¼-inch cut on that corner of the bag. It's best to start small and then make the opening bigger if needed.

Holding the bag perpendicular to the top of the cupcake, start piping from just inside the outside edge. Press the bag onto the cupcake and squeeze, moving the bag in a circle toward the center. When you get to the center, press the bag down and then draw the bag up as the frosting comes out. This will create a dome of frosting on the cupcake. Sprinkle with mini chocolate chips, crushed chocolate cookies, etc. of a contrasting color. Pretty!

JUST DON'T DO IT

Under no circumstances is it okay to mess up one corner of the bag and then cut the *other* corner, thinking you can just squeeze to the other side. This does not work. Not that I know from experience (and ending up covered in Peanut Butter Frosting) or anything. No, I would never try that.

Chocolate Cake

With a double dose of melted chocolate and cocoa powder, this cake, rich with chocolate flavor, is for true chocolate lovers. The applesauce not only lightens the cake, but also makes it incredibly moist.

Yield:	Prep time:	Cook time:	Serving size:
1 (9×13-inch) cake or 18 cupcakes	30 minutes	25 to 30 minutes for cake; 18 to 24 minutes for cupcakes	1 piece or 1 cupcake

½ cup chopped dark chocolate or ½ cup dark chocolate chips

½ cup unsalted butter

½ cup unsweetened applesauce

1 cup cocoa powder

1 cup whole-wheat pastry flour

½ cup rolled oats, ground to course meal

1½ tsp. baking powder

1 tsp. baking soda

½ tsp. Cinnamon Sugar (recipe in Chapter 7)

1½ tsp. salt

4 large eggs, at room temperature

2 tsp. vanilla extract

1 cup unprocessed sugar

1 cup Greek Yogurt (recipe in Chapter 3)

1. Preheat the oven to 350°F. Grease and flour a 9×13-inch cake pan or a cupcake pan.

2. In a small bowl, combine dark chocolate, unsalted butter, applesauce, and cocoa powder. Microwave for 20 seconds, and stir. Repeat until chocolate is melted. Mixture will not be smooth.

3. In a medium bowl, whisk together whole-wheat pastry flour, rolled oats, baking powder, baking soda, Cinnamon Sugar, and salt.

4. In a large bowl, whisk eggs until frothy.

5. Add vanilla extract to eggs, and whisk to combine. Whisk in unprocessed sugar, followed by chocolate mixture.

6. Slowly stir flour mixture into egg mixture.

7. Fold in Greek Yogurt until combined, and pour batter into the prepared pan.

8. For a 9×13 cake, bake for 25 to 30 minutes or until a toothpick inserted in cake comes out with just 1 or 2 crumbs. For cupcakes, bake for 18 to 24 minutes or until a toothpick inserted in cupcake comes out with just 1 or 2 crumbs.

9. Cool cake or cupcakes in the pan on a rack until room temperature.

10. Frost as desired, and store in a covered container at room temperature for up to 3 days or in the refrigerator for up to 5 days.

Variation: For **Chocolate Almond Cake,** replace 1 teaspoon vanilla extract with almond extract.

CHOCOLATE CAKE PAIRINGS

This cake is fantastic topped with fresh strawberries. Or try it with the Peanut Butter Frosting—with mini chocolate chips as a topping and/or chopped peanuts. For a sugar topping, combine 2 parts confectioners' sugar with 1 part cocoa and 1 part Cinnamon Sugar. Yum.

Vanilla Cake

Don't be alarmed by the deep golden color of this cake. It comes from the egg yolks, and it makes for an incredibly rich and colorful crust. The Whole-Wheat Cake Flour keeps this cake spongy with a tight crumb. This is a cake for every baker's repertoire. It's as classic as a little black dress, a string of pearls, or a dirty martini.

Yield:	Prep time:	Cook time:	Serving size:
1 (9×13-inch) cake or 24 cupcakes	20 minutes	25 to 30 minutes for cake; 18 to 24 minutes for cupcakes	1 piece or 1 cupcake

2½ cups Whole-Wheat Cake Flour (recipe in Chapter 3)

2½ tsp. baking powder

½ tsp. salt

¾ cup Yogurt Cheese (recipe in Chapter 3)

¾ cup milk

1½ sticks (12 TB.) unsalted butter, softened

1 cup unprocessed sugar

4 large eggs, at room temperature

1 TB. vanilla extract

1. Preheat the oven to 350°F. Grease and flour a 9×13-inch pan or a cupcake pan.

2. In a medium bowl, whisk together Whole-Wheat Cake Flour, baking powder, and salt.

3. In a small bowl, whisk together Yogurt Cheese and milk.

4. In a large bowl, and using an electric mixer on medium speed, cream unsalted butter for about 2 minutes or until light and fluffy.

5. Add unprocessed sugar, and cream for about 1 minute.

6. Add eggs, one at a time, and beat until well combined.

7. Add vanilla extract, and beat to combine.

8. Reduce mixer speed to low, and add milk mixture and flour mixture, alternating between the two, until well combined. Pour batter into the prepared pan.

9. For a 9×13 cake, bake for 25 to 30 minutes or until a toothpick inserted in cake comes out with just 1 or 2 crumbs. For cupcakes, bake for 18 to 24 minutes or until a toothpick inserted in cupcake comes out with just 1 or 2 crumbs.

10. Cool cake or cupcakes in the pan on a rack until room temperature.

11. Frost as desired, and store in a covered container at room temperature for up to 3 days or in the refrigerator for up to 5 days.

Variation: For **Orange Vanilla Cake,** reduce the vanilla extract to 2 teaspoons and add 3 teaspoons orange zest.

VANILLA CAKE PAIRINGS

Fresh raspberries are wonderful with this cake. For frosting, I suggest the Chocolate Cheese Frosting or the Dairy-Free Coconut Cocoa Cream. For a sugar topping, mix 2 parts confectioners' sugar with 1 part cocoa and 1 part Cinnamon Sugar (recipe in Chapter 7).

Blueberry Cake

You know how they always say that muffins are just an excuse to eat cake for breakfast? Not only do I completely agree, but I also think we should take this one step further. Why settle at muffins? If the people want cake, let them eat cake—blueberry cake, to be exact.

Yield:	Prep time:	Cook time:	Serving size:
1 (9×13-inch) cake or 24 cupcakes	20 minutes	30 to 40 minutes for cake; 15 to 25 minutes for cupcakes	1 piece or 1 cupcake

2¾ cups whole-wheat pastry flour

3 tsp. baking powder

2 tsp. ground cinnamon

½ tsp. salt

1½ sticks (12 TB.) unsalted butter, at room temperature

1 cup unprocessed sugar

4 large eggs

2 tsp. vanilla extract

1½ cups milk

3½ cups fresh blueberries

Zest of 1 small lemon (1 TB.)

1. Preheat the oven to 350°F. Grease and flour a 9×13-inch pan or a cupcake pan.

2. In a medium bowl, whisk together 2½ cups whole-wheat pastry flour, baking powder, 1 teaspoon cinnamon, and salt.

3. In a large bowl, and using an electric mixer on medium speed, cream unsalted butter for about 2 minutes or until light and fluffy.

4. Add sugar, and cream for about 1 minute.

5. Add eggs, one at a time, and beat until well combined.

6. Add vanilla extract, and beat to combine.

7. Reduce mixer speed to low, and add milk and flour mixture, alternating between the two, until well combined.

8. In the medium bowl, toss blueberries with remaining ¼ cup flour, remaining 1 teaspoon cinnamon, and lemon zest. Fold berries into cake batter, and pour into the prepared pan.

9. For a 9×13 cake, bake for 30 to 40 minutes or until a toothpick inserted in cake comes out with just 1 or 2 crumbs. For cupcakes, bake for 15 to 25 minutes or until a toothpick inserted in cupcake comes out with just 1 or 2 crumbs.

10. Cool cake or cupcakes in the pan on a rack until room temperature.

11. Frost as desired, and store in a covered container at room temperature for up to 3 days or in the refrigerator for up to 5 days.

BLUEBERRY CAKE PAIRINGS

For more fruity goodness, serve this cake topped with fresh strawberries. If you're looking for a winning frosting, try the Dairy-Free Coconut Cream. And for a eye-catching glaze, combine 3 parts confectioners' sugar with 1 part fresh lemon juice and drizzle over the top.

Angel Food Cake

Angel food is the most fun cake you can bake. It's magical how the egg whites transform into shiny white foam. Be sure you have a very large bowl for the egg whites. I learned this the hard way the first time I made it. Luckily, Manatee was home, so together we juggled the mixture into two other bowls before finding one big enough—and we still never lost a beat with the mixer! Continuous egg white beating through a four-bowl exchange was the product of great teamwork … and made a huge mess. Note with this recipe you can make angel food *cupcakes*. They're not the most attractive cupcakes I've ever made, but I love having single-serving angel food cakes. It makes it so much easier to have multiple servings ….

Yield:	Prep time:	Cook time:	Serving size:
1 Bundt cake or 12 cupcakes	15 minutes	45 to 50 minutes for cake; 20 to 30 minutes for cupcakes	1 piece or 1 cupcake

1 cup Whole-Wheat Cake Flour (recipe in Chapter 3)	12 large egg whites, at room temperature
1 tsp. Cinnamon Sugar (recipe in Chapter 7)	$\frac{1}{2}$ tsp. salt
$1\frac{1}{2}$ cups unprocessed sugar	$1\frac{1}{2}$ tsp. cream of tartar
	$1\frac{1}{2}$ tsp. vanilla extract

1. Preheat the oven to 350°F. Grease and flour a Bundt, angel food pan, or cupcake pan.

2. Using a fine strainer or a flour sifter, sift together Whole-Wheat Cake Flour, Cinnamon Sugar, and $\frac{1}{2}$ cup unprocessed sugar into a medium bowl.

3. In a very large glass bowl, and using an electric mixer on medium-high, beat egg whites for about 2 minutes or until white and foamy.

4. Add salt and cream of tartar, and continue beating until soft peaks form (when you gently lift up the mixer and peaks form in the foam).

5. Slowly add remaining 1 cup unprocessed sugar and vanilla extract, beating after each addition until well combined and stiff peaks form (they hold on their own after you pull up mixer). Pour batter into the prepared pan.

6. For cake, bake for 45 to 50 minutes or until a toothpick inserted into cake comes out with just 1 or 2 crumbs. For cupcakes, bake for 20 to 30 minutes or until a toothpick inserted into cupcake comes out with just 1 or 2 crumbs.

7. Cool cake or cupcakes upside down for 30 to 45 minutes. Remove from the pan, and eat immediately. Store in an airtight container in the refrigerator for up to 3 days.

ANGEL FOOD CAKE PAIRINGS

Any kind of fresh berry is the perfect partner for light and fluffy angel food cake. If you want frosting, use the Dairy-Free Coconut Cream along with fresh berries or the Dairy Free Coconut Cocoa Cream with mini chocolate chips and fresh berries. For a sugar topping, combine 2 parts confectioners' sugar with 1 part Cinnamon Sugar and fresh berries. Did I mention you should try fresh berries with this cake? You should.

Pumpkin Chocolate Cake

I came up with this recipe on a day when I couldn't decide what I was craving more: pumpkin or chocolate. With all the rationale I could muster, I decided I would just have to combine them into one perfect fall dessert. Because I do have some willpower, I did my best to keep this recipe as clean as possible, hence the applesauce, oats, honey, and reduced sugar. But don't worry; you'll never be able to tell it's healthy by the taste.

Yield:	Prep time:	Cook time:	Serving size:
1 (9×13-inch) cake or 24 cupcakes	20 minutes	25 to 35 minutes for cake; 15 to 25 minutes for cupcakes	1 piece or 1 cupcake

2 cups whole-wheat pastry flour

¼ cup rolled oats, ground to coarse meal

1 TB. Pumpkin Pie Spice (recipe in Chapter 7)

2 tsp. baking powder

1 tsp. baking soda

2 tsp. salt

½ cup unprocessed sugar

⅓ cup honey

½ cup unsweetened applesauce

½ cup Pumpkin Butter (recipe in Chapter 6) or unsweetened applesauce

4 large eggs, at room temperature

1 (15.5-oz.) can pumpkin purée

½ cup chopped dark chocolate or ½ cup dark chocolate chips

1. Preheat the oven to 350°F. Grease and flour a 9×13-inch pan or a cupcake pan.

2. In a medium bowl, whisk together whole-wheat pastry flour, rolled oats, Pumpkin Pie Spice, baking powder, baking soda, and salt.

3. In a large bowl, and using an electric mixer on medium-high speed, beat together unprocessed sugar, honey, applesauce, and Pumpkin Butter for 3 minutes.

4. Beat in eggs, 1 at a time.

5. With the mixer still on, add pumpkin purée.

6. Beat in flour mixture, and fold in chocolate. Pour batter in the prepared pan.

7. For a 9×13 cake, bake for 25 to 30 minutes or until a toothpick inserted in cake comes out with just 1 or 2 crumbs. For cupcakes, bake for 15 to 25minutes or until a toothpick inserted in cupcake comes out with just 1 or 2 crumbs.

8. Cool cake or cupcakes in the pan on a rack until room temperature.

9. Frost as desired, and store in a covered container at room temperature for up to 3 days or in the refrigerator for up to 5 days.

PUMPKIN CHOCOLATE CAKE PAIRINGS

This cake stands on its own, no frosting required. But if you must, try it with the Chocolate Cheese Frosting. It will be a rich, decadent dessert, worthy of Manatee's thirtieth birthday celebration, anniversaries, or really rough weeks (and in those cases, it's best with a good red wine and a gaggle of friends for sharing).

Carrot Cake

I was going to call this The Ultimate Carrot Cake, but then I realized it was just *my* ultimate carrot. This cake is everything I've ever loved in a carrot cake, and I love carrot cake. It's my ideal of what carrot cake should be. Poppy seeds, apricots, plump raisins, spices, apple butter, orange zest, creamy cheese frosting, and toasted walnuts—all my favorite carrot cake attributes in a four-layered tower of comfort food.

Yield:	Prep time:	Cook time:	Serving size:
1 half-sheet cake	20 minutes	15 to 20 minutes	1 piece

½ cup raisins or golden raisins

2½ cups whole-wheat pastry flour

1 cup unprocessed sugar or sucanat

2 TB. poppy seeds

2½ tsp. ground cinnamon

2 tsp. baking soda

½ tsp. ground nutmeg

¼ tsp. ground ginger

⅛ tsp. ground cloves

1 tsp. salt

3 large eggs, at room temperature

⅓ cup dried apricots blended in a blender or food processor with 2 TB. hot water

4 large carrots, shredded (2½ cups)

Zest of 1 large orange (2 TB.)

¾ cup Apple Butter (recipe in Chapter 6)

Creamy Cheese Frosting (recipe later in this chapter)

1 cup toasted walnuts

1. Preheat the oven to 350°F. Grease and flour a half-sheet baking pan.

2. Place raisins in a small bowl, and cover with hot water. Set aside to soak.

3. In a medium bowl, whisk together whole-wheat pastry flour, unprocessed sugar, poppy seeds, cinnamon, baking soda, baking powder, nutmeg, ginger, cloves, and salt.

4. Drain raisins, and place in a large bowl. Add eggs, apricots, carrots, orange zest, and Apple Butter, and stir to combine.

5. Add flour mixture to egg mixture, and stir to combine. Pour batter in the prepared pan.

6. Bake for 15 to 20 minutes.

7. Let cake cool completely in the pan on a rack. When cool to the touch, cut cake into 4 rectangles.

8. Place 1 rectangle on a large square plate or platter. Spread Creamy Cheese Frosting on top of rectangle, place second rectangle on top, and repeat frosting and cake rectangles until you have 4 layers of carroty goodness. Spread frosting on top, but leave sides bare so you can see all the layers. Top with toasted walnuts, and serve. Store in a covered container at room temperature or in the refrigerator for up to 3 days.

TOASTING WALNUTS

Don't be intimated by the thought of toasting walnuts. It's easy. Preheat the oven to 350°F. Spread walnuts in a single layer on a rimmed baking sheet, and bake for 10 to 15 minutes or until fragrant and golden. Allow to cool to room temperature before adding to cake.

Creamy Cheese Frosting

This is my version of cream cheese frosting, using rich, decadent Yogurt Cheese. If you haven't made Yogurt Cheese, you should. Or you can substitute cream cheese.

Yield:	Prep time:	Serving size:
2 cups	1 hour, 10 minutes	¼ cup

2 cups Yogurt Cheese (recipe in Chapter 3), at room temperature

2 TB. honey

2 tsp. ground cinnamon

3 TB. milk

1. In a large bowl, and using an electric mixer on medium speed, beat together Yogurt Cheese, honey, and cinnamon.

2. Reduce speed to low, slowly add milk, and blend until well combined.

3. Chill for at least 1 hour before using.

4. Store in an airtight container in the refrigerator for up to 5 days. Take out 10 minutes before spreading.

Chocolate Cheese Frosting

This is rich, thick, chocolate extravagance. This is frosting that needs to be spread. I think I actually heard it laugh a low, knowing, belly laugh at me when I tried to put in a bag and pipe it. I think it said: "You think you can squeeze me?" A little goes a long ways, so you might have some leftover. Never fear, it also goes great with Clean Graham Crackers (recipe in Chapter 14), with fresh strawberries, or just as a treat on a spoon.

Yield:	Prep time:	Cook time:	Serving size:
2 cups	1 hour, 15 minutes	1 minute	2 or 3 tablespoons

1½ cups dark chocolate, chopped, or 1½ cups dark chocolate chips

2 TB. coconut oil

1½ cups Yogurt Cheese (recipe in Chapter 3)

½ cup unsalted butter (1 stick), softened

⅛ tsp. orange zest (optional)

1 tsp. salt

¾ cup confectioners' sugar

1. In a medium glass bowl, combine dark chocolate and coconut oil. Melt in the microwave by heating for 20 seconds, stirring, and repeating until chocolate is smooth.

2. Place melted chocolate in a large bowl, and using an electric mixer on medium-high speed, beat well and gradually add Yogurt Cheese.

3. With the mixer running, add unsalted butter, orange zest (if using), and salt, and beat until combined.

4. Gradually add confectioners' sugar, and continue beating until combined.

5. Chill for at least 1 hour before using.

6. Store in an airtight container in the refrigerator for 4 or 5 days.

Peanut Butter Frosting

Remember when I said I wasn't a frosting person except for a few exceptions? This is the exception. This is by far my favorite frosting in the world. It's sweet peanut butter cream and perfect for chocolate cake. Just be prepared for people to not believe you when you tell them you made the frosting (and the cupcakes) from scratch. They'll continually ask what bakery you went to and roll their eyes when you insist you really did make them yourself. Don't blame them; it's not their fault. Blame the frosting. It's just that good.

Yield:	Prep time:	Serving size:
2 cups	1 hour, 10 minutes	⅓ cup

¼ cup unsalted butter, softened

1 cup Creamier Peanut Butter
(variation in Chapter 6)

6 TB. milk or unsweetened nondairy
milk (almond or soy)

1 tsp. vanilla extract

¼ tsp. salt

3 cups confectioners' sugar

1. In a large bowl, and using an electric mixer on medium-high speed, combine unsalted butter and ¼ cup Creamier Peanut Butter.

2. Add milk, vanilla extract, and salt, and beat until combined.

3. Gradually add confectioners' sugar and remaining ¾ cup Creamier Peanut Butter, alternating between the two and continuing to beat with the mixer until combined.

4. Chill for at least 1 hour before using.

5. Store in an airtight container in the refrigerator for up to 5 days.

Dairy-Free Coconut Cream

It's hard to believe you can create something so good with only two ingredients. By chilling the coconut milk in the freezer, the water in the can separates from the thick, coconut decadence. You need to use full-fat coconut milk in this recipe for the best results. Use this cream to frost cakes, as a vegan whipping cream, or as a dip for fruit or Clean Graham Crackers (recipe in Chapter 14).

Yield:	Prep time:	Serving size:
1½ cups	2 hours, 15 minutes	¼ cup

1 (14-oz.) can full-fat coconut milk	½ to 1 cup confectioners' sugar

1. Do not shake the can of coconut milk. Open the can, and put it in the freezer for 2 to 2½ hours or until chilled and starting to freeze. If it's frozen solid, let sit on the counter until it softens.

2. Remove the can from the freezer, and pour milk into a medium bowl. Do not add any coconut water from the can. Using an electric mixer on medium-high speed, beat until light and fluffy.

3. Gradually add confectioners' sugar, beating it into milk each time. Confectioners' sugar will give cream structure but also make it sweeter. Let your tastes dictate the amount of sugar you add.

4. Use immediately, or store in the refrigerator for up to 2 days. You might need to whisk it before using it if it's been in the fridge for more than 2 hours.

DESSERT TIP

This is a very delicate frosting. Spread it on the cake just before serving. Store the frosted cake in a cool place or in the fridge.

Dairy-Free Coconut Cocoa Cream

Just when you thought Dairy-Free Coconut Cream couldn't get any better, we add chocolate to get light, fluffy, chocolate puffs of frosting. Like the coconut cream, this goes great with Clean Graham Crackers (recipe in Chapter 14) or on its own.

Yield:	Prep time:	Serving size:
1½ cups	2 hours, 15 minutes	¼ cup

1 (14-oz.) can full-fat coconut milk	¼ cup cocoa powder
½ cup confectioners' sugar	½ tsp. ground cinnamon

1. Do not shake the can of coconut milk. Open the can and put it in the freezer for 2 to 2½ hours or until chilled and starting to freeze. If it's frozen solid, let sit on the counter until it softens.

2. Remove the can from the freezer and pour milk into a medium bowl. Do not add any water. Using an electric mixer on medium-high speed, beat until light and fluffy.

3. In a small bowl, whisk together confectioners' sugar, cocoa powder, and cinnamon.

4. Gradually add sugar mixture, beating it into milk each time. Confectioners' sugar will give cream structure but also make it sweeter. Let your tastes dictate the amount of sugar you add.

5. Use immediately, or store in the refrigerator for up to 2 days. You might need to whisk it before using it if it's been in the fridge for more than 2 hours.

NOTES ON FROSTING

This makes a great standalone dessert. Simply serve in small dishes, and garnish with fresh berries or mini chocolate chips.

Fantastic Frozen Desserts  16

Normally frozen desserts are for summertime. Not in the Badger Girl and Manatee household! We shiver and slurp our ice pops and gobble our dairy-free ice cream year-round. These treats are so good, you'll want to do the same.

The Ice Pop Obsession

Manatee is a healthy-eating super hero. He joyfully eats bowl after bowl of spinach, snacks on raw almonds, lunches on hard-boiled egg whites, and has no trouble saying no to desserts in public. But like any caped crusader, he has his weakness. For Superman, it was kryptonite; for Manatee, it's sugar-free ice pops.

In March 2012, he decreed he had bought his last box of ice pops. At the end of April, I became suspicious. Memorial Day weekend, I questioned him. In June, I told him I was going to build a shrine. Jesus was able to multiply fishes and loaves: Manatee has somehow multiplied ice pops. Every night he eats a few, but miraculously, the box never empties.

I created the ice pop recipes in this chapter as a way to thwart his one unclean habit. With so many chemicals in boxed ice pops, my fruity ice pops are a welcome relief. I've reduced the sugar so all you taste is the fruit. By puréeing and then straining the mixture, you can have the texture of a store-bought pop without all the nasty chemicals.

FRESH OR FROZEN?

You'll get the best results with ice pops if you use fresh fruit. If you do use frozen, thaw the fruit first and squeeze out any excess moisture before using.

The World of Dairy-Free Ice Creams

All the ice creams in this chapter are dairy-free. As someone who is lactose intolerant, I thought bowls of ice cream were a dream of the past or a stomachache in the future.

Thanks to the revolutionary work of Dreena Burton, a prolific vegan cookbook writer, I found an equation that produces rich and creamy dairy-free ice cream. I've modified it through my own experiments, but I credit her with the combination of coconut milk, coconut butter, and guar gum. It's a winning combo, and I have yet to see it anywhere else.

You can find guar gum at most health stores, or you can order it online—even sites like Amazon.com carry it. Store it at room temperature in your pantry for up to 1 year.

Coconut butter might be hard to find in stores, but you can order it online. Believe me, it's worth the hassle. It's creamy and salty, and it keeps the ice cream from getting too icy.

Blackberry and Lime Ice Pops

Fresh, sweet blackberries couple with tangy limes and very little added sweeteners. As soon as blackberries are in season, I stock up so I can make these pops.

Yield:	Prep time:	Serving size:
8 ice pops	4 to 6 hours	1 ice pop

5 cups fresh blackberries

1½ cups water

¼ cup agave nectar

Juice of 2 small limes (¼ cup)

1. In a blender, purée blackberries until smooth.

2. Strain berry purée through a fine-mesh strainer into a large bowl. Use a ladle or a large spoon to push purée through the strainer so you get the most berry for your buck.

3. Stir in water, agave nectar, and lime juice. Mixture should taste a little too sweet. That's normal, and it will lose some sweetness when it freezes.

4. Pour purée into pop molds, leaving ¼ inch at the top for expansion.

5. Freeze for 4 to 6 hours. Unmold by placing the molds in warm water or running warm water over the bottom of the molds.

6. Store in the freezer for up to 3 weeks.

Strawberry and Peach Ice Pops

I'm not a huge fan of peaches, but I love how the peaches complement the strawberries in these pops. If you're a peach fan, feel free to add more peaches in place of some of the strawberries.

Yield:	Prep time:	Serving size:
8 ice pops	6 hours	1 ice pop

4 cups fresh strawberries, hulled and quartered

3 medium peaches, pitted and quartered

Juice of 3 small limes (¼ cup plus 2 TB.)

½ cup water

2 TB. agave nectar

1. In a blender, purée strawberries, peaches, and lime juice. You might need to do multiple batches.

2. Strain fruit purée through a fine-mesh strainer into a large bowl.

3. Stir in water and agave nectar.

4. Pour purée into pop molds, leaving ¼ inch at the top for expansion.

5. Freeze for at least 6 hours. Unmold by placing the molds in warm water or running warm water over the bottom of the molds.

6. Store in the freezer for up to 3 weeks.

Pineapple and Tangerine Ice Pops

As I was trying to lure Manatee away from store-bought pops, I began to take note of his favorite processed flavor and found that he favored pineapple. I'm happy to say this pop beat out the store-bought pops in no time. The tangerine keeps the pineapple from getting too sweet. These are perfect after spending a day in the sun, whether it's the hot summer sun or crisp winter sun.

Yield:	Prep time:	Serving size:
6 ice pops	6 hours	1 ice pop

1 medium pineapple, skin and stem removed

Juice of 2 small tangerines (¼ cup)

½ cup water

2 TB. agave nectar

1. In a blender, purée ½ pineapple, 2 tablespoons tangerine juice, and ¼ cup water.

2. Strain purée through a fine-mesh strainer into a large bowl.

3. Repeat with remaining ½ pineapple, remaining 2 tablespoons tangerine juice, and remaining ¼ cup water.

4. Stir in agave nectar.

5. Pour purée into pop molds, leaving ¼ inch at the top for expansion.

6. Freeze for at least 6 hours. Unmold by placing the molds in warm water or running warm water over the bottom of the molds.

7. Store in the freezer for up to 3 weeks.

CORE AND ALL

You might have noticed I didn't tell you to core the pineapple. Because you'll be puréeing the pineapple, there's no need to deal with coring it.

Mango and Apricot Ice Pops

The mango in these pops makes them seem exotic. These pops make a great dessert for a summer barbecue or after eating a spicy Indian curry.

Yield:	Prep time:	Serving size:
6 ice pops	4 to 6 hours	12 ice pops

5 small apricots, pitted

1 large mango, cut into strips

Juice of 4 medium oranges (1 cup)

¼ cup water

2 TB. agave nectar

1. In a blender, purée apricots, mango, and orange juice.

2. Strain fruit purée through a fine-mesh strainer into a large bowl. Use a ladle or large spoon to push purée through the strainer.

3. Stir in water and agave nectar.

4. Pour purée into pop molds, leaving ¼ inch at the top for expansion.

5. Freeze for 4 to 6 hours. Unmold by placing the molds in warm water or running warm water over the bottom of the molds.

6. Store in the freezer for up to 3 weeks.

THE SKINNY

You might have noticed I'm not telling you to peel many of the fruits. Because you're straining, you don't need to skin the fruits first. If you choose not to strain the fruits, you might want to skin the peaches, apricots, and mango.

Dairy-Free Chocolate Ice Cream

This is the type of chocolate ice cream dreams are made of—creamy and chocolaty with just a hint of coconut. You can keep it plain, but check out some of my suggested add-ins at the end of the recipe for a twist on a classic. My favorite? Roasted almonds and white chocolate chips. Or is it the cayenne? Peanut butter? Try all of them. You won't be sorry.

Yield:	Prep time:	Serving size:
4 or 5 cups	2 to 4 hours	1 cup

1 (13.5-oz.) can full-fat coconut milk, shaken

½ cup unsweetened chocolate almond or soy milk

¼ cup coconut butter

⅓ cup cocoa powder

⅓ cup unprocessed sugar

½ tsp. guar gum

¼ tsp. salt

2 tsp. vanilla extract

1. In a blender, purée coconut milk, chocolate almond milk, coconut butter, cocoa powder, unprocessed sugar, guar gum, salt, and vanilla extract until smooth.

2. Follow your ice-cream maker's manufacturers' instructions for making ice cream. In general, turn on the machine and then pour in purée. After 20 to 25 minutes, ice cream should resemble soft serve.

3. Transfer to an airtight freezer-safe container, and freeze for 2 to 4 hours. Remove ice cream from the freezer 10 to 15 minutes before serving.

4. Store in the freezer for up to 3 weeks.

Variations: For **Dairy-Free Roasted Almond Double Chocolate Ice Cream,** add ⅓ cup roasted almonds and ¼ cup white chocolate chips to the ice-cream maker 5 minutes before the mixture reaches soft serve consistency. For **Dairy-Free Cayenne Chocolate Ice Cream,** add 2 teaspoons ground cinnamon and ½ to 1 teaspoon cayenne to the coconut milk mixture in the blender. For **Dairy-Free Chocolate Peanut Butter Ice Cream,** reduce the coconut butter to 3 tablespoons and add 2 tablespoons peanut butter to the coconut milk mixture in the blender. Also add 6 tablespoons peanut butter, ¼ cup chopped peanuts, and ¼ cup mini chocolate chips to the ice-cream machine 5 minutes before mixture reaches soft serve consistency.

COCONUT BUTTER, NOT OIL

For me, there was some confusion about coconut oil versus coconut butter. These are two different things. Coconut butter is coconut oil mixed with dried coconut flesh. For the ice-cream recipes, you need coconut butter. Coconut oil won't work. For more information on these two ingredients, check out the glossary.

Dairy-Free Vanilla Ice Cream

Sometimes vanilla ice cream is the perfect ticket. I love it with warm pies or crumbles or topped with Chocolate Sauce (recipe later in this chapter).

Yield:	Prep time:	Serving size:
4 or 5 cups	2 to 4 hours	1 cup

1 (13.5-oz.) can full-fat coconut milk, shaken

½ cup unsweetened vanilla almond or soy milk

¼ cup coconut butter

⅓ cup unprocessed sugar

½ tsp. guar gum

¼ tsp. salt

3 tsp. vanilla extract

1. In a blender, purée coconut milk, vanilla almond milk, coconut butter, unprocessed sugar, guar gum, salt, and vanilla extract until smooth.

2. Follow your ice-cream maker's manufacturers' instructions for making ice cream. In general, turn on the machine and then pour in purée. After 20 to 25 minutes, ice cream should resemble soft serve.

3. Transfer to an airtight freezer-safe container, and freeze for 2 to 4 hours. Remove ice cream from the freezer 10 to 15 minutes before serving.

4. Store in the freezer for up to 3 weeks.

Variations: For **Dairy-Free Vanilla Chocolate Chip Ice Cream,** add ¼ cup Chocolate Sauce (recipe later in this chapter) or mini chocolate chips to the ice-cream maker 5 minutes before mixture reaches soft serve consistency. For **Dairy-Free Roasted Almond Vanilla Ice Cream,** increase the salt to ½ teaspoon and add ½ cup chopped roasted almonds to the ice-cream maker 5 minutes before mixture reaches soft serve consistency.

ROASTING ALMONDS

Roasting almonds brings really brings out their flavor—and it's easy to do. Just preheat the oven to 350°F, line a rimmed baking sheet with a silicone mat and parchment paper, and arrange almonds in a single layer on the baking sheet. Bake for 10 to 15 minutes or until almonds are fragrant. Almonds will crisp as they cool.

Dairy-Free Cinnamon Ice Cream

Growing up, Manatee watched his older brother "make" cinnamon ice cream by mashing cinnamon into store-bought ice cream and stirring it until it resembled soft serve. Can you guess what Manatee's favorite ice cream is? You guessed it: Steve's Cinnamon Ice Cream. As soon as we got our ice-cream maker, I knew what I had to do. This ice cream has quickly become my favorite as well. The cinnamon adds a warmth you normally don't find in ice cream complemented by the extra vanilla. Thank goodness for older brothers!

Yield:	Prep time:	Serving size:
4 or 5 cups	2 to 4 hours	1 cup

1 (13.5-oz.) can full-fat coconut milk, shaken

¾ cup unsweetened vanilla almond or soy milk

¼ cup coconut butter

½ cup unprocessed sugar

½ tsp. guar gum

¼ tsp. salt

¼ cup ground cinnamon

3 tsp. vanilla extract

1. In a blender, purée coconut milk, vanilla almond milk, coconut butter, unprocessed sugar, guar gum, salt, cinnamon, and vanilla extract until smooth.

2. Follow your ice-cream maker's manufacturers' instructions for making ice cream. In general, turn on the machine and then pour in purée. After 20 to 25 minutes, ice cream should resemble soft serve.

3. Transfer to an airtight freezer-safe container, and freeze for 2 to 4 hours. Remove ice cream from the freezer 10 to 15 minutes before serving.

4. Store in the freezer for up to 3 weeks.

Dairy-Free Strawberry Ice Cream

I'll be first to admit I'm not one for fruit ice creams. Give me something chocolate or salty any day. Strawberries break the rule, though, and this is the perfect way to use berries you don't think you'll be able to eat fast enough. You can use 2 to 4 cups of strawberries in this recipe—that's a huge range! If you use 2 cups, the vanilla flavor will be equal to the strawberry. As you increase the berries, the berry taste intensifies. Adjust the amount of sugar to the sweetness of the berries. If you have super-sweet berries, you won't need as much sugar.

Yield:	Prep time:	Serving size:
4 or 5 cups	2 to 4 hours	1 cup

1 (13.5-oz.) can full-fat coconut milk, shaken	2 to 4 cups fresh strawberries, hulled and quartered
½ cup unsweetened vanilla almond or soy milk	½ tsp. guar gum
¼ cup coconut butter	¼ tsp. salt
⅓ to ½ cup unprocessed sugar	3 tsp. vanilla extract

1. In a food processor fitted with a chopping blade, purée coconut milk, vanilla almond milk, coconut butter, unprocessed sugar, strawberries, guar gum, salt, and vanilla extract until smooth.

2. Follow your ice-cream maker's manufacturers' instructions for making ice cream. In general, turn on the machine and then pour in purée. After 20 to 25 minutes, ice cream should resemble soft serve.

3. Transfer to an airtight freezer-safe container, and freeze for 2 to 4 hours. Remove ice cream from the freezer 10 to 15 minutes before serving.

4. Store in the freezer for up to 3 weeks.

Variation: For **Dairy-Free Chocolate-Dipped Strawberry Ice Cream,** pour ¼ cup Chocolate Sauce (recipe later in this chapter) or mini chocolate chips into the ice-cream maker 5 minutes before mixture reaches soft serve consistency.

Dairy-Free Mint Chocolate Chip Ice Cream

I love mint chocolate-chip ice cream. When I started looking at recipes, I was shocked that so many relied on mint extract and (*gasp!*) green food coloring. Have we sunk so low that we need to use green chemicals instead of fresh mint? This ice cream takes a little patience and a lot of fresh mint, but it's *so* worth it. Get it started around noon, let it seep throughout the afternoon, and that night you'll be able to enjoy totally natural and amazing mint ice cream. So what it if it isn't green?

Yield:	Prep time:	Cook time:	Serving size:
4 or 5 cups	4½ hours	2 hours	1 cup

4½ cups fresh mint, chopped

1 (13.5-oz.) can full-fat coconut milk, shaken

½ cup plain or vanilla unsweetened almond or soy milk

1 TB. vanilla extract

¼ cup coconut butter

⅓ cup unprocessed sugar

½ tsp. guar gum

¼ tsp. salt

¼ cup Chocolate Sauce (recipe later in this chapter) or mini chocolate chips

1. In a medium saucepan over medium-high heat, combine 4 cups mint, coconut milk, almond milk, and vanilla extract. Bring to a simmer, remove from heat, cover, and let seep for 2 hours.

2. In a blender, purée mint–coconut milk mixture, coconut butter, unprocessed sugar, guar gum, salt, and remaining ½ cup mint until smooth.

4. Follow your ice-cream maker's manufacturers' instructions for making ice cream. In general, turn on the machine and then pour in purée. After 20 to 25 minutes, ice cream should resemble soft serve. After 15 to 20 minutes, check the consistency. Right before it reaches soft serve consistency, add Chocolate Sauce.

5. Transfer to an airtight freezer-safe container, and freeze for 2 to 4 hours. Remove ice cream from the freezer 10 to 15 minutes before serving.

6. Store in the freezer for up to 3 weeks.

Variation: For **Dairy-Free Mint Chocolate-Chip Almond Ice Cream,** add ⅓ cup chopped roasted almonds to the ice-cream maker when you add Chocolate Sauce.

Chocolate Sauce

Who needs a store-bought, chemical-laden chocolate sauce when you can make a rich and chocolaty sauce at home in less than a minute? Dark chocolate chips and rich coconut oil make this a tropical indulgence.

Yield:	Prep time:	Cook time:	Serving size:
¼ cup	2 minutes	2 minutes	2 tablespoons

¼ cup dark chocolate chips　　　　　　　　1 tsp. coconut oil

1. In a small glass bowl, combine dark chocolate chips and coconut oil.

2. Microwave on high for 15 seconds. Stir, and heat for 5 to 8 more seconds. Stir, and repeat until chocolate has melted and mixture is smooth.

3. Serve immediately.

Beverages for All Ages  17

Hello, my name is Badger Girl, and I used to be a diet soda-a-holic.

I started every day with a diet soda and peanut butter toast. I loved how the first gulp of soda burned down my throat. For snacks, I loved how the chemically induced sweetness of the fake chocolate icing on a certain cream-filled cupcake paired with overly salty processed potato chips.

Even when I gave up processed foods, I had a hard time letting go of soda. Was it the caramel color I craved? What about the NutraSweet? The caffeine? No, I just needed a break from water.

I drink a ton of water throughout the day and night. During college, I called myself a thespian, and we actors, in addition to being loud, attention-grabbing, overly emotional people, are also part camel. We were taught to pee clear and were not allowed in class without a full water bottle or out of class without an empty bottle. Old habits die hard, but even I get tired of water. Don't you?

Put down that soda, and come with me on a tour of other possibilities: lemonades, infusions, homey hot liquids, sophisticated cocktails, and even our own healthy sodas. Why drink boring old diet soda when there's so much more out there?

Easy Homemade Beverages

After struggling to perfect my ratios, I've started viewing homemade beverages in a different light. For many of the recipes in this chapter, I use three parts:

- A base
- A sweetener
- A mixer (water or sparkling water)

This cuts down on fridge space—and disagreements about how strong it should be, how sweet it should be, whether or not it should be carbonated, or how to keep carbonated lemonade fizzy for more than one drink.

SODASTREAM

Sodastream machines add carbonation to regular tap water. If you like sparkling water, invest in one. If you don't like sparkling water (like me), but like to jazz up your homemade beverages, invest in one. Everything tastes better with bubbles.

Infused Vodkas

How can you not like infused vodkas? There couldn't be an easier or more impressive way to serve homemade fare at a party.

I'm a firm believer in signature cocktails for parties. I'm also a firm believer in reducing the amount of work I need to do during a party. After all the cleaning and cooking, I want to be sure I can actually enjoy the night (or afternoon) ahead. So how do I reconcile these conflicting schools of thought? Infused vodkas.

Prep your infusing material days or weeks ahead of time, and on the day of the party, your only job is to pour, suggest mixers, and be sure your guests understand that even though it may be packed with flavor, it's really just vodka.

DON'T TOSS THE BOTTLE!

When infusing vodkas, keep the vodka bottle. It's great for storing the infused vodka.

Lemonade

You know the saying: when life gives you lemons …. In my sheltered childhood, I refused to grasp the relationship with the sugary drink I called lemonade and the tart origin. Manatee's family, on the other hand, *lives* on homemade lemonade. When she was 10 years old, my niece Olivia taught me the family recipe. I swapped out the sugar with agave nectar, but I have her to thank for this refreshing little number.

Yield:	Prep time:	Serving size:
1 quart	15 minutes	½ cup

Juice of 8 small lemons (1 cup)
Juice of 1 medium orange (¼ cup)
2¾ cups water

¼ cup plus 2 TB. agave nectar
Sparkling water or more water

1. Into a quart mason jar, pour lemon juice, orange juice, water, and agave nectar. Add the lid, and shake to mix.

2. To serve, pour ½ cup Lemonade into a glass. Top with ½ cup sparkling water or water to dilute. Adjust according to your taste.

3. Serve immediately. If you don't add sparkling water, you can store it in the refrigerator for up to 4 days. Stir before serving. Sparkling water will lose its bubbles within 1 day.

PERSONALIZE IT

If you like stronger lemonade, add less water. For a lighter lemonade, use more water. This method allows you to customize each glass.

Orange Lemonade

By adding more orange juice to your lemonade, you get the natural sweetness of the orange and a more complex flavor.

Yield:	Prep time:	Serving size:
1 quart	15 minutes	½ cup

Juice of 8 small lemons (1 cup)
Juice of 4 medium oranges (1 cup)
2 cups water

3 TB. agave nectar
Sparkling water or more water

1. Into a quart mason jar, pour lemon juice, orange juice, water, and agave nectar. Add the lid, and shake to mix.

2. To serve, pour ½ cup Orange Lemonade into a glass. Top with ½ cup sparkling water or water to dilute. Adjust according to your taste.

3. Serve immediately. If you don't add sparkling water, you can store it in the refrigerator for up to 4 days. Stir before serving. Sparkling water will lose its bubbles within 1 day.

SPARKLING ORANGE LEMONADE

For parties, serve with vodka and just a little sparkling water.

Berry Purée

In the summer months, it's hard to resist all the delicious berries at the market. I like to keep a jar of berry purée in the refrigerator. It's great for making some all-natural drinks (like Berry Lemonade or Strawberry Soda) or topping ice cream. It's also a great way to use berries that are too ripe for eating. The recipe calls for strawberries, but you can use your favorite fresh berry instead.

Yield:	Prep time:	Serving size:
1 quart	20 minutes	1 cup

6 cups fresh strawberries   ½ cup water

1. In a blender, purée 3 cups strawberries with ¼ cup of water until smooth. Repeat for a second batch with remaining 3 cups strawberries and ¼ cup water.

2. Strain purée through fine-mesh strainer into a pitcher or bowl.

3. Store in an airtight container in the refrigerator for up to 1 week.

Berry Lemonade

Don't be tempted by the bottled pink lemonades in the store. You can make your own at home using Berry Purée. Real berry sweetness wins out over fake colors and chemicals any day in my book.

Yield:	Prep time:	Serving size:
1 quart	25 minutes	1 cup

1 cup Berry Purée (recipe earlier in this chapter)

Juice of 8 small lemons (1 cup)

Juice of 1 medium orange (¼ cup)

1 cup water

6 TB. agave nectar

Sparkling water or more water

1. Into a quart mason jar, pour Berry Purée, lemon juice, orange juice, water, and agave nectar. Add the lid, and shake to mix.

2. To serve, pour ½ cup berry lemonade into a glass. Top with ½ cup sparkling water or water to dilute. Adjust according to your taste.

3. Serve immediately. If you don't add sparkling water, you can store it in the refrigerator for up to 4 days. Stir before serving. Sparkling water will lose its bubbles within 1 day.

Variation: You can replace the strawberry purée with any other berry purée for a different flavor.

Berry Lemonade Ice Cubes

My mother's secret to summertime entertaining: lemonade ice cubes in the freezer, lemonade in the refrigerator, and lemons on the counter—at all times. She would pour the lemonade in the pitcher with the special lemonade ice cubes so the lemonade wouldn't ever get watered down, and she'd garnish each glass with a slice of fresh lemon. Simple, classy, and smart—just like her. Of course, it took me years to finally take her advice, but I guess that's typical of any daughter.

Yield:	Prep time:	Serving size:
12 to 16 ice cubes	2 hours	3 ice cubes

1 or 2 cups Berry Lemonade (recipe earlier in this chapter; amount varies depending on ice cube size)

1. Pour Berry Lemonade into ice-cube trays.

2. Freeze for at least 2 hours.

Variations: For **Double Berry Lemonade Ice Cubes,** add strawberries, blackberries, or blueberries to the ice-cube mold before pouring in the lemonade. When the ice cubes thaw in the drink, your guests will have frozen berries to enjoy. For **Lemonade Ice Cubes,** replace the Berry Lemonade with the Lemonade or Orange Lemonade (recipes earlier in this chapter). For **Citrus Lemonade Ice Cubes,** instead of adding berries in the Double Berry Lemonade Ice Cubes, add small slivers of limes or lemons.

Cucumber Infusion

Fruit-infused waters are great for the summer months when you need something just a little more than water to quench your thirst. On a hot day, nothing is more refreshing than a light and salty glass of cucumber water. You can decide whether or not to remove the cucumber seeds. They add a salty taste to the water that I, for one, really enjoy.

Yield:	Prep time:	Serving size:
2 quarts	2 to 8 hours	1 cup

3 cups sliced cucumber	2 qt. water

1. Place cucumbers in a pitcher, and pour in water.

2. Infuse for at least 2 hours before serving. Store in the refrigerator for 1 day.

Variation: For **Citrus Cucumber Water,** replace 1 or 2 cups cucumber with orange, lemon, and/or lime slices.

INFUSION PITCHERS

Special pitchers are available that separate the cucumber (or fruits) from dissolving into water. If you don't mind the water being a little cloudy, just throw the cuke in a pitcher of water and let nature do the rest.

Lemon Infusion

If you like tart drinks, this infusion is for you! Tart and crisp, cool and refreshing, this drink is a great way to change up your water routine. The day before a running race or triathlon, I add a sprinkle of salt to my lemon water to help me stay hydrated the next day.

Yield:	Prep time:	Serving size:
2 quarts	4 to 8 hours	1 cup

5 small lemons, ends removed and sliced (4 cups)	2 qt. water

1. Place lemon slices in a pitcher, and pour in water.

2. Infuse for at least 4 hours before serving. Store in the refrigerator for 1 day.

Strawberry Infusion

The berries impart a gentle sweetness to the water, making this fruity infusion the perfect counter to sugary fruit drinks. The water will turn pink, so you might want to strain it through cheesecloth if you're serving it to guests.

Yield:	Prep time:	Serving size:
2 quarts	6 to 12 hours	1 cup

3 cups fresh strawberries, hulled and halved	2 qt. water

1. Place strawberries in a pitcher, and pour in water.

2. Infuse for at least 6 hours before serving. Store in the refrigerator for 1 day.

Variation: Feel free to substitute your favorite berry for the strawberries. You can also add lime slices for a sweet and tangy infused water.

Clean and Simple Syrup

Simple syrup is, well, *simple* to make. You boil a sweetener and water together until the sugar dissolves. The remaining syrup is great for sweetening drinks. The normal ratio for simple syrup is 1 cup water to 1 (or more) cups sugar. To clean up this tried-and-true recipe, I opted for agave nectar so I could use a sweetener that wouldn't spike sugar levels and I could reduce the amount of the sweetening agent, as agave nectar is sweeter-tasting than sugar.

Yield:	Prep time:	Cook time:	Serving size:
1½ cups	1 minute	35 minutes	2 tablespoons to ⅓ cup

1 cup water	½ cup agave nectar

1. In a small saucepan over medium heat, combine water and agave nectar. Bring to a rolling boil, remove from heat, and allow to return to room temperature.

2. Store in a sealable container in the refrigerator for up to 3 weeks.

Orange Simple Syrup

This syrup is perfect for making orange soda or for imparting any beverage with a sweet, orange taste.

Yield:	Prep time:	Cook time:	Serving size:
1½ cups	5 minutes	35 minutes	2 tablespoons to ⅓ cup

3 medium oranges	½ cup agave nectar
1 cup water	

1. Remove orange peel using a vegetable peeler, pressing gently with the peeler to reduce the amount of white pith you remove with the peel. Set oranges aside for later use.

2. In a small saucepan over medium heat, combine orange peels, water, and agave nectar. Bring to a rolling boil, remove from heat, and allow to return to room temperature.

3. Strain syrup through a fine-mesh strainer into a sealable container. Store in the refrigerator for up to 3 weeks.

Lime Simple Syrup

This syrup is great for adding a light lime flavor to your sparkling water.

Yield:	Prep time:	Cook time:	Serving size:
1½ cups	5 minutes	35 minutes	2 tablespoons to ⅓ cup

3 small limes
1 cup water

½ cup agave nectar

1. Remove lime peel using a vegetable peeler, pressing gently with the peeler to reduce the amount of white pith on you remove with the peel. Set limes aside for later use.

2. In a small saucepan over medium heat, combine lime peels, water, and agave nectar. Bring to a rolling boil, remove from heat, and allow to return to room temperature.

3. Strain syrup through a fine-mesh strainer into a sealable container. Store in the refrigerator for up to 3 weeks.

Ginger Simple Syrup

When I started making simple syrups, this was the first one on my list. I love ginger-flavored drinks, so I knew I wanted to be able to make my own at home. As the syrup cools, it will fill your kitchen with the smell of fresh ginger.

Yield:	Prep time:	Cook time:	Serving size:
1½ cups	5 minutes	35 minutes	2 tablespoons to ⅓ cup

1 (4-in.) piece fresh ginger, peeled
and sliced

1 cup water
½ cup agave nectar

1. In a small saucepan over medium heat, combine ginger, water, and agave nectar. Bring to a rolling boil, remove from heat, and allow to return to room temperature.

2. Strain syrup through a fine-mesh strainer into a sealable container. Store in the refrigerator for up to 3 weeks.

FRESH AND FROZEN GINGER

To peel fresh ginger, don't bother trying to use a vegetable peeler. It's much easier (and less aggravating) to cut it off with a paring knife. To store leftover fresh ginger, remove the skin, slice into discs or mince, and freeze in an airtight container for up to 6 months. Use frozen ginger as you would fresh.

Orange Soda

My grandmother always bought different fruit sodas. This was a strange departure for me because I was accustomed to my beloved diet soda (even at a young age), but I loved trying them all anyway. My favorite was the orange—syrupy sweet and perfectly carbonated. This is a no-guilt, adult version of that childhood favorite.

Yield:	Prep time:	Serving size:
1½ cups	10 minutes	1½ cups

Juice of 2 or 3 medium oranges (½ cup)

¼ cup Orange Simple Syrup (recipe earlier in this chapter)

¾ cup sparkling water

1. Strain orange juice through a fine-mesh strainer, and pour into a glass.

2. Add Orange Simple Syrup and sparkling water, and stir gently to mix. Adjust the ratio of syrup to water to suit your taste.

3. Serve immediately.

Strawberry Soda

This soda is refreshing on a hot day or makes a sweet treat after dinner. The lime helps brighten the taste, and because you're are using agave nectar, it's a totally guilt-free sweet drink.

Yield:	Prep time:	Serving size:
1½ cups	5 minutes	1½ cups

¼ cup Berry Purée (recipe earlier in this chapter)

2 TB. Clean and Simple Syrup (recipe earlier in this chapter)

1 cup sparkling water

Juice of 1 small lime (1 TB.)

1. Into a tall glass, pour Berry Purée, Clean and Simple Syrup, sparkling water, and lime juice, and stir gently to mix.

2. Adjust the ratio of syrup to water to suit your taste.

3. Serve immediately, or store in the refrigerator for up to 1 day.

Variation: For **Blackberry Soda,** use blackberry purée and increase the lime juice to 2 tablespoons.

Ginger Lime Soda

I hate to pick favorites, but that's never stopped me before—this is my favorite homemade soda. The lime is refreshing, and you don't catch the ginger until the aftertaste. It's comforting to an upset stomach, refreshing on a hot day, and a very welcome break from water *and* diet soda.

Yield:	Prep time:	Serving size:
1¼ cups	5 minutes	1¼ cups

2 TB. Ginger Simple Syrup (recipe earlier in this chapter)

Juice of 1 small lime (1 TB.)

1 cup sparkling water

1. Into a tall glass, pour Ginger Simple Syrup, lime juice, and sparkling water, and stir gently to mix.

2. Adjust the ratio of syrup to water to suit your taste.

3. Serve immediately.

Variations: For **Lime Soda,** replace the Ginger Simple Syrup with Clean and Simple Syrup. For **Lemon Lime Soda,** replace the Ginger Simple Syrup with Clean and Simple Syrup, and replace 1 tablespoon lime juice with 1 tablespoon lemon juice.

Pomegranate Fizzes

This was the first drink I made when I bought my Sodastream machine. Talking with other soda makers, many talked about adding "Pom" juice to sparkling water. I went home, tried it, and immediately spit it out. No one told me how sour it was! It took some experimenting, but by adding some simple syrup and a splash of lime juice, I think I've come up with a great drink perfect for holiday parties and fall days. Now when I tell soda makers about this drink, I always mention how important it is to add some sweetener.

Yield:	Prep time:	Serving size:
1½ cups	5 minutes	1½ cups

¼ cup pomegranate juice

2 TB. Lime Simple Syrup or Clean and Simple Syrup (recipes earlier in this chapter)

1 cup sparkling water

Juice of 1 small lime (1 TB.)

1. Into a tall glass, pour pomegranate juice, Lime Simple Syrup, sparkling water, and lime juice, and stir gently to mix.

2. Adjust the ratio of syrup to water to suit your taste.

3. Serve immediately.

POMEGRANATE JUICE

Pomegranate juice is a rich, tart juice you can find in the produce section. It's a little pricey, but a little goes a long way.

Hot Cranberry Cider

Did you know the cranberry is Wisconsin's state fruit? Or that Wisconsin is the leading U.S. producer of cranberries? How about that I grew up next to one of the oldest family-run cranberry marshes in the world? Okay, I bet you didn't know the last one, but it's totally true. I grew up with the Detlefsen family of Whittlesey Cranberries, established in 1871. Needless to say, they have some great cranberry recipes. Our neighbor, Jo Anne, kept us supplied with Hot Cranberry Cider through the winter, and I never realized this wasn't a staple in every household. Let's work to change that, shall we?

Yield:	Prep time:	Cook time:	Serving size:
2 quarts	5 minutes	1 hour, 15 minutes	1 cup

1 qt. no-sugar-added cranberry juice	2 tea bags
⅔ cup unprocessed sugar	6 cups boiling water
1 (3-in.) stick cinnamon	Juice of 1 small lemon (1 TB.)
8 to 10 whole cloves	

1. In a large saucepan over medium heat, combine cranberry juice, sugar, cinnamon stick, and cloves. Heat for 1 hour. Do not let boil.

2. Place tea bags in a heat-resistant bowl. Pour boiling water over tea bags, and let sit for 5 to 8 minutes. Remove and discard tea bags.

3. Add tea to cranberry mixture, and stir in lemon juice.

4. Serve warm with cinnamon sticks. Store in an airtight container in the refrigerator for 2 or 3 weeks.

MORE REASONS TO LOVE IT

I always have a pot of this on the stove or in a slow cooker at all our holiday parties. Keep it on a low simmer, and stir it occasionally. Place a ladle, mugs, cinnamon sticks, and instructions ("Enjoy me with a cinnamon stick!") nearby. This also makes a great hostess gift during the holiday season. Pour some into a nice jar, and tie a ribbon with a bundle of cinnamon sticks to it. In my previous life as a corporate worker, I would keep a small bottle in the fridge so I could enjoy a cup of hot cider during the afternoons. If I haven't convinced you yet to try it, you should also know that your house will smell amazing when you make it. Now will you try it?

Hot Cocoa Mix

When I realized I was lactose intolerant, I had to let go of hot cocoa. Most premixed packs include some kind of milk or dairy derivative, as well as many chemicals and not-so-good-for-you ingredients. At the time, it was a tragedy, but now I realize it was the best thing to happen to my hot beverage repertoire. Hot cocoa can be so much more than hot water-y, bland hot chocolate with little fake marshmallows. Add some cinnamon and cayenne to round out the heat and some mini chocolate chips for some extra chocolate goodness, and don't even get me started on all the types of high-quality cocoas available.

Yield:	Prep time:	Serving size:
1 pint	5 minutes	1½ to 2 tablespoons

1 cup cocoa powder	¼ tsp. ground cinnamon
2 tsp. cornstarch	⅛ tsp. cayenne
1½ cups confectioners' sugar	½ cup mini chocolate chips
1 tsp. salt	

1. In a medium bowl, whisk together cocoa powder, cornstarch, confectioners' sugar, salt, cinnamon, cayenne, and mini chocolate chips.

2. Serve with hot milk, using 1½ to 2 tablespoons per 1 cup milk.

3. Store in an airtight container for up to 1 month.

MIXER OPTIONS

By making your own Hot Cocoa Mix, you control what goes inside and you can also control your liquid mixer. If you can do dairy, by all means, have some milk. For the rest of us, use your favorite nondairy milk. Unsweetened vanilla almond milk is my favorite, but experiment with different ones. Just don't use water. It won't be nearly as creamy and delicious.

All-Natural Mimosa

In the realm of cocktails, I think this is as healthy as you can get. Fresh-squeezed orange juice paired with sweet champagne. When you drop a berry in the bottom, it soaks in the champagne, leaving you with a post-drink treat.

Yield:	Prep time:	Serving size:
½ cup	10 minutes	½ cup

Juice of 1 or 2 medium oranges (¼ cup)

1 fresh blackberry

¼ to ⅓ cup champagne or sparkling wine

1. Strain orange juice through a fine-mesh strainer, and pour into a champagne flute. Drop blackberry into the bottom of the glass, and top with champagne.

2. Serve immediately.

Variations: For a **Strawberry Mimosa,** replace the orange juice with ¼ cup puréed strawberries and omit the blackberry. For a **Cranberry Orange Mimosa,** add a splash of cranberry juice.

Pineapple-Infused Vodka

More than any other infused vodka, this one should come with a warning. The last time we served it, our party started at noon and didn't end until the wee hours of the next morning. Afterward, we found a pair of sunglasses in our tomato plants and Manatee woke up with a sidewalk scrape on his ear we suspect happened during a lawn game. Not to mention, our guests couldn't stop raving about this drink. Consider yourself warned.

Yield:	Prep time:	Serving size:
1 liter	7 to 12 days	1 shot

1 pineapple	1 l vodka

1. Peel and slice pineapple into 1- to 2-inch-thick strips. Don't bother coring it.

2. Place pineapple strips in an airtight container, pour in vodka, and seal the container.

3. Place in a cool spot, out of direct sun. After 7 days of infusing, start tasting vodka daily. Vodka is done when you can only taste a hint of vodka through the sweetness of pineapple. The infusion time varies, depending on the sweetness of pineapple.

4. To serve, you can remove pineapple or leave it in. Transfer pineapple and vodka to a pitcher for a striking presentation, or remove pineapple and pour vodka back into its original bottle.

PUT DOWN THE PINEAPPLE!

You might think snacking on the vodka-infused fruit would be a good idea. Think again. Although the vodka has taken on all the sweetness of the pineapple, the pineapple has taken on the vodka. Yes, after a few drinks, we may have encouraged guests to try the fruit, but that was just to see what kind of horrible faces they'd make before they spit it out.

Orange-Infused Vodka

Perfect with cranberry juice or sparkling water, this is a sweet and refreshing vodka infusion. It's also one of the fastest infusions to make. In just a few days, it's ready to go.

Yield:	Prep time:	Serving size:
1 liter	3 or 4 days	1 shot

Peel of 5 medium oranges (1½ cups)	1 l vodka

1. Place orange peels in an airtight container, pour in vodka over, seal the container, and agitate.

2. Place in a cool spot, out of direct sun. After 2 days of infusing, start tasting vodka daily. Vodka should be ready in 3 or 4 days.

3. Strain orange peel from vodka, and store in original vodka bottle.

Ginger-Infused Vodka

I love ginger because it can play both hot and cold seasons. In the fall and winter, it can warm you from the inside out, but it can also refresh you during the summer. Try this vodka with a splash of lime juice or with some sparkling wine or water. When all else fails, sip it as an after-dinner drink to take the nip out of the cold.

Yield:	Prep time:	Serving size:
1 liter	5 to 10 days	1 shot

1 (4- or 5-in.) piece fresh ginger, peeled and sliced into ¼ to ⅛ inch slices (¼ cup)	1 l vodka

1. Pour 1 tablespoon vodka out of the bottle. Add sliced ginger to the bottle, seal, and agitate.

2. Place in a cool spot, out of direct sun. After 5 days of infusing, start tasting vodka daily. Vodka is done when the warmth of ginger overrides vodka flavor.

3. You can leave ginger in the bottle when you serve it.

Cranberry Vodka

I've had my share of vodka cranberry cocktails in the past, but nothing compares to a vodka cranberry made with cranberry-infused vodka. Did I mention I'm from cranberry country?

Yield:	Prep time:	Serving size:
1 liter	8 to 14 days	1 shot

1 (12-oz.) pkg. frozen cranberries   1 l vodka

1. Place frozen cranberries in an airtight container (frozen berries speed up the infusion process), pour in vodka, seal the container, and agitate.

2. Place in a cool spot, out of direct sun. After 7 days of infusing, start tasting vodka daily. When vodka has captured cranberry essence, strain out berries and return vodka to its original container. (It won't negatively affect the taste to keep berries in vodka, so if you like how festive that looks, feel free to keep them.)

BOUNCING BERRIES

Try this test on a fresh cranberry to see if it's a good one: drop it on the floor and watch to see if it bounces. A bouncing berry is a good berry.

Glossary

agave nectar   A low-glycemic sweetener from the blue agave plant, a spiky plant that resembles a cactus.

al dente   Italian for "against the teeth," this term refers to pasta or rice that's neither soft nor hard but just slightly firm against the teeth.

all-purpose flour   Flour that contains only the inner part of the wheat grain. It's suitable for everything from cakes to gravies.

allspice   A spice named for its flavor echoes of several spices (cinnamon, cloves, nutmeg) used in many desserts and in rich marinades and stews.

almond milk   A nondairy milk made by soaking walnuts in water and then puréeing the nuts and remaining liquid together.

antipasto   A classic Italian-style appetizer that includes an assortment of meats, cheeses, and vegetables, such as prosciutto, capicolla, mozzarella, mushrooms, and olives.

arborio rice   A plump Italian rice used for, among other purposes, risotto.

artichoke heart   The center part of the artichoke flower, often found canned in grocery stores.

arugula   A spicy-peppery green with leaves that resemble a dandelion and have a distinctive and very sharp flavor.

bake   To cook in a dry oven. Dry-heat cooking often results in a crisping of the exterior of the food being cooked. Moist-heat cooking, through methods such as steaming, poaching, etc., brings a much different, moist quality to the food.

baking powder   A dry ingredient used to increase volume and lighten or leaven baked goods.

balsamic vinegar   Vinegar produced primarily in Italy from a specific type of grape and aged in wood barrels. It's heavier, darker, and sweeter than most vinegars.

basil A flavorful, almost sweet, resinous herb delicious with tomatoes and used in all kinds of Italian- and Mediterranean-style dishes.

baste To keep foods moist during cooking by spooning, brushing, or drizzling with a liquid.

beat To quickly mix substances.

Belgian endive *See* endive.

blacken To cook something quickly in a very hot skillet over high heat, usually with a seasoning mixture.

blanch To place a food in boiling water for about 1 minute or less to partially cook the exterior and then submerge it in or rinse it with cool water to halt the cooking.

blend To completely mix something, usually with a blender or food processor; slower than beating.

boil To heat a liquid to the point where water is forced to turn into steam, causing the liquid to bubble. To boil something is to insert it into boiling water. A rapid boil is when a lot of bubbles form on the surface of the liquid.

bok choy A member of the cabbage family with thick stems, crisp texture, and fresh flavor. It's perfect for stir-frying.

bouillon Dried essence of stock from chicken, beef, vegetables, or other ingredients. It's a popular starting ingredient for soups because it adds flavor (and often a lot of salt).

braise To cook with the introduction of some liquid, usually over an extended period of time.

brine A highly salted, often seasoned, liquid used to flavor and preserve foods. To brine a food is to soak, or preserve, it by submerging it in brine. The salt in the brine penetrates the fibers of the meat and makes it moist and tender.

broil To cook in a dry oven under the overhead high-heat element.

broth *See* stock.

brown To cook in a skillet, turning, until the food's surface is seared and brown in color, to lock in the juices.

brown rice A whole-grain rice, including the germ, with a characteristic pale brown or tan color. It's more nutritious and flavorful than white rice.

bruschetta (or **crostini**) Slices of toasted or grilled bread with garlic and olive oil, often with other toppings.

bulgur   A wheat kernel that's been steamed, dried, and crushed, and is sold in fine and coarse textures.

butter lettuce   A small head of sweet lettuce that can be used to make lettuce wraps. Also known as Boston lettuce.

cake flour   A high-starch, soft, and fine flour used primarily for cakes.

canapé   A bite-size hors d'oeuvre usually served on a small piece of bread or toast.

caper   The flavorful bud of a Mediterranean plant, ranging in size from *nonpareil* (about the size of a small pea) to larger, grape-size caper berries produced in Spain.

caramelize   To cook sugar over low heat until it develops a sweet caramel flavor, or to cook vegetables (especially onions) or meat in butter or oil over low heat until they soften, sweeten, and develop a caramel color.

caraway   A distinctive spicy seed used for bread, pork, cheese, and cabbage dishes. It's known to reduce stomach upset, which is why it's often paired with foods like sauerkraut.

cardamom   An intense, sweet-smelling spice used in baking and coffee and common in Indian cooking.

carob   A tropical tree that produces long pods from which the dried, baked, and powdered flesh—carob powder—is used in baking. The flavor is sweet and reminiscent of chocolate.

cayenne   A fiery spice made from hot chile peppers, especially the cayenne chile, a slender, red, and very hot pepper.

ceviche   A seafood dish in which fresh fish or seafood is marinated for several hours in highly acidic lemon or lime juice, tomato, onion, and cilantro. The acid "cooks" the seafood.

chevre   A creamy-salty soft goat cheese. Chevres vary in style from mild and creamy to aged, firm, and flavorful.

chickpea (or **garbanzo bean**)   A roundish yellow-gold bean used as the base ingredient in hummus. Chickpeas are high in fiber and low in fat.

chile (or **chili**)   Any one of many different "hot" peppers, ranging in intensity from the relatively mild ancho pepper to the blisteringly hot habanero.

chili powder   A warm, rich seasoning blend that includes chile pepper, cumin, garlic, and oregano.

Chinese five-spice powder   A pungent mixture of equal parts cinnamon, cloves, fennel seed, anise, and Szechuan peppercorns.

chive   A member of the onion family with a light onion flavor. Chives grow in bunches of long leaves that resemble tall grass or the green tops of onions.

chop   To cut into pieces, usually qualified by an adverb such as "*coarsely* chopped" or by a size measurement such as "chopped into ½-inch pieces." "Finely chopped" is much closer to minced.

chutney   A thick condiment often served with Indian curries made with fruits and/or vegetables with vinegar, sugar, and spices.

cider vinegar   A vinegar produced from apple cider.

cilantro   A member of the parsley family used in Mexican dishes (especially salsa) and some Asian dishes. Use in moderation because the flavor can overwhelm. The seed of the cilantro plant is the spice coriander.

cinnamon   A rich, aromatic spice commonly used in baking or desserts. Cinnamon can also be used for delicious and interesting entrées.

clove   A sweet, strong, almost wintergreen-flavor spice used in baking.

coconut butter   Dried coconut flesh that's mixed with coconut oil to create a thick, smooth butter you can use in smoothies, in baking, and to make dairy-free ice cream. It's 100 percent coconut with very little processing and no added ingredients.

coconut milk   A nondairy milk made from the grated meat of a coconut used in many South Asian dishes and curries as well as desserts.

coconut oil   A no-trans-fat oil that's safe at high temperatures and renowned in the vegan world for creating flaky crusts and offering an all-natural, nondairy form of fat. In the 1990s, the highly processed version had a bad reputation for its high saturated fat content. Now, virgin coconut oil is gaining in popularity and offers a healthy fat with an indulgent taste.

coriander   A rich, warm, spicy seed used in all types of recipes, from African to South American, from entrées to desserts.

cornstarch   A thickener used in baking and food processing. It's the refined starch of the endosperm of the corn kernel. To avoid clumps, it's often mixed with cold liquid to make into a paste before adding to a recipe.

couscous   Granular semolina (durum wheat) that's cooked and used in many Mediterranean and North African dishes.

cream   To beat a fat such as butter, often with another ingredient such as sugar, to soften and aerate a batter.

crimini mushroom   A relative of the white button mushroom that's brown in color and has a richer flavor. The larger, fully grown version is the portobello. *See also* portobello mushroom.

crudité   Fresh vegetables served as an appetizer, often all together on one tray.

cumin   A fiery, smoky-tasting spice popular in Middle Eastern and Indian dishes. Cumin is a seed; ground cumin seed is the most common form used in cooking.

cure   To preserve uncooked foods, usually meats or fish, by either salting and smoking or pickling.

curry   Rich, spicy, Indian-style sauces and the dishes prepared with them. A curry uses curry powder as its base seasoning.

curry powder   A ground blend of rich and flavorful spices used as a basis for curry and many other Indian-influenced dishes. Common ingredients include hot pepper, nutmeg, cumin, cinnamon, pepper, and turmeric. Some curry can also be found in paste form.

custard   A cooked mixture of eggs and milk popular as a base for desserts.

dash   A few drops, usually of a liquid, released by a quick shake.

deglaze   To scrape up bits of meat and seasoning left in a pan or skillet after cooking. Usually this is done by adding a liquid such as wine or broth and creating a flavorful stock that can be used to create sauces.

devein   To remove the dark vein from the back of a large shrimp with a sharp knife.

dice   To cut into small cubes about ¼-inch square.

Dijon mustard   A hearty, spicy mustard made in the style of the Dijon region of France.

dill   A herb perfect for eggs, salmon, cheese dishes, and, of course, vegetables (pickles!).

dollop   A spoonful of something creamy and thick, like sour cream or whipped cream.

double boiler   A set of two saucepans designed to nest together, one inside the other, and provide consistent, moist heat for foods that need delicate treatment. The bottom pot holds water (not quite touching the bottom of the top pot); the top pot holds the food you want to heat.

dredge   To coat a piece of food on all sides with a dry substance such as flour or cornmeal.

drizzle   To lightly sprinkle drops of a liquid over food, often as the finishing touch to a dish.

edamame Fresh, plump, pale green soybeans, similar in appearance to lima beans, often served steamed and either shelled or still in the pod.

emulsion A combination of liquid ingredients that don't normally mix well (such as a fat or oil with water) that are beaten together to create a thick liquid. Creating emulsions must be done carefully and rapidly to ensure the particles of one ingredient are suspended in the other.

endive A green that resembles a small, elongated, tightly packed head of romaine lettuce. The thick, crunchy leaves can be broken off and used with dips and spreads.

entrée The main dish in a meal.

evaporated cane juice Sugar crystals that remain after evaporating cane juice. Compared to white sugar, evaporated cane juice goes through less processing.

extra-virgin olive oil *See* olive oil.

extract A concentrated flavoring derived from foods or plants through evaporation or distillation that imparts a powerful flavor without altering the volume or texture of a dish.

falafel A Middle Eastern food made of seasoned, ground chickpeas formed into balls, cooked, and often used as a filling in pitas.

fennel In seed form, a fragrant, licorice-tasting herb. The bulbs have a mild flavor, a celery-like crunch, and are used as a vegetable in salads or cooked recipes.

flaxseed A seed very high in omega-3s. To get the health benefits from flaxseeds, you must grind them. Ground flaxseed can be mixed with warm water to create a vegan egg substitute.

flour Grains ground into a meal. Wheat is perhaps the most common flour, but oats, rye, buckwheat, soybeans, chickpeas, etc. can also be used. *See also* all-purpose flour; cake flour; wholewheat flour.

fold To combine a dense mixture with a light mixture using a circular action from the middle of the bowl.

frittata A skillet-cooked mixture of eggs and other ingredients that's not stirred but is cooked slowly and then either flipped or finished under the broiler.

fry *See* sauté.

garlic A member of the onion family, a pungent and flavorful vegetable used in many savory dishes. A garlic bulb contains multiple cloves. Each clove, when chopped, provides about 1 teaspoon garlic.

ginger   A flavorful root available fresh, dried, or ground that adds a pungent, sweet, and spicy quality to a dish.

Greek yogurt   A strained yogurt that's a good natural source of protein, calcium, and probiotics. Greek yogurt averages 40 percent more protein per ounce than traditional yogurt.

handful   An unscientific measurement, it's the amount of an ingredient you can hold in your hand.

hearts of palm   Firm, elongated, off-white cylinders from the inside of a palm tree stem tip.

herbes de Provence   A seasoning mix of basil, fennel, marjoram, rosemary, sage, and thyme commonly used in the south of France.

hoisin sauce   A sweet Asian condiment similar to ketchup; made with soybeans, sesame, chile peppers, and sugar.

hors d'oeuvre   French for "outside of work" (the "work" being the main meal), an hors d'oeuvre can be any dish served as a starter before a meal.

horseradish   A sharp, spicy root that forms the flavor base in condiments such as cocktail sauce and sharp mustards. Prepared horseradish contains vinegar and oil, among other ingredients. Use pure horseradish much more sparingly than the prepared version, or try cutting it with sour cream.

hummus   A thick, Middle Eastern spread made of puréed chickpeas, lemon juice, olive oil, garlic, and often tahini.

infusion   A liquid in which flavorful ingredients, such as herbs, have been soaked or steeped to extract their flavor into the liquid.

Italian seasoning   A blend of dried herbs, including basil, oregano, rosemary, and thyme.

jicama   A juicy, crunchy, sweet, large, round Central American vegetable. If you can't find jicama, try substituting sliced water chestnuts.

julienne   A French word meaning "to slice into very thin pieces."

kalamata olive   Traditionally from Greece, a medium-small, long black olive with a rich, smoky flavor.

Key lime   A very small lime known for its tart taste; grown primarily in Florida.

knead   To work dough to make it pliable so it holds gas bubbles as it bakes. Kneading is fundamental in the process of making yeast breads.

kosher salt   A coarse-grained salt made without any additives or iodine.

lentil   A tiny lens-shape pulse used in European, Middle Eastern, and Indian cuisines.

liquid smoke   A liquid created by collecting condensed smoke in a tube placed above wood-burning chips.

mandoline   A cutting instrument consisting of a diagonal platform with a sharp razor embedded in it. You slide the food item across the platform to get consistent and often razor-thin slices.

maple syrup   A natural sweetener made from the sap of a maple tree. In the United States, there are four grade levels: Grade A Light Amber, Grade A Medium Amber, Grade A Dark Amber, and Grade B. In general, the lighter the color, the milder the flavor.

marinate   To soak meat, seafood, or another food in a seasoned sauce (a marinade) that's high in acid content. The acids break down the muscle of the meat, making it tender and adding flavor.

marjoram   A sweet herb, cousin of and similar to oregano; popular in Greek, Spanish, and Italian dishes.

meld   To allow flavors to blend and spread over time. Melding is often why recipes call for overnight refrigeration and is also why some dishes taste better as leftovers.

meringue   A baked mixture of sugar and beaten egg whites, often used as a dessert topping.

mesclun   Mixed salad greens, usually containing lettuce and other assorted greens, such as arugula, cress, and endive.

millet   A tiny, round, yellow nutty-flavored grain often used as a replacement for couscous.

mince   To cut into very small pieces, smaller than diced, about $1/8$ inch or smaller.

miso   A fermented, flavorful soybean paste, key in many Japanese dishes.

mouthfeel   The overall sensation in the mouth resulting from a combination of a food's temperature, taste, smell, and texture.

nutmeg   A sweet, fragrant, musky spice used primarily in baking.

nutritional yeast flakes   A deactivated strain of yeast packed with vitamin B, used to impart a cheesy taste to foods, and popular with vegans and those wishing to avoid dairy. Also known as *nooch*.

oat   The flake from oat groats. *See also* rolled oat.

oat flour   A gluten-free flour made out of ground oats.

olive   The fruit of the olive tree commonly grown on all sides of the Mediterranean. Black olives are also called ripe olives. Green olives are immature, although they're also widely eaten. *See also* kalamata olive.

olive oil   A fragrant liquid produced by crushing or pressing olives. Extra-virgin olive oil—the most flavorful and highest quality—is produced from the first pressing of a batch of olives; oil is also produced from later pressings.

oregano   A fragrant, slightly astringent herb used in Greek, Spanish, and Italian dishes.

orzo   A rice-shape pasta used in Greek cooking.

oxidation   The browning of fruit flesh that happens over time and with exposure to air. Minimize oxidation by rubbing the cut surfaces with lemon juice.

paella   A Spanish dish of rice, shellfish, onion, meats, rich broth, and herbs.

paprika   A rich, red, warm, earthy spice that lends a rich red color to many dishes.

parboil   To partially cook in boiling water or broth.

parsley   A fresh-tasting, green leafy herb, often used as a garnish.

pesto   A thick spread or sauce made with fresh basil leaves, garlic, olive oil, pine nuts, and Parmesan cheese.

pilaf   A rice dish in which the rice is browned in butter or oil and then cooked in a flavorful liquid such as a broth, often with the addition of meats or vegetables. The rice absorbs the broth, resulting in a savory dish.

pinch   An unscientific measurement for the amount of an ingredient—typically, a dry, granular substance such as an herb or seasoning—you can hold between your finger and thumb.

pine nut   A nut that's rich (high in fat), flavorful, and a bit pine-y. Pine nuts are a traditional ingredient in pesto and add a hearty crunch to many other recipes.

pita bread   A flat, hollow wheat bread often used for sandwiches or sliced pizza style. They're terrific soft with dips or baked or broiled as a vehicle for other ingredients.

pizza stone   A flat stone that when preheated with the oven, cooks crusts to a crispy, pizza-parlor texture.

poach   To cook a food in simmering liquid, such as water, wine, or broth.

polenta   A mush made from cornmeal that can be eaten hot with butter or cooked until firm and cut into squares.

porcini mushroom   A rich and flavorful mushroom used in rice and Italian-style dishes.

portobello mushroom   A mature and larger form of the smaller crimini mushroom. Brown, chewy, and flavorful, portobellos are often served as whole caps, grilled, or as thin sautéed slices. *See also* crimini mushroom.

preheat   To turn on an oven, broiler, or other cooking appliance in advance of cooking so the temperature will be at the desired level when the assembled dish is ready for cooking.

purée   To reduce a food to a thick, creamy texture, typically using a blender or food processor.

quinoa   A nutty-flavored seed that's extremely high in protein and calcium.

reduce   To boil or simmer a broth or sauce to remove some of the water content, resulting in more concentrated flavor and color.

render   To cook a meat to the point where its fat melts and can be removed.

reserve   To hold a specified ingredient for another use later in the recipe.

rice vinegar   Vinegar produced from fermented rice or rice wine, popular in Asian-style dishes. (It's not the same thing as rice *wine* vinegar.) You can buy plain or seasoned rice vinegar. Seasoned rice vinegar contains sugar and spices.

risotto   A popular Italian rice dish made by browning arborio rice in butter or oil and then slowly adding liquid to cook the rice, resulting in a creamy texture.

roast   To cook something uncovered in an oven, usually without additional liquid.

rolled oat   An oat groat that has been steamed, rolled, and flaked.

rosemary   A pungent, sweet herb used with chicken, pork, fish, and especially lamb. A little goes a long way.

roux   A mixture of butter or another fat and flour used to thicken sauces and soups.

saffron   An expensive spice made from the stamens of crocus flowers. Saffron lends a dramatic yellow color and distinctive flavor to a dish. Use only tiny amounts.

sage   An herb with a musty yet fruity, lemon-rind scent and "sunny" flavor.

sauté   To pan-cook over lower heat than what's used for frying.

savory   A popular herb with a fresh, woody taste. Can also describe the flavor of food.

scald   To heat milk just until it's about to boil and then remove it from heat. Scalding milk helps prevent it from souring.

scant   An ingredient measurement directive not to add any extra, perhaps even leaving the measurement a tad short.

sear   To quickly brown the exterior of a food, especially meat, over high heat.

sesame oil   An oil made from pressing sesame seeds. The clear version is tasteless, and the brown version is aromatic and flavorful.

shallot   A member of the onion family that grows in a bulb somewhat like garlic but has a milder onion flavor. When a recipe calls for shallot, use the entire bulb.

shellfish   A broad range of seafood, including clams, mussels, oysters, crabs, shrimp, and lobster.

shiitake mushroom   A large, dark brown mushroom with a hearty, meaty flavor. It can be used fresh or dried, grilled, as a component in other recipes, and as a flavoring source for broth.

short-grain rice   A starchy rice popular in Asian-style dishes because it readily clumps, making it perfect for eating with chopsticks.

silicone mat   A nonstick mat made of silicone used for baking.

simmer   To boil a liquid gently so it barely bubbles.

skillet (also **frying pan**)   A generally heavy, flat-bottomed, metal pan with a handle designed to cook food over heat on a stovetop or campfire.

skim   To remove fat or other material from the top of liquid.

soy sauce   A liquid prevalent in Asian cooking made from soy and wheat that's fermented. It adds salt and depth to a dish.

spelt flour   An ancient whole-grain flour with a nutty, rich taste that can substituted 1:1 with all-purpose flour.

steam   To suspend a food over boiling water and allow the heat of the steam (water vapor) to cook the food. This quick-cooking method preserves a food's flavor and texture.

steep   To let sit in hot water, as in steeping tea in hot water for 10 minutes.

stew   To slowly cook pieces of food submerged in a liquid. Also, a dish prepared by this method.

sticky rice   *See* short-grain rice.

stir-fry   To cook small pieces of food in a wok or skillet over high heat, moving and turning the food quickly to cook all sides.

stock   A flavorful broth made by cooking meats and/or vegetables with seasonings until the liquid absorbs these flavors. The liquid is strained, and the solids are discarded. Stock can be eaten alone or used as a base for soups, stews, etc.

strata   A savory bread pudding made with eggs and cheese.

sucanat   Pure dried cane sugar. It has the nuttiness and molasses taste of brown sugar but the texture of white sugar. You can find sucanat in the baking aisle by the sugar.

tahini   A paste made from sesame seeds used to flavor many Middle Eastern recipes.

tamarind   A sweet, pungent, flavorful fruit used in Indian-style sauces and curries.

tapas   A Spanish term meaning "small plate" that describes individual-size appetizers and snacks served cold or warm.

tapenade   A thick, chunky spread made from savory ingredients, such as olives, lemon juice, and anchovies.

tarragon   A sweet, rich-smelling herb perfect with seafood, vegetables (especially asparagus), chicken, and pork.

tempeh   An Indonesian food made by culturing and fermenting soybeans into a cake, sometimes mixed with grains or vegetables. It's high in protein and fiber.

teriyaki   A Japanese-style sauce composed of soy sauce, rice wine, ginger, and sugar that works well with seafood as well as most meats.

thyme   A minty, zesty herb.

tofu   A cheeselike substance made from soybeans and soy milk.

turmeric   A spicy, pungent yellow root used in many dishes, especially Indian cuisine, for color and flavor. Turmeric is the source of the yellow color in many prepared mustards.

tzatziki   A Greek dip traditionally made with Greek yogurt, cucumbers, garlic, and mint.

vegetable steamer   An insert with tiny holes in the bottom designed to fit on or in another saucepan to hold food to be steamed above boiling water. *See also* steam.

vinegar   An acidic liquid widely used as a dressing and seasoning, often made from fermented grapes, apples, or rice. *See also* balsamic vinegar; cider vinegar; rice vinegar; white vinegar; wine vinegar.

wasabi   Japanese horseradish, a fiery, pungent condiment used with many Japanese-style dishes. It's most often sold as a powder to which you add water to create a paste.

water chestnut   A white, crunchy, and juicy tuber popular in many Asian dishes. It holds its texture whether cool or hot.

whisk   To rapidly mix, introducing air to the mixture.

white mushroom   A button mushroom. When fresh, white mushrooms have an earthy smell and an appealing soft crunch.

white vinegar   The most common type of vinegar, produced from grain.

whole grain   A grain derived from the seeds of grasses, including rice, oats, rye, wheat, wild rice, quinoa, barley, buckwheat, bulgur, corn, millet, amaranth, and sorghum.

whole-wheat flour   Wheat flour that contains the entire grain.

wild rice   Not a rice at all, this grass has a rich, nutty flavor and serves as a nutritious side dish.

wine vinegar   Vinegar produced from red or white wine.

yeast   Tiny fungi that, when mixed with water, sugar, flour, and heat, release carbon dioxide bubbles, which, in turn, cause the bread to rise.

zest   Small slivers of peel, usually from a citrus fruit such as a lemon, lime, or orange.

Resources  B

There's nothing better than finding like-minded people and reading about others who have made similar commitments to a whole-food, clean-eating lifestyle. In this appendix, I've collected some resources you might find helpful and encouraging.

Books

Now that you've learned more about whole foods and clean eating, here are some other books you might enjoy.

Aziz, Michael. *The Perfect 10 Diet: 10 Key Hormones That Hold the Secret to Losing Weight and Feeling Great-Fast!* Naperville, IL: Cumberland House, 2010.

Bittman, Mark. *Food Matters: A Guide to Conscious Eating with Over 75 Recipes.* New York, NY: Simon and Schuster, 2009.

Pollen, Michael. *In Defense of Food: An Eater's Manifesto.* New York, NY: Penguin, 2008.

———. *The Omnivore's Dilemma: A Natural History of Four Meals.* New York, NY: Penguin, 2006.

Reno, Tosca. *The Eat-Clean Diet Recharged!* Toronto, ON: Robert Kennedy Publishing, 2009.

———. *Just the Rules.* Toronto, ON: Robert Kennedy Publishing, 2011.

Scarbrough, Mark, and Bruce Weinstein. *Real Food Has Curves: How to Get Off Processed Foods, Lose the Weight, and Love What You Eat.* New York, NY: Gallery Books, 2010.

Welland, Diane. *The Complete Idiot's Guide to Eating Clean.* Indianapolis, IN: Alpha Books, 2009.

Magazines

Clean Eating magazine

cleaneatingmag.com

Recipes and articles pertaining to clean eating

KIWI Magazine

kiwimagonline.com

Recipes and articles for parents who want to raise their kids on whole, clean foods

Living Without magazine

livingwithout.com

Recipes and articles for those living with food allergies or intolerances

Websites and Blogs

Badger Girl Learns to Cook

learntocookbadgergirl.com

Recipes and lifestyle blog posts for those trying to maintain a clean, whole-foods diet. Recipes are mostly dairy-free, kind of vegan, a little bit paleo, and always healthy.

LocalHarvest

localharvest.org/csa

Log on to find a CSA near you.

Slow Food International

slowfood.com

An international, grassroots movement focused on eating and celebrating local foods. Many cities have their own chapters and offer opportunities to meet other people who appreciate good food and volunteer opportunities to make healthy, local fare available to all.

Index

X–Y–Z